A FACING HISTORY AND OURSELVES PUBLICATION

THE
NANJING
ATROCITIES

CRIMES OF WAR

FACING
HISTORY
AND
OURSELVES

Facing History and Ourselves is an international educational and professional development organization whose mission is to engage students of diverse backgrounds in an examination of racism, prejudice, and antisemitism in order to promote the development of a more humane and informed citizenry. By studying the historical development of the Holocaust and other examples of genocide, students make the essential connection between history and the moral choices they confront in their own lives. For more information about Facing History and Ourselves, please visit our website at http://www.facinghistory.org.

Copyright © 2014 by Facing History and Ourselves National Foundation, Inc.

All rights reserved.

Facing History and Ourselves® is a trademark registered in the US Patent & Trademark Office.

ISBN-13: 978-1-940457-05-5

ISBN-10: 1-940457-05-X

Facing History and Ourselves is a global nonprofit organization founded in 1976 by educators who wanted to develop a more effective and rewarding way to engage students. We're guided by the belief that the lifeblood of democracy is the ability of every rising generation to be active, responsible decision makers who've learned to value compassion as much as reason.

By integrating the study of history and literature with ethical decision making, innovative teaching strategies, and extraordinary resources, professional development opportunities, and coaching, our program enables secondary school teachers to promote students' historical understanding, critical thinking, and social and emotional learning, and to facilitate transformative dialogue in their classrooms.

From the failure of democracy in Germany and the events leading to the Holocaust, to struggles for civil rights from the United States to South Africa, we trust students to wrestle with complex moments in human history, and work to help them understand the range of human behavior. We encourage students to reflect on the choices they confront in their own lives, and to consider how they can make a difference today.

ACKNOWLEDGMENTS

Primary Writer: Fran Sterling

The publication of *The Nanjing Atrocities: Crimes of War* has been an extraordinarily collaborative effort within Facing History and Ourselves. We extend our deepest gratitude to all who contributed to the development of this resource.

In particular we would like to thank Anla Cheng, Chair of the Facing History and Ourselves China Project, Cecilia Chan, Michelle Koo, Hui Li, Alice Mong, Tracy Palandjian, Florence Sloan, Michael Tse, Charlene Wang, Shirley Wang, members of the China Project, and China Overseas Holdings Limited for their vision, generous support and ongoing commitment to share the history of the Nanjing Atrocities in classrooms around the world.

While writing this resource, Facing History and Ourselves greatly benefited from the historical scholarship, guidance, and friendship of Joshua A. Fogel, Canada Research Chair and Professor of Chinese History. We would also like to thank Professor Bob Tadashi Wakabayashi of York University in Toronto, Professor Rana Mitter of Oxford University and Fan Ho of Nanjing University for their editorial support and scholarly contributions. We want to extend our gratitude to former Nuremberg prosecutor Ben Ferencz for his long time friendship and for his personal and insightful foreword to this resource. Thank you to author Gish Jen for her honest conversations on the role of culture and identity and to Chief Prosecutor of the International Criminal Court Luis Moreno Ocampo who greatly informed our understanding of the Tokyo Trials and their legacy today. Special thanks are extended to many scholars who generously contributed their expertise throughout the writing of this resource. These include Director Zhu Chengshan of the Nanjing Massacre Memorial Museum, Steven Ting and Professor Liu Haiping, Chair of the Dept. of Foreign Studies at Nanjing University, Professor Su, Shanghai Normal University, Professor Richard Wasserstrom, University of California, Davis, Professor Frank Dikköter, University of Hong Kong, Professor Zhang, Nanjing University, Professor Zhang Lianhong, Nanjing Normal University and Professor Margaret Wells, University of Toronto. This resource would not have been lifted off the ground without the many contributions of several research interns who provided invaluable support to the publication: Shira Bartov, who greatly enhanced the section on the Nanjing Safety Zone, and Jason Kingdon and Jackson Tse, who researched and located essential documents during the early stages of this project.

Special thanks go to Judy Katz and Grant Rhodes, John Zeljo from Teaching East Asia at the University of Colorado, and Karen Jungblut from the Shoah Visual History Foundation for their valuable insights, scholarship and contributions to the final resource book.

Lastly, Facing History and Ourselves would like to acknowledge and express its gratitude to the tremendous effort of the staff who dedicated their time and expertise in order to support the research, writing, and publication of this text. First, to Adam Strom, who read every word of the book many times and was a genuine partner from the very beginning of the book's inception to its end. To the editorial team of Dimitry Anselme, Juan Castellanos, Karen Murphy, Marty Sleeper, Marc Skvirsky, and Margot Stern Strom: the book greatly benefited from your constructive criticism, contributions, and guidance along the way. A great deal of gratitude is extended to Pam Haas, Erin Lee, Ellen Lempereur-Greaves, Kathleen Shugrue, and Brooke Harvey for their project leadership and organization of the overall project. Catherine O'Keefe, Samantha Landry, Ariel Perry, and our various editorial and design consultants graciously turned the page into a visually engaging resource for print and digital formats. Erin Kernen ensured that all licensing was intact. Tracy O'Brien provided ongoing research and publication support throughout the entire length of the project. Our communications team, led by Anne Burt, spread the word about the importance of this publication. We would also like to acknowledge the work of Wilkie Cook, Alexia Prichard, and Rob Tokanel as they developed the website and companion videos to accompany the book.

FOREWORD BY BENJAMIN B. FERENCZ   1

INTRODUCTION   4

CHAPTER 1: IDENTITY, HISTORY, AND CULTURE   13

     Introduction   14

Reading 1   Connecting to Our Past   16

Reading 2   To Carry History   18

Reading 3   Culture and Identity: East and West   20

Reading 4   Women, Tradition, and Social Custom   23

Reading 5   Honor   26

Reading 6   Learning About Difference   30

Reading 7   Coming of Age during War   34

CHAPTER 2: EMERGING NATIONS: 1868–1911   37

     Introduction   38

Reading 1   Meiji Period in Japan   43

Reading 2   Shinto and Japanese Nationalism   49

Reading 3   Education and Nation Building in Japan   51

Reading 4   Seeds of Unrest: The Taiping Movement   55

Reading 5   Self-Strengthening Movement in China   59

Reading 6   Reforms   60

Reading 7   Rebels: The Boxer Rebellion   62

Reading 8   The Birth of the First Chinese Republic   65

Reading 9   An End of Two Millennia   67

     Primary Sources: 72

     (1) The Treaty of Nanking (summary); (2) The Boxer Protocol (summary); (3) Pamphlet, The Revolutionary Army (1903) (excerpt); (4) Newspaper Article Reporting on the Proclamation of the First Chinese Republic; (5) Edict of Abdication; (6) The Articles of Favorable Treatment [of the Great Qing Emperor After His Abdication]

     Map: Spheres of Influence (1850–1914)   81

CHAPTER 3: PRELUDE TO WAR: 1911–1931   **83**

Introduction   84

Reading 1   **Expressions of Imperialism**   90

Reading 2   **Competition for the Region: The Russo-Japanese War**   94

Reading 3   **New Ways of Thinking: Racial Purity**   96

Reading 4   **Taisho Democracy in Japan: 1912–1926**   98

Reading 5   **Strengthening the Japanese Nation**   102

Reading 6   **First Decades of the Chinese Republic: 1911–1931**   105

Reading 7   **Internal Strife in China**   108

Reading 8   **Exclusion and Humiliation**   111

Reading 9   **Restoring the Status of Asia**   115

Reading 10   **Japan's Expansion into Manchuria**   118

Reading 11   **Preparing for War: Alliances with Germany**   122

Reading 12   **Political Conflicts within China**   126

Reading 13   **The Road to War**   127

Primary Sources: 132

(1) Treaty of Shimonoseki/Treaty of Maguan (excerpt);
(2) National Anthem Kimagayo—Japan's National Anthem;
(3) Newspaper Article "Rich Land is Goal for Japanese Army";
(4) Excerpts of the Covenant of the League of Nations; (5) A
Case for Japanese Expansion (close reading)

Map Japanese Empire Building (1870–1942)   143

CHAPTER 4: THE NANJING ATROCITIES   **145**

Introduction   146

Reading 1   **The Coming of War and Terror to Nanjing**   152

Reading 2   **December 13, 1937**   154

Reading 3   **A Failure of Leadership**   158

Reading 4   **Frontline Headlines**   160

Reading 5   **Wartime Stories**   165

Reading 6   **Voices of Soldiers**   167

Reading 7   **"I Will Never Forget": Voices of Survivors**   172

Reading 8   Hell on Earth: George Fitch   179

Reading 9   **Politics and the Atrocities**   183

Reading 10   **Women in War**   186

Reading 11   **The Conduct of Soldiers**   189

Reading 12   **Prisoners of War in Nanjing**   191

Reading 13   **Living Under the Occupation**   196

Reading 14   **Chinese Resistance**   200

             Primary Sources: 204

             (1) Song, "Eight Hundred Heroes"; (2) Secondary Source
             from Scholar—Dissenting Opinion of Radhabinod Pal (close
             reading); (3) Photograph, "100-Man Killing Contest"; (4) Eye-
             Witness Tells of Horror Seen in the Fall of Nanjing

CHAPTER 5: RESCUE AND RESISTANCE IN NANJING   **211**

             Introduction   213

             Map Nanjing and its Safety Zone (1937–1939)   218

Reading 1   **Conviction and Courage: Minnie Vautrin**   219

Reading 2   **Wrestling with the Reality of War: Tsen Shui-fang**   225

Reading 3   **A Simple Sense of Outrage: Dr. Robert O. Wilson**   230

Reading 4   **A Plea for Humanity: Miner Searle Bates**   234

Reading 5   **A Question of Morality: John Rabe**   237

Reading 6   **Rescue Outside the Safety Zone**   243

             Primary Sources: 246

             (1) Time Line, Nanjing Safety Zone, August 1937–
             February 1938; (2) Notice for Chinese Refugees Issued by
             the Nanjing Safety Zone Committee

CHAPTER 6: AFTERMATH AND JUDGMENT   **249**

             Introduction   250

Reading 1   **Accepting Defeat**   253

Reading 2   **War Criminals and Aggressive War**   258

Reading 3   **"The Future Emerges"**   263

Reading 4   **Rebuilding**   268

Reading 5   **The History Problem**   272

Reading 6   **Responsibility of Command**   276

Reading 7   **A Warning to the Rest of the World**   282

Reading 8   **Rape as a Weapon of War**   285

Primary Sources: 289

(1) Potsdam Declaration (excerpt); (2) Text of the
Instruments of Surrender of Japan (close reading);
(3) Fact Sheet, International Military Tribunal for the Far East;
(4) Preamble of the 1947 Japanese Constitution (close
reading); (5) Summary of Treatment of Sexual Violence
in International Law; (6) Report of the United Nations'
Secretary General on the Protection of Civilians in Armed
Conflict (United Nations S/2007/643)

**CHAPTER 7: MEMORY, LEGACY, AND
CHOOSING TO PARTICIPATE**   **303**

Introduction   304

Reading 1   **A Nation's Past**   307

Reading 2   **What History Textbooks Leave Out**   310

Reading 3   **Refuting Denial**   314

Reading 4   **Museums and Memory**   317

Reading 5   **Soldiers and Reconciliation**   319

Reading 6   **Apology**   323

Reading 7   **What Is Enough?**   326

Reading 8   **Healing Historical Wounds**   333

Primary Sources: 336

(1) Speech by Japanese Prime Minister Tomiichi Murayama
on the 50th Anniversary of the War's End (close reading)

FOREWORD

There are deeds of such evil magnitude that the mind is incapable of grasping their full horror and cruelty without focusing on one particular person or event. Anne Frank, Auschwitz, Nanjing, and Hiroshima are names that help illuminate the dark picture of inhumanity. Yet similar cruelties continue to occur even to this very day. What can be done to move toward a more peaceful and humane world? My personal experiences may be instructive.

In the winter of 1921 my parents, together with their two infant children, fled from poverty and persecution in Romania and settled in New York. I decided upon a career in crime prevention having grown up in a crime-infested neighborhood in that state. In 1941 Harvard Law School awarded me a scholarship, and during my tenure there I was employed as a student adviser and researcher for a professor who was writing a book on war crimes. After Japan's attack against the United States at Pearl Harbor, I enlisted in the US army. In 1945 I was discharged as a sergeant of infantry and awarded five battle stars for having survived the major battles of the war. Not all wounds are visible.

My final orders were to report to the headquarters of General George Patton and to start gathering evidence of German atrocities so that perpetrators might be brought to justice. As a war crimes investigator my duties required me to disinter bodies of Allied flyers who had been shot down and then beaten to death by German mobs. I collected evidence of incredible atrocities as we liberated several Nazi concentration camps filled with emaciated prisoners who were dead or dying. The scenes of sorrow and suffering are indescribable. I had peered into hell. The grisly assignment changed the course of my life.

I returned home after the war but was soon persuaded to return to Germany to assist with the war crimes trials taking place in Nuremberg. The war department gave me the simulated rank of a full colonel. I had entered into what was described as "the biggest murder trial in history." Twenty-two high-ranking Nazi officers, many with doctoral degrees, commanded Nazi extermination squads [Einsatzgruppen] that systematically slaughtered more than a million innocent and helpless people, including thousands of children shot one at a time. All Jews, "gypsies," and others were murdered simply because they did not share the race, religion, or ideology of their executioners.

The case I presented was "a plea of humanity to law" to uphold "the right of all persons to live in peace and dignity regardless of their race or creed." I was then 27 years old and it was my first case. I remained constant to the ideals of my youth. I repeated the same appeal when invited to make the final statement for the prosecution in the first case of the new International Criminal Court in The Hague on 25 August 2011. I was then in my 92nd year.

My law work almost invariably related to seeking justice for the oppressed. In August of 1991 I was invited to visit Tokyo to meet with a large number of Chinese, Korean, and Indonesian women who were rape victims or sex slaves of the Japanese army during the war years. They had learned that I had been influential in obtaining German compensation for the victims of Nazi crimes and sought my help in persuading the Japanese to do likewise. I admired the Japanese volunteers who organized the campaign. However, not all Japanese citizens shared the same view. I believe that remorse is the beginning of wisdom.

In addition to thousands of women raped in Nanjing during the occupation, the army itself organized so-called comfort stations where comfort women were provided for the sexual pleasure of Japanese soldiers. I looked into the tired eyes of surviving victims as they recounted the conditions under which they had to live and work. I was outraged at the designation of sex slaves as comfort women. There is nothing comfortable about being raped. Initially the post-war official apologies from Japan were too often weak or evasive. Compensation was all but nonexistent. In contrast, the new German government's effort to make monetary amends to the victims of persecution has helped bring Germany back into the fold of the world community. Failure by the Japanese government to acknowledge a moral or legal obligation to the women violated by Japanese soldiers will remain a stain on the nation's history, although the country has made recent efforts to forge amends.

To deter abhorrent deeds of such magnitude that it shocks the conscience of decent people everywhere requires a very widespread and profound change of heart and mind. The glorification of war must be ended and replaced by a glorification of peace. Since time immemorial wars have been hailed as the path to power, riches, and glory. It must be recognized that there has never been a war without atrocities. The only way to eliminate the crimes of war is to eliminate war itself. Many people believe it is not possible to reverse entrenched thinking in a short period of time; but I am convinced that it can be done!

I am encouraged by the fact that we now have a functioning International Criminal Court that was considered an idle dream not long ago. It must be recognized in national and international courts that the illegal use of armed force is a crime against humanity. Of course every accused is entitled to be presumed innocent pending a fair trial. If the force is not in self-defense and proportionate, or approved by the United Nations Security Council in accordance with the UN Charter, it is illegal. No person or group should be immune from prosecution for acts which the Nuremberg tribunals condemned as the supreme international crime of illegal war (aggression) which incorporates all the other crimes. My esteemed supreme commander in war, General Dwight D. Eisenhower, when he was president of the United States tried to warn the nation and the world: "In a very real sense the world no longer has a choice between force and law. If civilization is to survive, it must choose the rule of law."[1]

One of the most significant, yet frequently overlooked, conclusions derived from war crimes trials after World War II at Nuremberg, Tokyo, and elsewhere is that crimes are committed by individuals and not by nations, cities, groups, or other entities but by individuals. Those white-collar criminals who plan and direct criminal activities and never fire a shot may be even more culpable than direct perpetrators. Law must apply equally to everyone—including those who sit in judgment. No nation should be vilified or condemned for the evil deeds of a few miscreant or misguided leaders and individuals.

The current system of resolving unsettled disputes between nations or violent groups by sending young people out to kill other young people they don't even know and who have done them no harm is too absurd and too dangerous to continue. Powerful nations already possess the military ability to destroy all life on earth. Hopefully they also have the intelligence and determination to prevent it from happening.

The voice of young people who must bear the burdens and risks must also be heard. New communication technologies hold out the hope that the current inequities that give rise to violent conflicts will, in time, be alleviated. It must be recognized that you cannot kill an ideology with a gun. Tolerance, compassion, and compromise are vital components of a more peaceful planet. New generations must be taught to view with abhorrence all actions that fail to respect the human dignity of all peoples.

The progress I have witnessed during my lifetime convinces me that with patience and determination rational people will recognize that law is always better than war—even if there be occasional miscarriages of justice. The logo on my website is "Law. Not War!" Hopefully, it may serve as a useful guide to a more humane and peaceful world.

Benjamin B. Ferencz, Nuremberg war crimes prosecutor, JD, Harvard 1943

---

1   Dwight D. Eisenhower, "Freedom Under Law," *Department of State Bulletin* 38, no. 986, (May 19, 1958): 831.

INTRODUCTION

In the foreword of *The Nanjing Atrocities: Crimes of War* Ben Ferencz, war crimes investigator and chief prosecutor at the Nuremberg Trials, writes, "It must be recognized that there has never been a war without atrocities." In August 1937 Hosaka Akira, a Japanese army medical doctor assigned to the Shanghai Expedition Army, began a diary. As his unit arrived on the outskirts of Nanjing, China at the end of November, Hosaka writes:

> At 10:00 on 29 November 1937 we left to clean out the enemy in Chang Chou and at noon we entered the town. An order was received to kill the residents and eighty (80) of them, men and women of all ages, were shot to death [at dusk]. I hope this will be the last time I'll ever witness such a scene. The people were gathered in one place. They were all praying, crying, and begging for help. I just couldn't bear watching such a pitiful spectacle. Soon the heavy machine guns opened fire and the sight of those people screaming and falling to the ground is one I could not face even if I had had the heart of a monster. War is truly terrible. [Allied Translator and Interpreter translation.][2]

Hosaka's diary ends abruptly on December 7. One week later on December 13, 1937, Nanjing (Nanking),[3] the then capital city of China, was captured by Japanese imperial forces. Immediately soldiers of the Imperial Army ran riot in the captured city in a spree of rape and murder of barbaric scale. Roughly 80% of the infrastructure of the capital city was also destroyed between mid-December and February 1938, which encompassed the height of the violence.[4] The atrocities committed in and around the immediate surroundings of Nanjing remain as one of the greatest war crimes during World War II. They also mark the opening phase of Japan's war in China.[5]

Historian Rana Mitter believes studying what occurred in Nanjing during these several months is immensely important for several reasons. First, it is one historical event that has too long been misunderstood or ignored and second, because it tells us a great deal about the contemporary politics of China and Japan. He goes on to explain:

> First of all it [Nanjing] is worth studying because it shows us what happens in a situation where an imperialist society which has decided to turn against democracy and has militarized in a very inward looking and brutal way is allowed to exercise what it feels

are its rights of conquest in a neighboring country. The atrocities that were committed against the Chinese people in Nanjing and the deaths of so many people were not the product of a cold calculated plan, but rather they were the victims of a violent outburst of a feeling of imperialist entitlement by a country that had created a narrative about its own role in Asia which its Chinese neighbors resolutely did not share. . . .

Also important is how this event [the Nanjing Atrocities] has been treated in the East Asia of today because one would like to say that the memory of these horrific events has brought China and Japan closely together. But the fact is that it hasn't, or it hasn't yet. . . .

Now we should be clear. There are very many people in Japan who have done a great deal to publicize the horrors of the massacre and we should be very grateful to many efforts by Japanese scholars and politicians who have apologized for the massacre, and have also acknowledged that Japan has to come to terms with it. At the same time there is too much in the public sphere in Japan which does not spend time to understand why those events have happened.

And the fact is that outside a sphere of those who really read history and understand the complexity of the relationship between those two societies, we are in the danger of being in a world where there are two very different interpretations of the [history] on either side of the East China Sea. It is clearly important to understand the reality of what happened at the time and why it matters so that we can bring together a shared understanding that is important, not just for China and Japan, but for the wider world including the West, that has to deal with those two immensely important nations.[6]

The Nanjing Atrocities: Crimes of War asks students to consider what occurred in Nanjing within the larger context of examining the relationship between war and war time atrocities. By framing this event in this manner, we hope students can reach a deeper understanding of the dangers that can arise when nationalism and militarism remain unchecked, and when institutions within a nation are manipulated to foster climates of superiority, intolerance, and dehumanization.

The resource book begins decades before the war erupted on mainland China. As China and Japan confronted the colonial ambitions of Western nations, both were forced to adopt and adapt to new ways of thinking and governing in order to survive. Beginning this resource at this juncture in history is not intended to suggest that the Nanjing Atrocities were inevitable or a direct a result of a single cause, person, or cultural element. Rather, the Nanjing Atrocities, and Japan's war in China, were the result of an escalation of many factors that scholars continue to debate to this day. This resource will allow students to weigh these many forces by considering the following questions:

- Were there developments in nineteenth- and early twentieth-century China and Japan that foreshadow the possibility of war atrocities during World War II?

- Why did some members of the Japanese Imperial Army perpetuate some of the most barbaric and violent acts during World War II?

- Why was sexual violence and rape used as a weapon of war in China?

- What are the legacies of the Nanjing Atrocities?

This resource also attempts to shift what many historians of East Asia argue is a grave imbalance in understanding the history of the twentieth century. For decades following the war, Western classrooms have accorded a great deal of attention to the study of World War II on the European continent. Little if any attention has been directed to the study of Japan's war in China. After all, it was during the years 1937 through 1945 that Japan and China were embroiled for the first time in a global conflict. Each suffered great losses in military and civilian populations and experienced dramatic internal migration and shifts in their political, economic, and cultural lives.[7] Two years before Germany invaded Poland and four years before the United States entered the war in 1941, China experienced the full aggression of Japanese power with very little international support. Historian Diana Lary notes:

> [The] names of battles and generals are unknown to most Westerners—as unknown as the war in Asia itself. The Asian names that Westerners do recognize from the war in Asia- Singapore, Bataan, Iwo Jima, Hiroshima are places where Westerners were involved and are from parts of Asia other than China. . . . And yet the all-out war that started in China with the Japanese invasion in 1937 and lasted until 1945 was the longest conflict of any in the warfare that then engulfed the world—World War II.[8]

The war was the last of a long series of foreign invasions that started in the 1840s with the Opium Wars. . . . China's encounter with imperialism started with Western aggression, but the Japanese invasion and occupation almost a century later were by far the greatest foreign assaults that China suffered in her modern history. The ultimate external assault on China came not from the West, but from an Asian country, part of the world that China had dominated so long herself.[9]

The Nanjing Atrocities will follow Facing History and Ourselves' approach to the study of history—our scope and sequence.[10] The first chapter of the book explores the relationship between society and the individual. It asks readers to explore the ways culture and history affect the development of our identities and subsequently how individuals see themselves and others as a result. Author Gish Jen explores the cultural differences between the East and the West, and considers the influences of family and identity on the way individuals see themselves in relation to their community and nation.

Chapters Two and Three focus on the historical and cultural context of two nations most directly involved in the Nanjing Atrocities, China and Japan. Readings in these chapters explore the way these two traditional empires evolved to modern nations and the way that different leaders in different times thought about who belonged and who did not, and ultimately look at the conflict that arose between Chinese nationalism and Japanese imperialism. These chapters also consider the particular forces shaping one's national identity, the effects of these influences, and consequently how countries understood one another as a result. From there, exploring the political motivations underlying such decisions can follow in a more grounded historical foundation.

For Japan, nation building began with the end of the shogunate and the beginning of the Meiji era: the restoration of imperial rule in 1868. Reinstating rule by emperor went side-by-side with adopting more modern and more "Western" models of organizing, protecting, and educating the nation. In order to survive in this increasingly global market, Japan understood it had three choices—join with the other global powers of the day, build an empire and remain sovereign, or fall under colonial rule. This perception contributed to Japan's industrial and military push as well as its motivation to embark on and be victorious in its own colonial wars, first against the Chinese during the Sino-Japanese War (1894–1895) and a decade later against Czarist Russia (1904–1905) during the Russo-Japanese War.

At the same time of Japan's ascent, in China the Qing Empire declined. The fall of Qing rule did not happen quickly but followed decades of corruption. In 1911 the Xinhai Revolution began, initiating the end of over three centuries of Qing rule and establishing the first Chinese republic. While the new Chinese republic made tremendous strides in establishing many modern reforms in education and the military, once the last emperor had abdicated, the lack of political unity remained an obstacle to unification and modernization within the nation.

Three years later in 1914, World War I began on the European continent. Japan was poised to be a dominant Asian player in the war as a result of its 40-plus years of reforms, while the new republic in China remained politically fragmented with large regions still under warlord rule. China's lack of internal political unity coupled with the challenges of its size, its many languages, and high illiteracy contributed to its inability to effectively protect and organize itself against foreign aggression. In response, China experienced both political unrest and a sudden rise of nationalism. The Nationalist Party, in power since 1912, offered one vision of China while the Chinese Communist Party, established in 1921, offered another. Several times the Nationalists and Communists attempted to create a united political coalition. But by the early 1930s, political fragmentation and disorder remained a reality in China while Japan's military strength was unrivaled in the region and expansionist ambitions continued. The first Japanese advance occurred in 1931 when Japanese imperial forces successfully occupied Manchuria and created the puppet state of Manchukuo. Six years later in July 1937, the Marco Polo Bridge Incident outside Beijing began pitting Japan's imperial forces against China's Revolutionary Army in what became, in the Chinese heartland, the start of World War II. This was soon followed by a major Japanese invasion into the Shanghai-Nanjing region.

Chapters Four and Five focus in depth on the Japanese occupation of the then capital city of Nanjing and examine the atrocities that occurred, through a range of individual perspectives. To better understand this history, the readings use a range of sources, from speeches to diplomatic correspondence, transcripts from the postwar trials, journalistic accounts, diary entries, and personal testimonies from victims, perpetrators, and witnesses. Chapter Five, in particular, focuses on rescue and resistance and the courageous efforts and dilemmas facing a handful of foreign businessmen and missionaries who chose to remain and establish a demilitarized safety zone, the Nanjing Safety Zone, for those Chinese remaining in the city.

Chapter Six addresses issues of judgment and legacy in the years directly following the end of the war. Particular attention is given to the efforts to seek legal accountability for the perpetrators in Nanjing within the larger context of the end of World War II in Japan. What would be done with the leaders of Japan, particularly the emperor? How far up the chain of command should one go in seeking to hold people accountable for the violence? How should one balance the desire to bring Japan back into the community of nations with efforts to hold political leaders responsible for the wartime atrocities?

Finally, Chapter Seven looks at the challenge of bridging the legacy of the Nanjing Atrocities with the differing memories of what occurred. This chapter also features several contemporary stories which surround the historical accounting and memory of the Nanjing Atrocities today.

Several points of clarity are important to note at the onset of this resource book. Since the war's end, the mass violence that occurred Nanjing has been referenced with many names. At the time of the postwar trials in Tokyo beginning in 1946, the events were called the "Rape of Nanking." But mass rape was sadly only one of the crimes committed to demoralize, terrorize, and instill fear in the populace. The "Nanjing Massacre" has also served as a term of reference but again, massacre of civilians and prisoners of war was only one of the crimes. In order to avoid reducing the magnitude of the tragedy, this resource will adopt what York University historian Professor Bob Tadashi Wakabayashi recommends as a more accurate term of reference: atrocity. He states that by understanding the events from late 1937 through early 1938 collectively as atrocities, we avoid reducing the violence to one crime alone. Instead "the Atrocity" or in this resource the "Nanjing Atrocities" will be the term chosen to comprise the range of violence and brutality that occurred during this period of time. According to Professor Wakabayashi, "These comprised large-scale violent, inhumane acts including, but not limited to, rape, pillage, torture, arson, mass murders of prisoners of war (POWs) and civilians, and air raids on urban population centers."[12]

Another critical point that remains controversial concerns the numbers killed during the initial occupation of the city and the months that followed. To date no definitive consensus has been reached among scholars of this history on exact numbers of individuals killed or raped during the period of time from December 13, 1937 through March 1938. Depending upon how one defines the event, including the time period, the geography covered, and who is included as a victim, scholars have put forth a victim count just shy of 200,000 to upward of 300,000, which is the number carved on the wall of the Nanjing Memorial Hall Museum in Nanjing.[12] With evidence destroyed during and after the war, precise records of numbers killed may never be fully verifiable. However this ongoing uncertainty should not minimize the fact that large scale atrocities did occur and need to be recognized and acknowledged.

At the end of World War II there was great hope that out of the devastation from two world wars during the first decades of the twentieth century, a new era would begin with a blossoming of democracy and respect for human rights. By 1948 the world had learned of the countless acts of crimes against peace and war crimes during World War II, both in East Asia and in Europe. The war crimes trials at the International Military Tribunal of the Far East in Tokyo and those held in Germany were attempts by the international community to hold leaders accountable for the brutal war crimes and aggressive war waged with the hope of future prevention.[13] For people like Ben Ferencz, a veteran of battle himself, such high hopes remain unfulfilled to this day.

Human rights scholar and author Ian Buruma reminds us that mass violence is not inevitable: "There are no dangerous peoples; there are only dangerous situations, which are the result, not of laws of nature or history, or of national character, but of political arrangements. To be sure, these arrangements are affected by cultural and historical circumstances, but they are never determined by them."[14]

For Teachers: Using *The Nanjing Atrocities: Crimes of War*

Chinese Names and Places

Pinyin is the internationally recognized romanization system used today for Chinese. However, many of the readings and quotes throughout this resource predate the use of pinyin and use various alternate romanization schemes. For consistency, the romanizations from our readings are often used in the text. When multiple romanizations of the same Chinese word are presented, the alternative spelling is presented in parentheses: for example, Nanjing (Nanking) or General Tang Shengzhi (Tang Sheng-chih) Note that in Chinese names, the surname is presented first.

Japanese Names

As is the convention in East Asia, this resource will place the Japanese surname before the given name.

Overview of Chapter

Each chapter includes a historical overview framing the larger history of the readings included. This section also suggests chapter specific questions for both educator and student to consider.

Using Primary Source Documents

Primary source documents are included throughout this resource in order to build historical context and to facilitate deep historical inquiry. The primary sources selected have previously been translated into English. You will also notice that specific sources have been identified for close reading exercises.

Historical Maps

A selection of historical maps were created specifically to enrich teachers and students experience with this resource and to further build historical investigations. These maps will include both Chinese and Japanese names.

Deepening Historical Knowledge Online

At the Nanjing Atrocities website (www.facinghistory.org/nanjing-atrocities) educators and students will discover a robust collection of educational materials and media assets to further supplement the Nanjing Atrocities. These will include:

- *Connection Questions:* Following each reading are text based questions, discussion questions and writing prompts.

- *Video Resources:* To deepen the teacher's and student's historical understanding of the time period covered, a rich collection of classroom accessible videos have been created.

- *Image Galleries:* Image galleries provide visual touch points for use in the classroom.

- *Lesson Pathways:* The Nanjing Atrocity resource can be used in multiple disciplines and adopted into many educational environments. The Lesson Pathways section provides an interdisciplinary collection of lesson activities to greater facilitate the integration of this resource into secondary and higher education settings.

---

2   Daqing Yang, "Diary of a Japanese Army Medical Doctor, 1937," *Researching Japanese War Crimes: Introductory Essays* (Washington, DC: National Archives and Records Administration, 2006), ix, accessed May 23, 2014, http://www.archives.gov/iwg/japanese-war-crimes/introductory-essays.pdf.

3 Nanking was the spelling of the city at the time of its capture. For this resource we will use the current romanization of the city, Nanjing.

4 Huang Meizhen, *The Japanese and Puppet Plunder and Control of the Occupied Areas of Central China* (Beijing, 2004), 36.

5 Rana Mitter (professor, Oxford University), interview with the author, March 11, 2014.

6 Ibid.

7 Rana Mitter, Forgotten *Ally: China's World War II, 1937–1945* (Boston: Houghton Mifflin Harcourt, 2013), 5. While exact numbers are difficult to ascertain, Mitter quotes upward of 80–100 million Chinese who were displaced as a result of the Japanese occupation during the years 1937 to 1945.

8 Diana Lary, "Introduction: The Context of the War," in *China At War,* ed. Stephen R. MacKinnon, Diana Lary, and Ezra F. Vogel (Stanford: Stanford University Press, 2007), 1.

9 Diana Lary, *The Chinese People at War: Human Suffering and Social Transformation, 1937–1945* (Cambridge: Cambridge University Press, 2010), 1.

10 The term scope and sequence is used to describe a journey of discovery about oneself and others that is a key component of our pedagogy. It is a journey of investigation into some of the most terrible atrocities in human history and some of the most appalling examples of collective violence in our world today. It is also a journey into some of the most extraordinary examples of human courage and compassion.

11 Bob Tadashi Wakabayashi, "The Messiness of History," in *The Nanjing Atrocity 1937–38: Complicating the Picture,* ed. Bob Tadashi Wakabayashi (New York: Berghahn Books, 2007), 16.

12 Bob Tadashi Wakabayashi, ed., *The Nanjing Atrocity 1937–38: Complicating the Picture* (New York: Berghahn Books, 2007), 384. Some of the most contentious discussion about the Nanjing Atrocties remains embroiled on who should be included in the victim count. This resource will not examine the victim count in detail. Myron Cramer, the sole American prosecutor at the Tokyo Trials concluded after the trial that between 260,000-300,000 Chinese civilians were massacred in Nanjing. Fred L. Borch, "Sitting in Judgment: Myron C. Cramer's Experiences in the Trials of German Saboteurs and Japanese War Leaders," Prologue Magazine 41, Summer (2009): 34-40, accessed February 11, 2014, http://www.loc.gov/rr/frd/Military_Law/pdf/Sitting-in-Judgment.pdf.

13 The charter for the International Military Tribunal (IMT) at Nuremberg was signed on August 8, 1945, and on January 19, 1946, for the International Military Tribunal for the Far East (IMFTE) in Tokyo. For more information on the IMT see http://avalon.law.yale.edu/subject_menus /imt.asp#proc. For information on IMFTE see http://lib.law.virginia.edu/imtfe/.

14 Ian Buruma, *The Wages of Guilt: Memories of War in Germany and Japan* (New York: Farrar, Straus and Giroux, 1994), 295.

CHAPTER 1

IDENTITY, HISTORY, AND CULTURE

The readings in Chapter One explore individual voices of Chinese and Japanese people as they consider the impact history and culture have had on their sense of belonging. In doing so, they offer insights into the way different people think about their sense of agency—their ability to act and make choices that could influence the world around them. These readings also introduce ideas for students to consider as they learn the history of China and Japan leading up to the outbreak of World War II in 1937 and through its conclusion in 1945.

The readings ask students to consider the following questions:

- What factors influence how we see ourselves?
- What role does a nation's history play in shaping the way people see themselves and the way they see others?
- How does culture affect this process?
- How do all of these facets of identity influence the decisions individuals make?

For media and classroom materials such as discussion questions and additional primary sources, visit www.facinghistory.org/nanjing-atrocities.

INTRODUCTION

When you look at a mountain from different sides,
one side looks like rolling hills and the other side
looks like rugged peaks.

—CHINESE POET SU TUNG-PO, 1036–1101

We begin to learn our culture—the ways of our society—just after birth. This process is called socialization and it involves far more than schooling. It influences our values—what we consider right and wrong and how we understand ourselves in the world we live in. Family life, religious traditions, and beliefs, as well as our ethnic heritage and geography, all contribute to the way we know ourselves and others.

Knowing the history of where we live, "our past," deeply matters as well. Chapter One of *The Nanjing Atrocities: Crimes of War* introduces the experiences of individuals seeking to understand themselves within two neighboring countries and cultures, China and Japan. For centuries these countries exchanged language, ideas, and culture quite harmoniously, albeit in some matter of isolation. During an era of empire building and growing nationalism around the globe, individual Chinese and Japanese sought to find a place in their rapidly changing nation and world. Beginning in the mid-nineteenth century, the exchange turned increasingly competitive and hostile as each nation sought to survive, as well as ascend, as the leading power in Asia. That hostility contributed to the Japanese invasion of China during World War II and the Nanjing Atrocities.

Author Iris Chang believed that it was not just her own Chinese-American identity that would benefit from a reckoning with the wartime atrocities in Nanjing (Nanking). She believed a confrontation with this period in history would be helpful for both China and Japan. While some scholars were critical of her approach, she explained her thinking in the introduction to her book:

> In recent years sincere attempts to have Japan face up to the consequences of its actions have been labeled "Japan bashing." It is important to establish that I will not be arguing that Japan was the sole imperialist force in the world, or even in Asia, during the first third of the century. China itself tried to extend its influence over its neighbors and even entered into an agreement with Japan to

Ullstein Bild/The Granger Collection

Japanese troops march through a combat zone in China, September 1937.

delineate areas of influence on the Korean peninsula, much as the European powers divided up the commercial rights to China in the last century.

Even more important, it does a disservice not only to the men, women, and children whose lives were taken at Nanking but to the Japanese people as well to say that any criticism of Japanese behavior at a certain time and place is criticism of the Japanese as a people. This book is not intended as a commentary on the Japanese character or on the genetic makeup of a people who would commit such acts. It is about the power of cultural forces either to make devils of us all, to strip away that thin veneer of social restraint that makes humans humane, or to reinforce it. Germany today is a better place because Jews have not allowed that country to forget what it did nearly sixty years ago. The American South is a better place for its acknowledgement of the evil of slavery and the one hundred years of Jim Crowism that followed emancipation. Japanese culture will not move forward until it too admits not only to the world but to itself how improper were its actions just half a century ago.[1]

---

1 Iris Chang, *The Rape of Nanking: The Forgotten Holocaust of World War II* (New York: Penguin Books, 1997), 13–14.

CONNECTING TO OUR PAST

THE PAST

I have supposed my past is a part of myself.
As my shadow appears whenever I'm in the sun
the past cannot be thrown off and its weight
must be borne, or I will become another man.

But I saw someone wall his past into a garden
whose produce is always in fashion.
If you enter his property without permission
he will welcome you with a watchdog or a gun.

I saw someone set up his past as a harbor.
Wherever it sails, his boat is safe—
if a storm comes, he can always head for home.
His voyage is the adventure of a kite.

I saw someone drop his past like trash.
He buried it and shed it altogether.
He has shown me that without the past
one can also move ahead and get somewhere.

Like a shroud my past surrounds me,
but I will cut it and stitch it,
to make good shoes with it,
shoes that fit my feet.[2]

Connecting to our past can shape how we understand ourselves today.
The stories passed down from our parents or the relationships we have
with places, people, or culture can deeply influence our perspectives and
how we weigh decisions. The context in which we understand our past is
also critically important.

Chinese writer Jin Xuefei, who now writes under the pen name of Ha Jin, was born in 1956 and came of age during the tumultuous time of the Cultural Revolution.[3] In his poem "The Past," Jin writes of his connection with his past and with his home country of China. In 1986 Jin Xuefei came to the United States to complete his PhD. Following the Tiananmen Square protests in 1989, he decided to remain in the US with his wife and son.

Today Ha Jin consciously writes only in English as a way for him to "[create] a kind of distance . . . [and] write more objectively."[4] In 1999 he received the National Book Award for his novel *Waiting* and in 2002 he joined the English Department at Boston University as a full professor. In 2012 Ha Jin's novel *Nanjing Requiem* was published, which is based upon the lives of several individuals who survived the Nanjing Atrocities.

Charlene Wang, a Chinese American born in Hong Kong in the 1960s who now resides in New York City, shares another connection to her past more directly related to the Japanese occupation of China in the winter of 1937:

> My mother was born on December 14, 1937 in Guangdong as the Sino-Japanese war ravaged China and the Nanjing Atrocities were in full swing. Her childhood was to be shaped by the 8 years of war. The world was an unsafe place as the family suffered the death of her father as they fled as refugees to Hong Kong. Her memories as a little girl were that of starving people on the side of roads and frightening encounters with Japanese soldiers on the street. Her family lost most of the wealth they had and she and her 6 siblings were raised by her mother under these dire circumstances.
>
> The trauma of these early years set her in a state of depression that she could not shake off for the rest of her life. She had trouble being optimistic or hopeful, as the uncertainties of life were just too scary. Little did I know as a kid that these frames of reference could be passed on to the next generation. In turn, recollections of my childhood years bring back feelings of fearfulness and uncertainty even though there was no doubt about my mother's love. We were always told to be ready in case our world should collapse at any time. There was no protection from the elements that we could not control.

My mother has long passed away, but the reverberations of that war are still affecting my life as I know it. As I raise strong daughters of my own, I try to rediscover the little girl in me that never felt carefree. I have to reassure myself that the world is indeed safe, that life has a way of always moving towards a better place as long as hope is in the human spirit.[5]

---

2 Ha Jin, *Facing Shadows* (New York: Hanging Loose Press, 1996), 63.
3 See Facing History and Ourselves' study guide *Teaching "Red Scarf Girl"* to learn more about the Cultural Revolution.
4 "Writing without Borders: Chris GoGwilt interviews Ha Jin," *Guernica*, January 14, 2007, http://www.guernicamag.com/interviews/post-2/.
5 Charlene Wang, email to author, November 6, 2013.

READING 2

TO CARRY HISTORY

How does history impact the way we see ourselves and others? American author and civil rights activist James Baldwin often wrote about the way that the past impacted the present. He explained that:

> For history, as nearly no one seems to know, is not merely something to be read. And it does not refer merely, or even principally, to the past. On the contrary, the great force of history comes from the fact that we carry it within us, are unconsciously controlled by it in many ways, and history is literally present in all that we do. It could scarcely be otherwise, since it is to history that we owe our frames of reference, our identities, and our aspirations.

> And it is with great pain and terror that one begins to realize this. In great pain and terror, one begins to assess the history which has placed one where one is, and formed one's point of view. In great pain and terror, because, thereafter, one enters into battle with that historical creation, oneself, and attempts to recreate oneself according to a principle more humane and more liberat-

ing, one begins the attempt to achieve a level of personal maturity and freedom which robs history of its tyrannical power, and also changes history.

But, obviously, I am speaking as an historical creation which has had bitterly to contest its history, to wrestle with it and finally accept it, in order to bring myself out of it. [6]

Chinese American author Iris Chang carried her family's difficult history and heritage with her and it deeply shaped her professional life and her identity as an adult woman. In the introduction to her 1997 best-selling book *The Rape of Nanking*, she writes about the way she first learned about the atrocities:

I first learned about the Rape of Nanking when I was a little girl. The stories came from my parents, who had survived years of war and revolution before finding a serene home as professors in a midwestern American college town. They had grown up in China in the midst of World War II and after the war fled with their families, first to Taiwan and finally to the United States to study at Harvard and pursue academic careers in science. For three decades they lived peacefully in the academic community of Champaign-Urbana, Illinois, conducting research in physics and microbiology.

But they never forgot the horrors of the Sino-Japanese War, nor did they want me to forget. They particularly did not want me to forget the Rape of Nanking. Neither of my parents witnessed it, but as young children they had heard the stories, and they were passed down to me. . . . Their voices quivered in outrage, my parents characterized the Great Nanking Massacre, or *Nanjing Datusha,* as the single most diabolical incident committed by the Japanese in a war that killed more than 10 million Chinese people.

Throughout my childhood Nanjing Datusha remained buried in the back of my mind as a metaphor for unspeakable evil. But the event lacked human details and human dimensions. It was also difficult to find the line between myth and history. While still in grade school I searched the local public libraries to see what I could learn about the massacre, but nothing turned up. That struck me as odd. If the Rape of Nanking was truly so gory, one of the worst episodes of human barbarism in world history, as my parents insisted, then why hadn't someone written a book about it?[7]

---

6 James Baldwin, "Unnameable Objects, Unspeakable Crimes," Blackstate.com, accessed January 1, 2014, http://blackstate.com/baldwin1.html.
7 Iris Chang, *The Rape of Nanking: The Forgotten Holocaust of World War II* (New York: Penguin Books, 1997), 7–8.

READING 3

CULTURE AND IDENTITY: EAST AND WEST

Cultural psychologists Hazel Rose Markus and Alana Conner studied different ways of being, or what they term the *independent* and *interdependent* selves. Markus and Conner looked at a range of environments, from classroom participation to ways of parenting, between students from Eastern and Western cultures. While there are important variations and distinct differences within these regions and cultures, Markus and Conner shared some general observations:

> For many East Asians, and their children growing up in the West, listening, following the "right" way, fitting in, and keeping calm are not odd classroom behaviors; they are the very route to being a good person—a good interdependent self, Eastern style. But for their Western classmates and teachers, speaking up, choosing your own way, standing out, and getting excited are also ways of being a good person—but in this case, a good independent self, Western style. . . .
>
> Independent European-American parents and teachers say that a student should first choose what she wants to do, and then do it her own way. In the West, choice is perhaps the most important

act because it lets people realize all five facets of independence. Choice allows people to express their individuality and unique preferences, influence their environments, exercise their free will, and assert their equality.

But interdependent parents . . . lay out a different agenda: I show my child the right thing to do, and then help her *do it the right way.* In the East, following the right way is a central act because it lets people realize all five facets of interdependence: relating to others, discovering your similarities, adjusting yourself to expectations and the environment, rooting yourself into networks and traditions, and understanding your place in the larger world.[8]

Author Gish Jen feels the tension between cultures in very personal ways. In an interview conducted for Harvard University Press, Jen reflects on her individualistic, or independent, self that dominates in the West, especially America, and her collectivist, or interdependent, self that dominates in the East, including China. Jen first came to understanding this continuum in herself after reading her own father's autobiography:

I was not a narrative native. We didn't do this in my family. I was not asked what do you want, as if what I wanted was a very important thing or what do I like. I was not encouraged to think of myself as a unique individual whose uniqueness was really a very important thing. Quite the contrary. And so therefore it wasn't until I started reading that I realized that in the West . . . this was a foundational idea. That it started with pictures of you as a baby. I don't have any pictures of myself one minute after I was born. In fact, I have very few pictures of myself and there are few stories also about me as a child. As I started to get interested in this whole question of narrative difference, which is tied to a difference of self and difference in perception, I happened to start to work on my father's autobiography that he had written when he was 85.

When I first looked at it, it just made no sense at all to me. Here was this thing that was supposed to be an autobiography about his growing up in China, and yet he, himself, did not appear until page 8. This autobiography did not start with "I was born in such and such a year." No, no, no. It started way, way before that, thousands of years before that, and went through the generations. By the time my father gets to his birth, he mentions his birthday in parentheses, in conjunction with another event. I remember reading that and thinking, "How very interesting." I could both see that it was "weird" from a Western narrative point of view and yet of course there was something about it that was incredibly familiar to me. I understood this. I understood this diminishment of the self. One thing was something I knew with my left hand and another was something I knew with my right.[9]

In her book *Tiger Writing: Art, Culture, and the Interdependent Self,* Jen expands on the differences between the independent and interdependent self even further:

[T]he "independent," individualistic self stresses uniqueness, defines itself via inherent attributes such as its traits, abilities, values, and preferences, and tends to see things in isolation. The second—the "interdependent," collectivist self—stresses commonality, defines itself via its place, roles, loyalties, and duties, and tends to see things in context. Naturally, between these two very different self-construals [self-definitions] lies a continuum along which most people are located, and along which they may move, too, over the course of a moment. Culture is not fate; it only offers templates, which individuals can finally accept, reject, or modify, and do.[10]

---

8   Hazel Rose Markus and Alana Conner, *Clash!: 8 Cultural Conflicts That Make Us Who We Are* (New York: Hudson Street Press, 2013), 5-9.
9   "Gish Jen, Tiger Writing," YouTube video, 3:35, posted by "Harvard University Press," November 14, 2012, http://www.youtube.com/watch?v=ZLi08sq6qtM.
10 Gish Jen, *Tiger Writing: Art, Culture and the Interdependent Self* (Cambridge: Harvard University Press, 2013), 2–7.

WOMEN, TRADITION, AND SOCIAL CUSTOM

Social customs and practices tied to gender roles deeply shape our personal identity. They can also reflect the values and traditions within our culture. While gender roles continue to change over time, in historically traditional nations around the world, gender roles are deeply ingrained.

In China and Japan, shifts in gender roles began to significantly shift around the turn of the twentieth century when some women gained greater access to education. It was in this environment when women were exposed to opportunities to challenge and change their lives for the first time. One woman who reflects this dramatic shift in Chinese society was Qiu Jin. Born in 1875 in the city of Shaoxing in Zhejiang Province, Qiu Jin was the eldest daughter of a well-educated family. Her privileged childhood distinguished her from many Chinese girls during this time, but the choices she made during her life serve as a window into the dramatic social and political changes unfolding throughout China at the turn of the twentieth century.

Traditionally Chinese girls of this era, particularly those raised in privileged households, would be separated from boys at an early age. Girls were schooled in subjects such as cooking, embroidery, and other traditional arts, all with the intention of fulfilling their primary role in society as mothers and wives. In contrast, boys would be schooled in classic literature, history, and philosophy, aspiring to live as scholars, merchants, or possibly advisers in the imperial court. Qiu Jin's parents were both highly educated. They chose to defy tradition and provide all their children an equal education by hiring private tutors.

Qiu Jin in traditional male clothing

Within her home Qiu Jin studied Chinese classics alongside martial arts. She also discovered her gift in composing poetry. While her private education within her home opened up the world of learning, Qiu Jin still remained a

Xia Gongran/Xinhua Press/Corbis

young woman coming of age in a country with many long-standing traditions. One inescapable custom that visibly marked a Han woman, and one that was inflicted only on upper-class Han women of the period, was foot-binding. Girls would begin this process sometimes as early as 4 or 5 years old whereby their feet would be broken and bound in tight bandages for the next 10 to 15 years. The ultimate goal was to shape a "delicate" foot of three inches long that would fit into small slippers. This small size was deemed a true sign of beauty and high social status. It was also an important attribute for any successful marriage. In the privacy of her writing, Qiu Jin shares her experience and views of this custom in an excerpt from *Stones of the Jingwei Bird*:

> Bound feet have always been a disgrace! You torture your own body to make lotus-petal feet. With such painful broken bones and withered muscles, how can you walk anywhere freely? Because of these feet, we become frail and weak and even catch tuberculosis. How can we blame this on anything but our ignorance? We're unable to fend for ourselves since we can't even walk. . . . From morning until night, we sit still like statues, and if some calamity strikes, we're like prisoners who want to escape but can't move. . . .

Figure 1   **Figure 2**

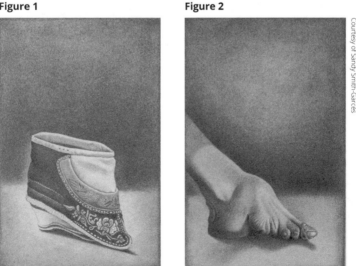

Courtesy of Sandy Smith-Garcés

These drawings depict the ancient Chinese tradition of foot-binding, showing a delicate, tiny shoe in Figure 1, and the woman's foot that has been disfigured to fit inside in Figure 2.

bands fancy little feet, they tie their bindings even tighter, into three inches which they boast are like lotus petals. When they walk, it's like a willow branch swaying in the wind, which they think is so attractive. . . .

What's the use of a pair of pointy feet? One day, civilization will spread throughout our land, And people will absolutely spurn little feet and regard them as a thing for animals.[11]

At the age of nineteen Qiu Jin obeyed her father's wishes and married the son of a wealthy merchant. The marriage was an unhappy one and by 1904, amidst the Russo-Japanese War, Qiu Jin arranged care for her children and ventured to Japan for further studies at the Jissen School for Women. By this time Qiu Jin had become a more vocal supporter of women's rights in China and a more prolific poet. At the time more than 10,000 Chinese students, men and women, were studying in Japan, which offered greater access to higher education for all students and had embraced greater educational reforms throughout the country. Some of the Chinese students coming to Japan were politically active in reform movements in China and, like Qiu Jin, sought out revolutionary political activities and organizations during this period.

Upon her return to China, Qiu Jin's commitment to political and social change for women in China was firm and she composed the following poem:

MAN JIANG HONG (SECOND VERSE)

Incessantly I've longed to ignite
The incense of freedom.
When, when can we avenge
Our country's humiliation?
My peers, let us
Exert ourselves as of today.
Peace and security for our race is our goal.
The prosperity we seek should exceed our own
showy jewelry and clothes.
Above all, the three-inch bow-slippers
have been all too disabling.
They must go.[12]

This commitment to political change was also the cause of her death. Once her plans for an uprising against the Qing court were discovered, Qiu Jin was executed by Manchu troops on July 12, 1907.

11 Amy D. Dooling and Kristina M. Torgeson, eds., *Writing Women in Modern China: An Anthology of Women's Literature from the Early Twentieth Century* (New York: Columbia University Press, 1998), 75-76.

12 Kang-I Sun Chang and Haun Saussy, eds., *Women Writers of Traditional China: An Anthology of Poetry and Criticism* (Stanford: Stanford University Press, 1999), 653–54.

READING 5

HONOR

Cultural values and practices can also be inherited and reflect the social hierarchy and interactions expected within a family, a community, or a nation over generations. In some societies, such as China and Japan, the value associated with honor is one such example. Honor can be both very personal and very universal. It can entail an individual's practice of "saving face," or upholding a place of status and power by following an entrenched set of cultural norms as well as honoring one's family, or filial piety. In practice, filial piety means respecting your elders, listening to your parents or guardians, and abiding by the rules established within your family.

Honor can also reach beyond your personal and familial life and include practices associated with places such as your nation. This could mean upholding your nation's laws, participating in national rituals such as raising a flag or singing an anthem, exercising your rights such as voting, following your leader's policies and values, or serving in the military.

In both Chinese and Japanese culture, honor remains a very important value and finds expression in many ways—personally, culturally, and nationally. In China, filial piety is one of the most enduring. For centuries, "The 24 Paragons of Filial Piety," a collection of Confucian parables written by fourteenth-century scholar Guo Jujing, was taught to convey moral values through stories.

Chinese author Yu Hua recalls reading these stories as a young boy coming of age in Communist China at a time when the official policy was to ban any materials that contained such content.[13] Yu Hua never forgot the lessons of one story in particular:

> In the Jin dynasty there was an exemplary son named Wu Meng,
> born to a family too poor to own a mosquito net. When the sting
> of mosquitoes made it difficult for his father to sleep, Wu Meng
> took off his shirt and sat by his parents' bed, letting the mosqui-
> toes bite him and never once swatting them away, so that they
> had no reason to leave him and bite his parents.[14]

In Japan, honor was associated with the high-status role of the samurai warriors. Samurai warriors served the shogun, who for centuries held the highest standing in society. Samurai followed a strict order of rules known as "The Way of the Warrior," or Bushido code, in which honor was one of the essential edicts to follow.

Felice Beato

This photograph shows Samurai from the 1860s. The Samurai warrior was a noble position that embodied the important Japanese cultural value of honor.

In the translated story below, we read of a young Japanese boy's impression of the idea and practice of honor through his father's life yet seen through the eyes of a young samurai boy:

> Suzuki Tarō was born a samurai in 1832. His father had been a samurai. His sons would be samurai. By then, the government of the *shogun*, or military governor based in Tokyo (then called Edo) had been in power for more than 200 years. It was shogunal policy to minimize change, to freeze Japanese society into a rigid social class structure. For this reason, little in Japan in 1832 was unpredictable.
>
> To grow up as a samurai meant learning the military arts, so Tarō spent many hours wrestling and fencing and riding and studying archery. But Japan had enjoyed nearly 200 years of peace, and in peacetime one needed other skills as well. So Tarō studied reading and writing and, as he grew older, began to read the Chinese classics.
>
> There were many things Tarō was not allowed to do simply because he was a samurai. For instance, at home he never saw a *samisen*, perhaps the most important musical instrument of this day. Why not? Because the music of the samisen was unworthy for samurai to hear. Townsmen, maybe, but not samurai.
>
> Tarō's family and almost all the other samurai families lived near the castle of the lord. The castle sat high on a hill with a moat, thick walls, and a tall tower. The lord himself and his two most trusted advisers lived in the castle. The rest of the samurai lived in the houses spread out around the lower slopes of the hill. The most important samurai families lived closest to the castle walls. Tarō's family was not very important and therefore lived down the hill, closer to the temples and stores of the town.
>
> As a samurai, Tarō was free to walk through the townsmen's quarter, and he did so often. . . . But townsmen were not so free to wander. They had to stay out of the samurai quarter, except when they had a specific reason for entering. . . . As Tarō walked on past the *tatami* [a Japanese mat] makers, he came to a border area between town and country. . . . Beyond the border area lay

Matsumoto Castle served as the home of the lord and the center of Japanese social structure.

the countryside, a checkerboard of small rice paddies with a tiny farm village every mile or so. On a fine June day, Tarō would find the fields full of farmers—men, women, and children—knee deep in mud, transplanting rice seedlings to be harvested in November. . . . Tarō thanked his lucky stars that he was a samurai when he saw how these farmers labored.

Tarō's father served his lord in the capacity of overseer of four farm villages, so Tarō had heard considerable discussion at home of the farmers and their problems. In theory, the farmers were a prized class: after all, they produced the rice crop that fed Japan and supported the government of the samurai. But Tarō knew that reality was something different. Taxes on farmers were very high. And last year had been a bad crop year: heavy rains had come just before the harvest and much of the crop had rotted in the fields.

Indeed Tarō remembered his father's anxiety during the winter, when one group of farmers had seemed on the point of lodging formal protest with the lord. In a year of bad crops, they wanted the tax rate lowered. Tarō's father had met with them and assuaged their anger, and the formal protest had not been made. That was certainly a good thing for Tarō's father, and perhaps also for the farmers.

Had the protest been made, Tarō's father might well have lost his job, been disgraced, and perhaps even driven to commit suicide as atonement. The lord expected his officials to control all matters within their jurisdiction. The fact that a group of farmers took political action—whatever the merits of their case—was enough to indicate that the official in charge was not fulfilling his duty. The farmers leading the protest might have been executed or deported, even if the lord determined their protest was justified, for such unauthorized political action was a challenge to the stability of the social order. Farmers, after all, were farmers. They grew rice, paid taxes, and obeyed the directions of their natural superiors. Samurai were samurai. Samurai ruled. There could be no mixing of functions.[15]

---

13 At the time when these stories were authored (fourteenth century), China's imperial dynasties stressed the importance of being loyal to one's ruler and dutiful to one's parents. In contrast, when the Communists came to power in 1949, they stressed loyalty only to the party.
14 Yu Hua, "When Filial Piety Is the Law," *New York Times*, July 7, 2013, accessed January 1, 2014, http://www.nytimes.com/2013/07/08/opinion /yu-when-filial-piety-is-the-law.html.
15 Miyabe Miyuki, *All She Was Worth*, trans. Alfred Birnbaum (New York: Houghton Mifflin, 1996), 101–06.

READING 6

LEARNING ABOUT DIFFERENCE

Michael David Kwan has strong memories of being excluded as a child. He was born on March 6, 1934, in Beijing to a Swiss-born mother and a Chinese father who held a high-ranking administrative position in one of China's major rail companies. When Kwan was two his mother ran off to Shanghai, leaving his father to raise his son alone. Several years later his father remarried another Westerner, this time a British-born woman living in China named Ellen. Under her care, Kwan spent the first 12 years of his childhood sheltered behind the privileged walls of the Legations Court at Beijing and in the British Concession in Tianjin, largely separated from everyday life and the everyday people of China.

During this period in China the expatriate and wealthy Chinese community was bound by a social hierarchy comprised of Chinese, foreigners/Westerners, and what was pejoratively called "mixed-blood Eurasians." They understood one another according to a prescribed ranking deeply rooted in their family ancestry. In China, Eurasians like Kwan were placed in the lowest category, and Chinese were at the top. At school Kwan was called a "half-caste" or "half-breed" by his peers, mocked because of his light brown hair and his "foreign nose."

Years later in 2000 Kwan recalls these early memories of dealing with feelings of difference:

> The first day, my father delivered me to school. The headmaster was expecting us. [He] propelled me into a classroom where thirty-six boys were seated at double desks. . . . On the back wall were pictures of Wang Jingwei [the Chinese leader who led the puppet government in Nanjing after the occupation] and of Tojo, prime minister of Japan. Over their heads were the crossed flags of the puppet Nanking government, five horizontal bars—red, yellow, blue, white and black—and Japan's red sun in a white sky. A banner that read "The Great and Glorious United Asia" was strung across the top. . . .

> The headmaster cleared his throat, folded his hands across his chest, and intoned, like an actor onstage, "This is your new classmate." He had already forgotten my name and had to consult a slip of paper tucked in his sleeve. "Kwan's father is an important man, so . . . what do you say?"

> "Welcome to our class!" piped the children. The teacher glowered at me behind his back. . . .

> I wandered into a corridor where the other boys horsed about. The only light came from two grimy windows, one at either end. The rest of the corridor was in permanent twilight. The air stank of the latrine down the hall. The floor was slick with spit and snot. The dingy walls, dark with soot and cobwebs near the ceiling, were covered with graffiti at eye level.

"There's the new one!" someone shouted.

Leering faces surrounded me.

"A foreigner!"

"Naw! Just a stinking half-caste!"

"His father's an important man!"

Someone hawked and spat in contempt.

They joked about my hair, my nose, jeering and jabbing at me. The teachers monitoring the corridor averted their eyes.

The bell finally rang, ending recess. The bird-like teacher reappeared and began a most curious lesson. In a strident voice she told the class, "Foreigners are evil. Especially the British, who poisoned our bodies with opium, and the Americans, who ruined our minds with their god and other silly ideas!"

The class chorused, "Evil! Evil! Evil!" as she beat time with her willow switch.

I found myself shouting with them in spite of myself, until the teacher's stick cracked down on my desk. There was an instant silence. Her eyes narrowed. "What are you yelling about?"

I was bewildered. The tip of her stick flicked my hair.

"What color is it?" she sneered.

"The color of s__t," someone said from the back of the room.

Everyone laughed. The teacher bared her teeth in a grin, and the tip of her stick travelled down my forehead to rest on the bridge of my nose.

"*Yang bi zhi,*" she spat, and "Foreign nose" became my nickname. My formal education had begun. . . .

My fellow students were all Chinese Catholics, supposedly from a better class than those I encountered at the school in Beijing. Xenophobia was just as strong, however, and often abetted by teachers. . . . Religion and war propaganda were spouted in the same breath. God's love and mercy seemed impotent in the face of the casual killings that sake-crazed Japanese soldiers indulged in daily in the streets. . . .

After the school in Beijing, I was leery about reaching out to other boys. I did make one friend, though, quite by chance. I had been made to kneel on the playground all afternoon for punishment for something or other. . . . A few days later, during recess, as I leaned against the building warming myself in the sunlight, trying to be inconspicuous, someone leaned against the wall beside me. I looked cautiously out of the corner of my eye. . . .

"French?" he said, barely moving his lips, meaning did I speak it.

"English," I whispered back. There was a pause. He shut his eyes and faced the sun.

"I guess we're birds of a feather," he said as though he was talking to the sun. Members of minority groups have uncanny ways of recognizing each other. I felt a particular rush of warmth as though all the blood had suddenly been squeezed out of my heart. He turned back to the sun, cushioning his forehead on folded arms pressed against the wall.

"Shao," he said, addressing his shoes.

"Kwan," I replied without moving.

Shao sauntered off, hands in his pockets.

I made no effort to get to know Shao. He was always surrounded by other boys, sometimes talking earnestly, sometimes jabbering like a crazed magpie, now and then running about in a fit of sheer exuberance. I looked on, wanting to be part of the group but afraid of making a fool of myself by approaching them.

My separateness made me an easy target. Once after benediction I was swarmed. I don't quite know how it started but Shao, coming out of the cathedral, intervened in the nick of time.

"Stop it," he said, driving his fist into the back of the boy nearest him.

"What did you do that for, Shao?" the boy whined.

"He's my friend," Shao replied evenly. "Understand?"

He put his arm around my shoulders, and stood there until the others drifted off. He took me under his wing from that moment.

"To live in this place, we have to be special," Shao explained. He had a Chinese father and a Belgian mother. A survivor, he sounded older than his years.[16]

---

16 Michael David Kwan, *Things That Must Not Be Forgotten: A Childhood in Wartime China* (New York: Soho Press, 2000), 19–20, 102–03, 115–16.

READING 7

COMING OF AGE DURING WAR

How do your childhood experiences shape your identity? For Japanese author and Nobel Laureate Oe Kenzaburo, World War II remains one of these memories and became a seminal part of his identity as an author. Oe was born in January 1935 in a small rural village in what is now Ehime Prefecture on the island of Shikoku. He was the third son in a family of seven.

When World War II ended in August 1945, he writes of this moment as an "unbridgeable break" with the past. Not only did Oe's father die during the war in the Pacific, but his nation's surrender shattered his youthful innocence. He recalls his ethics teacher asking him one day at school before Japan's surrender, "What would you do if the emperor asked you to die?" "I would die sir, I would cut open my belly and die," Oe recalls dutifully replying.[17]

Years later in an essay titled "Growing Up during the Occupation" Oe Kenzaburo wrote of his coming of age at this moment in time and the dramatic impact the war had on his entire life:

When the war ended I was only ten years old, a grade-school boy in a mountain village, and I couldn't understand what the Emperor was saying over the radio when he announced that we had surrendered. The grownups sat in front of the radio and cried. I watched them from the garden, which was bathed in strong summer sunlight. The room where the grownups sat crying was dark.

Soon I got bored and went out to play. As all the adults were inside, listening to the radio, there were only children on the village road. We gathered here and there in small groups and talked.

Not one of us knew exactly what had happened. We were most intrigued by the strange and somewhat disappointing fact that the Emperor had spoken in a human voice no different than any ordinary adult's. None of us understood what he had been saying, but we had certainly heard his voice. One of my friends was even able to imitate it very cleverly. We surrounded him, a boy in grimy shorts who spoke in the Emperor's voice, and we howled with laughter. . . .

My present image of the Emperor bears no resemblance to the awe-inspiring figure I imagined when I was an indiscriminating schoolboy. I feel no particular affection for the Emperor himself or for the Imperial Household. My mother, on the other hand, if she were given the opportunity, would hurry to the great square in front of the palace to do reverence to the Emperor as though he were a god, and seems keenly interested in all the doings of the Imperial Household.

But this attitude is not unique with my mother: at least half of the Japanese people demonstrate a keen interest in the Imperial Court. The feel of deep esteem for the Emperor himself also seems to be general all over Japan. . . .

I remember seeing a picture of some grade-school children parading and flag-waving in celebration of the Crown Prince's betrothal. This crowd of young cheering faces was rather a shock for me.

What made those children parade the streets with banners in their hands? Was it the influence of their parents and teachers? Was it the Emperor worship that remains embedded in some recess of

Time & Life Pictures/Getty Images

Emperor Hirohito, the Emperor of Japan from 1926–1989, visits factory workers after World War II had ended.

the Japanese consciousness? Or was it merely an innocent love of fun and parades?

As long as every Japanese is able to formulate for himself whatever image of the Emperor he pleases, the word *symbol* will denote something wholesome. But what if the power of journalism created that parade and set those voices cheering by forcing on the children some specific image of the Emperor?

Those grade-school boys and girls were wreathed in smiles, but when we were children, we passed before the Imperial portrait with frightened faces and bowed heads.[18]

---

17 John Rodden, "The Translator as Team Player: John Nathan," in *Performing the Literary Interview: How Writers Craft Their Public Selves* (University of Nebraska Press, 2007), 145.

18 Oe Kenzaburo, "Growing Up During the Occupation," in *Sources of Japanese Tradition*, ed. Wm. Theodore de Bary, Carol Gluck, and Arthur L. Tiedemann, 2nd edition, vol. 2 (New York: Columbia University Press, 2005), 1074–75.

CHAPTER 2

EMERGING NATIONS: 1868–1911

The readings in Chapter Two explore the relationship between modern nation building and nationalism in China and Japan, from 1868–1911. The years included in this chapter begin with the Meiji era in Japan in 1868 and end with the fall of Qing rule in China in 1911. During this time period reforms in both nations contributed to forging new national identities, resulting in the growth of nationalism in China and the expansion of empire in Japan.

The readings ask students to consider the following questions:

- How do external threats shape the way leaders think about their country and its place in the world?

- How do changes in the world impact the way communities view themselves?

- What choices can leaders make to help preserve and protect their nations' place in the world?

- How do these choices affect the way people see themselves and each other in the world?

For media and classroom materials such as discussion questions and additional primary sources, visit www.facinghistory.org/nanjing-atrocities.

INTRODUCTION

Like all communities around the world, Japan and China were isolated for centuries, sometimes by choice and sometimes by geographical realities. By the nineteenth century the self-imposed isolation began to lift. Eventually these countries were more dependent on other nations as their populations increased and the need for more resources, land, and access to economic trade grew.

Growth also led to an exposure to a variety of different cultures and styles of government. At times this variety was accepted, other times it was viewed cautiously, and sometimes the very existence of the variety was seen as a threat. One response was the rise of nationalism, and another was conflict. Sociologist Theodore Abel defines *nationalism* as "a strong positive feeling for the accomplishments of the nation, its position of power, the men and institutions and the traditions which are associated with the glorified events of its history."[1] While many of the reformers in China and Japan were motivated by feelings of nationalism and a desire to have their region viewed with more respect, particularly by those in the West, nationalism can also re-inforce ideas about who belongs in that nation and who doesn't. By creating a sense of "us" (e.g., Chinese or Japanese), nationalism can create a "them" (e.g., non-Chinese or non-Japanese). In the twentieth century, such ideas of belonging to a particular nation also laid the foundation for two world wars and an escalation of mass violence of enormous scale.

As we examine the path to war, we will explore the ways in which Chinese and Japanese national movements led to the development of nation-states in the region. A nation-state is defined as a sovereign territory of land with its own political structures and geographical boundaries. Some nation-states are united by a common language, customs, and cultures while others, especially those created as a result of war or conflict, have a variety of characteristics and share only a common geography. Different types of leadership and eco-nomic structures also developed as nation-states established themselves. But order was maintained by requiring people to identify with their leader, feel loyal to him, and feel that they belonged to the newly established nation.

In China and Japan the creation of the modern nation and nationalist ideals preceded the outbreak of war in 1937. China did not begin to modernize until Qing rule was dissolved in 1911 and the first Chinese republic was established. At this time China remained fragmented and the early years of the republic remained fragile. The nation's leaders had to contend with warlords, warring political factions and a diverse and vast geographic span, which only further fragmented the nation. A strong sense of unity as a Chinese nation was just beginning.

In Japan a modern centralized government began with the Meiji era in 1868. At this time the yoke of its feudal past was discarded and the nation began to rapidly industrialize, building a modern Western-style army and reforming the education system and civic administration. Over the span of just four decades Japan transformed itself and emerged as the foremost Asian nation in the region.

This woodblock print from an unknown artist created in 1870 depicts tensions in Meiji-era Japan as new customs and ideas competed with traditional ways of life.

One force affecting the development of these two nations came from outside the region itself—the Industrial Revolution in Europe and the United States during the mid-nineteenth century. The Industrial Revolution was a period of transition where new manufacturing processes were adopted and economies moved from being predominantly agrarian-based to largely industrial and urban. The demand for manufactured goods, labor, and raw materials continued to grow and as a result, populations swelled in cities throughout the industrializing world to meet the labor demand, and new markets were needed to obtain resources and to sell goods in profitable markets.

The fuel for this industrial machine became an ideology known as imperialism. Imperialism is the expansion of a nation's power and authority by occupying new regions and markets through military force and through the spread of ideas. Imperialism creates a paternalistic relationship, or an unequal power dynamic, between the colonizer (the imperial power) and the colonized nation (the occupied country). From the mid-1800s through the beginning of World War I the "Age of Imperialism" was at its height. Imperialism was always more than about economics; it was also a cultural process.[2] Beyond an unequal economic relationship, colonial rule and trade policies facilitated the transfer of ideas between the imperial power and the less powerful state. These relationships often came with assumptions about the superiority and inferiority of cultures and religious traditions that sometimes challenged traditional ideas about power and relationships between individuals, groups, and nations.

In parts of Asia, including China and Japan, the influences and pressures of imperialism affected the efforts of modern nation building. Large numbers of American and European missionaries came to the region in an effort to spread Christianity. While some may argue that educational and medical services improved in the regions with missionary efforts, others remain steadfast that such efforts came at a cost. Before the nineteenth century, both countries flourished while remaining largely isolated from the influences of outside countries. However, in the age of empire, China's vast geography, labor, and natural resources and Japan's strategic location and military prestige made both countries highly desirable in the eyes of the West.

More specifically, by the mid-nineteenth century European demand for Chinese exports such as teas, porcelain, and silks remained high while Chinese demand for European exports such as cotton, wool, tin, lead, or furs was less profitable. This caused an imbalance of trade, particularly between Great Britain and China. To mitigate this trade imbalance Great Britain capitalized on the demand for a highly desirable, addictive, and profitable drug in China: opium.[3]

At this time the Qing Empire in China had been in power for more than two centuries. Qing power was ruled by the Manchus, an ethnic minority in China. The Qing Empire was not what we know of as China today. It had no organized, empire-wide army or navy under a centralized command. Instead regional leaders controlled their own armies and fleets. Qing rule was opposed to the trade and use of opium yet Great Britain was able to exploit desire for the opiate by aggressively pushing for its trade and importation into China. Tensions increased between the two nations, eventually resulting in the First Opium War (1839–1842), pitting the British Empire against China. Orville Schell, director of the Center on U.S.-China Relations at the Asia Society, says of this moment:

> [T]he [first] Opium War marks a moment in modern Chinese
> history when the old cycles of dynasties rising and falling really
> encountered something else, something new and that was the

West. That experience was an extremely humbling one for China
because it was defeated again and again and again. . . . The [first]
Opium War ending in 1842, was really the beginning of this very
first stressful and humiliating time when they [China] were defeated, repetitively.[4]

A decade later the Second Opium War (1856–1860) erupted among the British Empire, the French Empire, and China. While both opium wars were essentially fought over foreign trade and more open diplomatic relations with China, over time the opium wars came to be about a great deal more. When the British Empire's superior naval fleet arrived in 1842, China had little choice but to concede to the imperial power's demands. Alongside the national humiliation of defeat, a series of unfair treaties were signed between China and Western powers as a result of these wars. The "unequal treaty system" led to the Treaty of Nanking (1842) and the Treaty of Tientsin (1858). The treaties granted full civil rights to Christians within China (this was particularly important for the missionary movement), opened more Chinese ports to British merchants, permitted Chinese indentured servants to be transported on British ships, and legalized the opium trade. It also resulted in the establishment of concessions throughout China by many of the more powerful colonial nations. A concession was a territory of land that was governed and occupied by a foreign power. Concessions strengthened Western powers' economic, political, and cultural "spheres of influence," including granting foreign residents in China extraterritoriality status, or the freedom from local legal jurisdiction. This colonial domination of China, at times referred to pejoratively as the "carving up of China," impaired its political, economic, and social sovereignty for the next century.[5]

China was not alone in navigating multiple Western incursions. Up until the nineteenth century, Japan had also remained largely isolated. During the Edo period (1615–1868), the sakoku policy prevented foreigners from entering the country and punished Japanese who left the country with the penalty of death. Missionaries were barred entrance and only allowed to trade with the Chinese and Dutch.[6] When US Commodore Perry first anchored his naval vessels in 1853 in Edo Bay and then six months later with a larger and more intimidating fleet, this policy began to change. Perry's official mission was to secure several agreements that would "open up" Japan to American trade and allow for American naval ships to dock for resupply. This gunboat diplomacy was negotiated through letters delivered by Perry and addressed to the Emperor asking for access to Japan's ports in order to resupply the American ships. In actuality, Emperor Komei wielded little power while the

Tokugawa *shogun*, or commander of the force, in Edo still held onto the reigns.

Initially the requests were denied and the shogun issued an edict to "expel the barbarians." However, over a short amount of time, Japanese leaders, as Chinese leaders were doing at the same time, submitted to a series of treaties acquiescing to American demands. Japanese leadership had witnessed the consequences of China's losses following both opium wars and aimed to avoid a similar fate. Many began to view Western military methods and armaments and Western models of states' institutions as attractive and necessary for Japan to survive and advocated for such changes.

Motivated by national pride, approximately 15 years after Commodore Perry's arrival, Japanese rebels launched an overthrow of the Tokugawa shogunate who ruled Japan since 1600. For hundreds of years Japan was organized by a warrior class known as the samurai, or "one who serves." The highest leader in this social order was known as the shogun, or "commander of the force," who yielded tremendous power throughout the country. While the emperor was recognized as the official head of the country and was said to "reign, not rule," it was the shogunate who controlled the feudal lords known in Japan as the daimyos, who governed regional areas throughout the country. The daimyos were largely an inherited class of leaders, meaning a father would pass the title and the land on to his son, or a shogunate could grant the title for services rendered to him. The rebels involved in the overthrow were low-level samurai who blamed the recent incursions and treaties with the West on the entrenched power of the shogunate. They sought to halt any further weakening of Japanese power through the restoration of imperial rule. This *ishin* (Japanese for "restoration" and "renovation") gave Emperor Komei's son Mutsuhito, who was a mere 15 years old at the time of his succession, a symbolic leadership role as the newly restored ruling emperor. As the centuries of shogunate power began to be dismantled, the new emperor took the name Meiji, or "enlightened rule," and the Meiji era in Japan was initiated.

By the turn of the twentieth century both China and Japan had experienced tremendous shifts. Both felt the hand of foreign threats, and colonial pursuits and reformers within each country began to develop new ideas about what it meant to be Chinese or Japanese and what would need to be done in order to survive in this newly globalized world.

---

1   Theodore Abel, *Why Hitler Came to Power* (Prentice-Hall, 1938), 29.
2   James L. Hevia, *English Lessons: The Pedagogy of Imperialism in Nineteenth-Century China* (Durham and London: Duke University Press, 2003), 3.
3   It is important to note that by the end of the nineteenth century Chinese producers and distribu-

~~of opium largely took over the market. After the first Republic of China was established in~~ 1911, different Chinese political power bases at the time—warlord, Nationalist, Communist—all relied on the revenue from opium as a key source to support their policies. So while initially, trading opium was dominated by foreigners who bought and sold the drug while pursuing their imperial aims, eventually the Chinese themselves controlled the market and profited from its lucrative sales. Bob Tadashi Wakabayashi (professor, York University), private correspondence with the author, January 1, 2014.

4   Orville Schell, "Wealth and Power: Introduction," Asia Society video, 1:43, accessed September 1, 2013, http://sites.asiasociety.org/chinawealthpower/chapters/introduction/.

5   The full extent of the restraints were not completely abolished until January 11, 1943, when the United States and Great Britain negotiated with China new treaties based upon more reciprocal and equitable relations. The most notable exception to the seclusion policy was the continued presence of Dutch and Chinese missions in the harbor of Nagasaki.

6   By 1853 sakoku policy was dismantled and Western nations established trade routes and exploited other economic interests in the region.

READING 1

MEIJI PERIOD IN JAPAN

Knowledge shall be sought throughout the world so as to strengthen the foundations of imperial rule.

—1868 MEIJI PLEDGE

With Emperor Meiji's ascension to the throne in 1867, Japan theoretically restored power to the emperor, but because he was only 15 years old he had little governing power. Instead, the power rested with the new government consisting of a small, close-knit cabinet of advisers. This new cabinet immediately began implementing a series of reforms to both strengthen and unify Japan. One of their largest concerns was that Japan would not be able to regain its sovereignty if it did not modernize. With the recent display of the superior armament of the United States military with Commodore Perry in 1853, such concerns were not unfounded.

The goals of the early leaders of the Meiji era were ambitious, as they established new economic, political, and social institutions that governed Japan through World War II. The majority of these reforms were greatly influenced by the West, but they never deviated significantly from Japan's cultural and historical roots. Perhaps most dramatically, it abolished the old system of a social hierarchy based on inherited status. For example, samurai, who historically were recognized as a warrior class, could now be farmers and engage in trade and commerce, and townspeople could now join Japan's new army.

The Meiji government communicated these changes to the country by publishing the Charter Oath in 1868. This brief document outlined the intentions and policies of the new government and laid the foundation for all the reforms that would follow in the coming decades. The original text is believed to have been written by Yuri Kimimasa, an official of the fief of Fukui.[7]

The Charter Oath of the Meiji Restoration (1868)

By this oath we set up as our aim the establishment of the national weal[8] on a broad basis and the framing of a constitution and laws.

Deliberative assemblies shall be widely established and all matters decided by public discussion.

All classes, high and low, shall unite in vigorously carrying out the administration of affairs of state.

The common people, no less than the civil and military officials, shall each be allowed to pursue his own calling so that there may be no discontent.

Evil customs of the past shall be broken off and everything based upon the just laws of Nature.

Knowledge shall be sought throughout the world so as to strengthen the foundations of imperial rule.[9]

Many early Meiji reformers believed such reforms were necessary for achieving diplomatic equality and military strength and to begin building a path toward democracy. The motto of the era was "Enrich the Country and Strengthen the Military" and at the helm of this effort was Emperor Meiji. He embraced these efforts both in practice and in appearance. He wore Western-style military clothing, styled his hair in a Western manner, and grew a kaiser mustache. The pervasive philosophy of "Civilization and Enlightenment" impacted social policy throughout Japan and aspired to "correct" Japanese culture and to cultivate the idea of "civilizing" the nation. For example, officials outlawed mixed bathing and excessive exposure of flesh in public.

Government officials also consolidated power among an elite band of oligarchs. They formed a close circle around the emperor and advised him on everything. Their first priorities included implementing land tax reforms and military conscription to strengthen the government. Over the next four decades, the emperor and his oligarchs made education compulsory and invested in everything from banks to railroads to modern printing presses that increased newspaper circulation. The military adopted

Emperor Meiji of Japan (1852–1912)

Western-style weapons and uniforms and took steps toward new models of military education. Some Japanese remained unaware of the changes taking place while others remained directly opposed to them. All of these changes, however, caused tremendous upheaval for a people ruled by a warrior class for centuries.

None of these far-reaching reforms were put into place overnight. The ideas for the reforms largely came about as a result of trips that Japanese officials took to the United States and Europe. Five years after the emperor was restored to the throne, Meiji adviser Iwakura Tomomi led a delegation of nearly 50 government officials on an 18-month diplomatic mission to Europe and the United States. Iwakura understood that Japan would maintain sovereignty only if it embraced a certain degree of modernization. The objectives of the Iwakura Mission, as it came to be known, were twofold: to hold preliminary discussions on a revision of the "unequal treaties" signed with the Western imperial powers beginning in the 1850s and to observe and study the public and private institutions of these Western powers. While Iwakura and his delegates were largely unsuccessful in renegotiating the provisions of the treaties, they were impressed by the culture and institutions of the West and brought back many ideas for the reforming of schools and universities, factories, power plants, cultural life, the police, military, and government.

The Eastern Culture Association

Members of the Iwakura Mission traveled to Europe and the United States to attend talks and observe Western institutions.

One member of the delegation was the statesman Ito Hirobumi. He documented everything, from currency systems to education and technology. Ito observed the role that the constitutions of various nations played in guiding the conduct and institutions of the nations he visited. After studying the Prussian and Austrian constitutions, Ito, Japanese leaders, and Western scholars began drafting the Meiji Constitution in 1881. Eight years later it was promulgated.[10] The document defined the roles and responsibilities of the emperor, the rights and obligations of all Japanese citizens, and the establishment of government institutions such as the Diet (Japanese legislature) and the judiciary. In essence, the rule of law became institutionalized in Japan. In order to maintain a link between past and present, essential to the preservation of order, the framers of the Meiji Constitution maintained the imperial system while becoming a modern nation-state. In fact, the day chosen for the Meiji emperor to announce the constitution to the Japanese people was February 11, 1889, the anniversary of the ascension of Jinmu, the mythical and purportedly first emperor of Japan, to the throne 2,349 years earlier.[11]

Excerpts of the preamble and several articles of the constitution highlighting these changes in Japan are included below:

Preamble

Having, by virtue of the glories of Our Ancestors, ascended the Throne of a lineal succession unbroken for ages eternal; desiring to promote the welfare of, and to give development to the moral and intellectual faculties of Our beloved subject, the very same that have been favored with the benevolent care and affectionate vigilance of Our Ancestors; and hoping to maintain the prosperity of the State, in concert with Our people and with their support, We hereby promulgate, in pursuance of Our Imperial Rescript of the 12th day of the 10th month of the 14th year of Meiji, a fundamental law of State, to exhibit the principles, by which We are to be guided in Our conduct, and to point out to what Our descendants and Our subjects and their descendants are forever to conform.

The rights of sovereignty of the State, We have inherited from Our Ancestors, and We shall bequeath them to Our descendants. . . .

Chapter 1: Emperor (excerpted 7 out of 17 articles)

Article I. The Empire of Japan shall be reigned over and governed by a line of Emperors unbroken for ages eternal.

Article II. The Imperial Throne shall be succeeded to by Imperial male descendants, according to the provisions of the Imperial House Law.

Article III. The Emperor is sacred and inviolable.

Article IV. The Emperor is the head of the Empire. . . .

Article XI. The Emperor has the supreme command of the Army and Navy.

Article XII. The Emperor determines the organization and peace standing of the Army and Navy.

Article XIII. The Emperor declares war, makes peace, and concludes treaties.

Chapter 2: Rights and Duties of Subject

(excerpted 4 out of 15 articles)

Article XVIII. The conditions necessary for being a Japanese subject shall be determined by law.

Article XX. Japanese subjects are amenable to service in the Army and Navy, according to the provisions of law.

Article XXIII. No Japanese subject shall be arrested, detained, tried or punished, unless according to law.

Article XXIX. Japanese subjects shall, within the limits of law, enjoy the liberty of speech, writing, publication, public meetings and associations.

Chapter 3: The Imperial Diet (excerpted 3 out of 22 articles)

Article XXXIII. The Imperial Diet shall consist of two Houses, a House of Peers and a House of Representatives.

Article XXXIV. The House of Peers shall, in accordance with the Ordinance concerning the House of Peers, be composed of the members of the Imperial Family, of the orders of nobility, and of those persons who have been nominated thereto by the Emperor.

Article XXXV. The House of Representatives shall be composed of Members elected by the people, according to the provision of the Law of Election.[12]

---

7   A *fief* is an estate of land held in feudal service.
8   A *weal* is a sound, healthy, prosperous state.
9   Wm. Theodore de Bary, Carol Gluck, and Arthur E. Tiedemann, eds., *Sources of Japanese Tradition*, 2nd edition, vol. 2 (New York: Columbia University Press, 2005), 672.
10 Paul Akamatsu, *Meiji 1868: Revolution and Counter-Revolution in Japan*, trans. Miriam Kochan (New York: Harper and Row, 1972), 278.
11 Jinmu is the mythical son of the Shinto sun goddess Amaterasu-Omikami and traditionally believed to be the first emperor of Japan. See Reading 2.2, "Shinto and Japanese Nationalism," for a further explanation.
12 de Bary, Gluck, and Tiedemann, *Sources of Japanese Tradition*, 745-47.

SHINTO AND JAPANESE NATIONALISM

Although many of the ideas for the Meiji government and its institutions were borrowed and adapted from the West, Japan's *Shinto* and its rituals were instrumental in shaping Japan's modern identity and its connection to its ancestral past. Shinto, Japan's indigenous religion, predates written historical records. Shinto means the "way of the gods," and legend tells that all emperors of Japan descend from an unbroken imperial line dating back to Japan's first emperor, Jinmu Tenno. With the restoration of the imperial line in the Meiji era, a connection to Japan's Shinto roots was reestablished and it became the official state religion. From this point forward, decisions of state and legitimacy of rule by emperor were inextricably linked to the deities, or the gods.

One of the most visible representations of the link between the Japanese government and religion is the Yasukuni shrine. A Shinto shrine is a structure whose main purpose is for the safekeeping of *kami*, or the sacred spirits. These kami are embodied in forms important to life such as elements found in nature—wind, air, water, and mountains. Human and human forms can also become kami after death and are revered by family members as ancestral kami. The kami of extraordinary people in Japan are preserved in hundreds of shrines throughout the country, including those for the imperial family, those dedicated to powerful clans, those for rice, and those who died during war in the service of the nation.[13]

The name *Yasukuni* originates from the classical Chinese text Zuo Zhuan and means "pacifying the nation." Emperor Meiji chose this name to commemorate Japan's victims of war and to connect the state to a sacred Shinto site. Emperor Meiji visited the Yasukuni shrine twice a year. This helped establish an association among the emperor, the shrine, and the sacrifice of dying in battle. Because those who died in battle were assured a sacred rest site at Yasukuni and ritual visitation from the emperor, dying for the emperor became one of the highest Japanese honors.

Japanese nationalist Katsuhiko Kakehi explained in 1933 in the journal *Contemporary Japan* what he believed was the relationship between Shinto and the Japanese people:

> Shinto is not a mere abstract concept; it is a system of faith which
> came into existence with the birth of the Japanese race. Shinto,

the proper sense of the word, is "the way of the gods." By the way of the gods is meant the way people should live in accordance with the divine will. It is a code of ethics founded upon examples set by the gods; it represents humanity and divinity combined into one. . . .

All the experience gained under every possible circumstance by the ancestors of mankind for long ages has been thoroughly tested by the Yamato [Japanese] race in order to form what is in effect a universal creed. It is not an artificial creation of the Japanese people; it is a natural realization of the will of the gods. From such divine manifestations the experience of the nation has been formed; in other words, the divine will has expressed itself through the life of the Yamato race. We accordingly believe that the national experience of the Japanese and the will of the gods are one and identical, and that the Japanese race was placed on earth as a realization of the life of the gods and is possessed of their divine attributes. . . .

The direct line of descent from the grandson of the Sun Goddess is the Imperial Family. It is on account of this that we call our Ruler . . . the Descendent of the Heavenly grandson. By having the divine offspring as their *Tenno* (Emperor), the people also participate in the glory of the Gods. . . . Shinto shrines are . . . the material expressions of the purity and gratitude of human minds in which the spirit of the gods dwell. There are numerous Shinto shrines in the country and these are united, with the grand Shrine of Isé as their head. . . .

Japanese faith in the gods is evinced in the shrine worship practiced everywhere throughout the country and [is] the fundamental nature of the Japanese nationality. It is not substantially based upon philosophical doctrines, actual historical facts, or formally written texts. The teachings of Shinto are unwritten traditions and legendary stories which have been preserved through generations. . . . The Japanese people as a whole have joined in establishing Shinto, their unique national religion, and in fostering its boundless growth. It is a religion, but at the same time it is the life of the nation.[14]

12 The construction of Yasukuni began in 1869 under orders from Emperor Meiji, who believed
 it would "console the spirits of those who sacrificed their lives to restore political power from
 the Tokugawa shogun to the emperor." When Emperor Meiji visited the site in 1874, he was so
 moved that he composed the following: "I assure those of you who fought and died for your
 country that your names will live forever in this shrine." Today the Yasukuni shrine is a site of
 controversy. Its current context is discussed in Chapter 7, Reading 7.1 "A Nation's Past."
14 Katsuhiko Kakehi, "An Outline of Shinto," *Contemporary Japan I,* no. 4 (March 1933): 584–93.
 For more information on the sun goddess Amaterasu-Omikami and the holiest of shrines in Japan,
 the Ise shrine, see http://orias.berkeley.edu/visuals/japan_visuals/shintoC.HTM.

READING 3

EDUCATION AND NATION BUILDING IN JAPAN

Japan's efforts to build a modern nation considered both its history and ad-
aptation of Western practices. This exposure to other nations paved the way
for a new openness with the rest of the world and allowed for the emergence
of a group of intellectuals who believed that adopting aspects of Western
culture would only strengthen Japan. Kido Takayoshi (1833–1877), one
delegate on the Iwakura Mission, wrote to his friend Sugiyama Takatoshi in
1873 and discussed the critical role of education in the United States:

> When it comes to things like schools and factories, it is impossi-
> ble to tell you everything, for it defies description. From now on,
> unless we pay a great deal of attention to the children, the pres-
> ervation of order in our country in the future will be impossible.
> . . . Maintaining a stable state will be difficult unless we consider
> social conditions and pay attention to social evils. Nothing is
> more important than schools for improving social conditions
> and uprooting social evils. The civilization we have in our country
> today is not a true civilization, and our enlightenment is not true
> enlightenment. To prevent trouble ten years from now, there is
> only one thing to do, and that is to establish schools worthy of the
> name. A long-range program for the stability of our country will
> never be carried out if we have only a small number of able peo-
> ple; we have to have universal adherence to the moral principles

> of loyalty, justice, humanity, and decorum. . . . Our people are not
> different from Americans or Europeans of today: It is all a matter
> of education or the lack of education.[15]

Another intellectual, Fukuzawa Yukichi (1835–1902), was a prominent Japanese thinker who pushed for the adoption of Western culture. In 1871 he penned the following discussion on the role education can play in human equality:

> Heaven does not set one man above the other, nor does heaven
> set one man below another, so it is said. If this is so, then when
> Heaven gives birth to men, all men are equal. At birth there is
> no distinction between noble and ignoble, high and low. . . .
> Nevertheless, when one looks broadly at this human society of
> ours today, there are wise people and there are stupid ones;
> there are poor and there are rich; there are men of high birth
> and there are men of low birth. Their respective conditions are as
> far apart as the clouds and the mud. Why is this? This answer is
> very clear. [It] is a matter of whether or not they have received an
> education.[16]

Such ideas were integrated into the first comprehensive education legislation in Japan, called the *Gakusei* (or school system). The changes to its education system included four years of compulsory elementary education for boys and girls and a gender-segregated secondary education and university system. Schools would also teach practical subjects to their children; for boys this included science, math, history, ethics, and Japanese language courses. Girls also learned these subjects, but less time was devoted to them so that they could also learn sewing and other domestic trades. The day before the legislation took effect, the preamble was issued:

> It is only by building up their characters, developing their minds,
> and cultivating their talents that people may make their way in the
> world, employ their wealth wisely, make their business prosper,
> and thus attain the goals of life. But people cannot build up their
> characters, develop their minds, or cultivate their talents without
> education. That is the reason for the establishment of the schools.
> Beginning with speech, writing, and arithmetic in everyday life and
> extending to military affairs, government, agriculture, trade, law,
> politics, astronomy, and medicine, there is not a single phase of
> human activity that is not based on learning. . . .

because learning was viewed as the exclusive prerogative of the samurai and courtiers, others—farmers, artisans, merchants, and women—have neglected it completely and have no idea what it is. Even those few samurai and courtiers who did pursue learning were apt to claim that it was for the state, not knowing that it was the very foundation of success in life. . . .

Accordingly, the Office of Education will soon establish an edu-cational system and will revise the regulations related to it from time to time so that in the future, there shall be no village with an uneducated family or a family with an uneducated person. Every guardian, acting in accordance with this, shall bring up his or her children with care and see to it that they attend school. . . . [17]

The idea that "there shall be no village with an uneducated family or a family with an uneducated person" had a unifying effect for the country. As more Japanese received an education, a more literate and more productive workforce for the nation emerged. More newspapers and magazines were circulated, allowing educated men and women to gain greater knowledge of their own nation and their world. As Article V of the Charter Oath declared, "Knowledge shall be sought throughout the world so as to strengthen the foundations of imperial rule."

By the 1880s officials began to put the ideals in the Gakusei preamble into practice. While education was seen as the foundation of imperial rule, sub-mission to the emperor was reinforced as well. A decade later officials issued "The Imperial Rescript on Education." This document was circulated widely and read aloud at all important school events. Students were required to memorize the text, prostrate themselves in front of a picture of the emperor and empress of Japan, and recite it in full.[18]

Know ye, Our Subjects:

Our Imperial Ancestors have founded Our Empire on a basis broad and everlasting, and have deeply and firmly implanted virtue; Our subjects ever united in loyalty and filial piety have from generation to generation illustrated the beauty thereof. This is the glory of the fundamental character of Our Empire, and herein also lies the source of Our education. Ye, Our subjects, be filial to your parents, affectionate to your brothers and sisters; as husbands and wives be harmonious, as friends true; bear yourselves in

The Imperial Rescript on Education was widely circulated through schools in Japan.

modesty and moderation; extend your benevolence to all; pursue learning and cultivate arts, and thereby develop intellectual faculties and perfect moral powers; furthermore, advance public good and promote common interests; always respect the Constitution and observe the laws; should emergency arise, offer yourselves courageously to the State; and thus guard and maintain the prosperity of Our Imperial state; and thus guard and maintain the prosperity of Our Imperial Throne coeval with heaven and earth. So shall ye not only be Our good and faithful subjects, but render illustrious the best traditions of your forefathers. . . .

The way here set forth is indeed the teaching bequeathed by Our Imperial Ancestors, to be observed alike by Their Descendants and the subjects, infallible for all ages and true in all places. It is Our wish to lay it to heart in all reverence, in common with you, Our subjects, that we may all attain to the same virtue.

October 30, 1890[19]

15 *Kido Takayoshi monjo* 4, 320, trans. adapted from Irokawa, The Culture of the Meiji Period, 54–55, quoted in de Bary, Gluck, and Tiedemann, *Sources of Japanese Tradition*, 678.
16 Richard Minear, trans., "Fukuzawa Yukichi, akumon no susume," *Fukuzawa Yukichi zenshü*, III, (Tokyo: Iwanami, 1969), 29–31.
17 Herbert Passin, *Society and Education in Japan*, quoted in de Bary, Gluck, and Tiedemann, *Sources of Japanese Tradition*, 765–66.
18 The ritual of prostration before the emperor is a holdover from earlier eras when commoners had to avert their gaze when high-ranking persons such as court nobles, daimyo, or shoguns passed by. Bob Tadashi Wakabayashi (professor, York University), personal communication with the author, January 1, 2014.
19 "The Imperial Rescript on Education [Official Document]," annotated by Brian Platt, Children and Youth in History, Item 136, accessed November 15, 2012, http://chnm.gmu.edu/cyh/primary-sources/136.

READING 4

SEEDS OF UNREST: THE TAIPING MOVEMENT

At the same time efforts of reform were under way in Japan in the mid-nineteenth century, China remained under the same dynasty that had ruled for more than 200 years. Qing rule, led by the ethnic minority Manchu people, were struggling to maintain China's wealth and prestige in East Asia.

The first emperor in power after the opium wars was Emperor Tongzhi (r. 1861–1875). At the age of five he had little power and instead, his mother, Empress Dowager Cixi, largely controlled the reigns. She promoted a movement called the Tongzhi Restoration to halt any further decline of Qing power by restoring the traditional sociopolitical order and strengthening Confucian culture. The damaging defeats by the British in the opium wars were partially a cause of domestic instability, but also partially a consequence. Although Qing leaders did not passively submit to Western imperialism, they held power when Western colonial powers gained an economic and political foothold in China. As a result, the legitimacy and effectiveness of their rule and the rule of the Manchu people was shaken, contributing to the further weakening of the Chinese nation.

While opium addiction and subsequent conflict over its trade continued, clashes between tradition and modernity also confronted China's imperial court. This set the stage for one of the bloodiest civil wars ever in world history, the Taiping War from the early 1850s up to 1864.[20] Until China's loss to Britain in the opium wars, Western traders were permitted to conduct trade and business only through an association of Chinese merchants known as cohong, 13 authorized merchants approved by the Chinese central government. *(See Source 1: The Treaty of Nanking [summary].)* The Treaty of Nanking, signed after China's defeat in the opium wars, ended this system and opened up new opportunities for European and American traders. This shifted the majority of China's economic activity from south to north. Massive job losses followed in the south, causing famine and severe economic depression. In the aftermath, the Chinese looked for a leader to guide them out of the crisis.

Hong Xiuquan (1813–1864) emerged as a leader under these conditions. Born into a peasant family, Hong received a strong classical education and was exposed to translated Christian tracts through foreign missionaries. Hong tried four times to pass the imperial examination. These formal imperial examinations were part of the great tradition of upward mobility in imperial China. If you were part of the very small percentage of people who succeeded in passing these very tough and very lengthy exams, you would have the opportunity of joining the bureaucracy and maybe even end up working at the imperial court and serving the emperor.

After his four unsuccessful attempts, Hong fell ill and into a coma in 1837. He reawakened several months later with a vision; he believed himself to be the younger brother of Jesus Christ, and his mission, and that of his followers, was to cleanse China of the Manchus and anyone else who stood in their way of creating a "Heavenly Kingdom of Great Peace" (Taiping Tianguo). In order to reach this desired place, the vision told him, the mantle of the Mandate of Heaven—the ancient Chinese philosophy determining the virtue of the emperor—must be removed from the emperor through the use of military power.

For the next 10 years Hong continued to study Christian texts, teaching in village schools, and sharing his knowledge with family and friends. For the most part his message was not well received. But in southern China, he found himself among the *Hakka,* a subethnicity of Chinese people who had traditionally been discriminated against by the ethnic majority. Possibly because the Hakka had always been economically marginalized, they proved more receptive to his message. Suddenly he found himself the leader of the "God Worshippers," a band of rebels who shared his political, economic, and religious beliefs. His number of followers grew, and eventually his band of followers not only wanted to hear his message but also helped him form an army. They called their new religion the Taiping, or "Great Peace" faith. It was based on Christianity and missionary teachings, but it was an unusual interpretation of Christianity based upon recognizing Hong as the younger brother of Jesus Christ. It soon developed into a religion whose idea of a sovereign deity challenged the existing Qing rule.

The Taipings used their religious zeal to exploit the insecurity caused by the social and economic conditions at the time. In their early years, the Taipings built their own militia and continued to indoctrinate others into their cause. Eventually, they formed a full army, forged alliances, recruited families, and joined together peasants and intellectuals who believed the Qing were weak and the cause of China's decline. Their militia had amazing success. When the Taipings put their swords together they discovered that in fact the Qing dynasty armies were not as strong and not as well organized as they had imagined. In 1850, after withstanding a large-scale assault by government troops, Hong publically proclaimed himself the King of the Heavenly Kingdom of Great Peace (Taiping Tianguo Tianwang) and launched the Taiping Rebellion the following year.

The Taiping cause had sweeping appeal. Politically and economically the movement appealed to the climate of anti-Manchu rule and to destitute peasants. Quickly they managed to occupy a great deal of desirable land including Nanjing, the former capital of China, which they made their capital. As one Taiping leader would recount:

> Each year they [the Manchus] transform tens of millions of China's gold and silver into opium and extract several millions from the fat and marrow of the Chinese people and turn it into rouge and powder. . . . How could the rich not become poor? How could the poor abide by the law?[21]

The Taiping movement also gained strength by spreading their religious and political messages through the printed page. Borrowing from practices of Christian missionaries, Hong and other Taiping leaders published upward of 44 books and numerous other policy proposals and political and religious tracts. The documents range in scope from treatises such as *The Ten Heavenly Commandments* to economic platforms outlining the blueprint for their entire society as well as social ideas such as the separation of men and women. The Taiping social program, the idea that land and property should be made collective, is one of the ideas that got a young man named Mao Zedong very inspired years later.

This scene depicts the Taiping Rebellion, a period of civil war and uprising in China that lasted from 1850–1864.

Despite this early success, the Taiping Rebellion was eventually beset by internal strife, lack of cohesion, autocratic leadership, and extreme religious dogma. The final battle, the third battle for the city of Nanjing, was particularly bloody with hundreds of thousands killed. The rebellion finally collapsed in 1864, when it was defeated by provincial Qing armies, known as the new armies, which had been given permission to be assembled by the dynasty to defeat the Taipings. These new armies, led by their provincial leadership, would eventually lead to a phenomenon critical for twentieth-century China that is often called warlordism.[22]

While there is no definitive death toll for the entire 13-year conflict, the estimated carnage is upward of 20 million Chinese killed during the years of the Taiping Rebellion.[23] In the end, the Taiping threat was finally ended, but at a great cost. The veneer of power held by the Qing began to fall apart as it became more clear that the central government no longer had the power to control things from Beijing (Peking).

---

20 Rana Mitter (professor, Oxford University), interview with the author, March 11, 2014.
21 Franz Michael, *The Taiping Rebellion* (Seattle: University of Washington Press, 1971), 3.
22 Warlordism is based on the idea that each province of China might have its own strong man in charge with his own independent army who would pay very little attention to the central government. Zeng Guofan was one such new army leader. He drew upon Western learning to train the new armies, but also believed in the idea of a Chinese spirit and essence to build morale.
23 Paul Cohen, *History in Three Keys: The Boxers as Event, Experience and Myth* (New York: Columbia University Press, 1997), 14.

READING 5

SELF-STRENGTHENING MOVEMENT IN CHINA

After the opium wars and 13 years of violence during the Taiping Rebellion, Chinese reformers could no longer ignore the need for change. The Qing court and the emperor had become so entrenched and ineffective they could no longer be relied upon to meet the needs of the populace. More and more Chinese supported efforts to identify their country's weaknesses, eliminate them, and learn how to best emulate the West and Japan without erasing the best aspects of Chinese culture.

China's leaders understood that modern reforms were necessary for China's survival. One of the most prominent movements that emerged became known as the self-strengthening movement. It advocated strengthening the imperial system by adopting Western economic and industrial practices and military technology but did not advocate for any large-scale social reforms. The slogan of the self-strengthening movement was "Learn the superior technology of the barbarian, in order to control him." The self-strengtheners were convinced of China's cultural superiority and only wanted to master the technology of the West, not adopt their culture.

One of the leaders of this movement was the high-ranking Qing minister Feng Guifen who wrote the following in 1860:

> We have only one thing to learn from the barbarians, and that is
> strong ships and effective guns. . . . In the end, the way to avoid
> trouble is to manufacture, repair, and use weapons by ourselves.
> Only thus can we pacify the empire; only thus can we become the
> leading power in the world; only thus can we restore our original
> strength, redeem ourselves from former humiliations, and main-
> tain the integrity of our vast territory so as to remain the greatest
> country on earth.[24]

---

24 Wm. Theodore de Bary and Richard Lufrano, eds., *Sources of Chinese Tradition*, 2nd edition, vol. 2 (New York: Columbia University Press, 2000), 235-37.

READING 6

REFORMS

As self-strengtheners promoted reforms, a transition in imperial rule was taking place. In 1875 the Tongzhi emperor died with no heir in line. Facing pressure from reformers, maintaining stability was important for the Qing to remain in power. In an unconventional move, the imperial family agreed that the empress dowager's four-year-old nephew would ascend to the throne, becoming the ninth Qing emperor to rule over China.[25] Emperor Guangxu (1871–1908) was adopted by the empress but did not exercise any real influence until he turned 18 in 1889. During the intervening years, the empress retained a firm grip on power and continued to resist reform. When Guangxu came of age, however, he immediately began enacting programs to modernize China, trying to emulate what he had learned about Japan's Emperor Meiji and the West.

Guangxu's reforms accelerated after China's loss to Japan in the Sino-Japanese War of 1894–1895. This loss was devastating. The Qing Empire was sizably larger, richer, and better equipped than Japan. Japan had been the despised land of eastern barbarians. But China's military, systems, strategy, and training remained underdeveloped. The loss to Japan was the ultimate wake-up call for dynastic reforms.

The Qing court asked well-respected scholar Kang Youwei to provide advice to the emperor at this critical moment. Kang believed self-strengthening did not go far enough to transform the institutions inhibiting China's growth. On June 16, 1898, he met with the emperor and told him:

> . . . all the laws and the political and social systems [must] be changed and decided anew, before it can be called a reform. Now those who talk about reform only change some specific affairs, and do not reform the institutions. . . . Most of the high ministers are very old and conservative, and they do not understand matters concerning foreign countries. If Your Majesty wishes to rely on them for reform it will be like climbing a tree to seek a fish.[26]

Extremely impressed with Kang, the emperor immediately appointed him to
the foreign ministry, initiating a series of far-reaching reform efforts known
as the Hundred Days' Reform. Led by reformers such as Kang Youwei and
Liang Qichao, an ambitious plan to restructure the political, economic,
and educational structures began. The reformers hoped to emulate Japan's
constitutional monarchy. Using the Japanese model they believed that they
could rid the government of the despotism and absolute power that had
corrupted the previous rulers. Kang and his allies felt that reorganizing
the Chinese army, improving military equipment, and enhancing military
education was a necessary first step toward larger changes in the political
organization of the empire. The Qing's recent loss to Japan (1894–1895)
only reinforced this claim. The New Army, as it was called by Qing reformers, embraced Western military operations, adopting their uniforms, drills,
and education system.[27]

The Hundred Days' Reform included a complete overhaul of the Chinese
educational system to mirror Western models. This included changing the
three-tiered civil service examination system; rather than test students in
their command of Confucian texts such as the Four Books and the Five
Classics, the emperor instead suggested current affairs be the focus.[28] The
empress dowager and her conservative officials condemned the efforts to reform the military and education system, claiming the efforts were too radical
and would weaken Qing rule. To prevent further change, the empress dowager and the conservative officials ignored the emperor's edicts and staged a
coup just three months after the Hundred Days' Reform was launched. She
took control of the government by announcing the emperor was seriously
ill and placing him under house arrest. Liang fled to Japan and Kang soon
followed. They continued to advocate for change even from Japan; however,
for the time being the tide of reform efforts had been temporarily halted.

---

25 *Dowager* is a term used to refer to a widow who has inherited property or a title from her de-
ceased husband. While the emperor died in 1871, the young emperor Guangxu did not ascend to
the throne until 1874.

26 Immanuel Hsu, *The Rise of Modern China,* 6th edition (New York: Oxford University Press,
2000), 372.

27 The New Army, or Beiyang Army, was the centerpiece of the Qing's dynasty military reconstruction in the late 19th century. It should not be confused with the provincial armies established
during the Taiping Rebellion.

28 However, the eight-legged essay exam remained in place. For approximately 600 years the exam
was administered to filter out the most literate and well-educated people in the country for civil
servant positions.

REBELS: THE BOXER REBELLION

The Hundred Days' Reform also coincided with an upsurge of anti-Western sentiment in the north of China directed, in part, at the growth of missionary settlements. Every major Christian denomination established a range of educational and church-affiliated institutions across the country after the Treaty of Nanking in 1842.

Beginning in the French and German Catholic missionary communities in Shandong, local Chinese felt the Western missionaries protected only the local Christian converts. When legal decisions needed to be made or family disputes arose, Western missionaries could bypass local authorities since they were exempt from various laws, which only compounded the animosity. The resentment was further deepened when the region experienced severe droughts, followed by disastrous floods and economic strife. With the building of railroads by Western investors, and other aspects of imperialism, the anger grew. This despair created the foundation for another civil rebellion composed largely of unemployed peasants and farmers, anti-foreign in belief and violent in action. They were called the Boxers by foreigners because of the martial arts many of the rebels practiced.

The beginning of the Boxer Rebellion can be traced to the 1899 killing of two priests by two Boxer members visiting a German missionary in Juye County, China. In response, Kaiser Wilhelm II, the German leader at the time, dispatched German troops to the scene of the crime, which further angered the rebels. The ongoing presence of foreign military to intimidate and attempt to control the local population ignited a spark of rebellion. By late October they occupied a Catholic church that had once been a temple to the Jade emperor and continued on their path of violence. "Support the Qing, destroy the foreigners" became their slogan as they continued to resist foreign military control.

Feng Jinyu and Li Mingde were interviewed in 1966 about their activities with the Boxers in their youth. They recall:

> Girls who joined the Boxers were called "Shining Red Lanterns" as they dressed all in red, held a little red lantern in one hand and in the other a red fan. All of them were unmarried girls about eighteen or nineteen years old. In every village there were girls who joined the Shining Red Lanterns but they did not want others to

~~see their rituals so they would practice only at night when it was~~
dark. There was a song then that went:

> Learn to be a Boxer, Study Red Lantern.
> Kill all the foreign devils and make churches burn.[29]

As the Chinese aversion and anger to foreigners escalated, their safety became increasingly precarious as the Boxers' armed struggle continued. One British newspaper gave the following account:

> Peking, May 20 [1900.] From all parts of the surrounding country news is constantly arriving of fresh atrocities committed by the "Boxers." On the 20th inst., at Shan-lai-ying, sixty miles from Peking three Christian families were murdered, only two persons escaping. . . .
>
> Besides this, much of the rolling stock was burned or otherwise damaged by the rioters, and some large godowns [warehouses] full of valuable merchandise were burned after their contents had been looted. The total amount of the damage is roughly estimated at half a million taels [a weight measurement in China.] Among the rolling stock destroyed was the Imperial Palace car, which alone cost 1,700 taels. . . .
>
> I am informed that the attack on the place was made by villagers living in the neighborhood, led by some of the "Boxers." This gives the affair an even more serious complexion, as it shows that the movement is more widespread than had been imagined.[30]

Initially Qing troops suppressed the Boxers, but in January 1900 the dynasty ordered that the Boxers should not be considered bandits. When the Boxer Rebellion reached Beijing's (Peking's) foreign legations (embassies) in the spring of 1900, more violence was unleashed against foreigners.[31] They burned Christian churches, killed Chinese Christians, and violently intimidated any Chinese official who attempted to suppress their revolt. The violence continued to escalate into what is known today as the "siege of the legations," or the occupation of foreign embassies. The empress dowager implored all foreigners to leave the city immediately, and when many remained barricaded out of fear for their lives, she declared war on all foreigners and allied herself with the Boxers. In response, the Eight-Nation Alliance (Austria-Hungary, France, Germany, Italy, Japan, Russia, the United Kingdom, and the United States) sent their own military forces to end the siege. The Boxers were overwhelmed. Fearing for her safety, the empress fled

Historica, Yamagawa shuppan

The Eight-Nations alliance included troops from Britain, the United States, the Australian colonies, British India, Germany, France, Austria-Hungary, Russia, Italy, and Japan.

to Xi'an, a safe location at the time, with her high-ranking Qing officials and remained there until a final peace agreement, the Boxer Protocol, was signed in 1901.[32]

The empress dowager and the Qing court had suffered another humiliating defeat. For the past 60 years, Western powers had slowly eroded Chinese sovereignty and undermined Qing legitimacy and power. By the turn of the twentieth century new leaders of resistance movements, such as the Boxers, introduced the possibility for their nation to be strong once again.

---

29 Pei-kai Cheng, Michael Lestz, and Jonathan D. Spence, eds., *The Search for Modern China: A Documentary Collection* (New York: W. W. Norton & Company, 1999), 186.

30 "The Boxer Rebellion as reported in the UK papers—extracts—in the main with an attempt to give a naval flavor," Late 18th, 19th and early 20th Century Naval and Naval Social History website, accessed June 8, 2014, http://www.pbenyon.plus.com/Boxer/Boxer.html.

31 Legations in Beijing at the time included the United Kingdom, France, Germany, Italy, Austria-Hungary, Spain, Belgium, the Netherlands, Russia, Japan, and the United States.

32 "Boxer Protocol, Peking 7. September 1901 Peace Agreement between the Great Powers and China," 100jia website, accessed January 1, 2014, http://www.100jia.net/china1900/ereignisse /boxerprotokoll.htm.

THE BIRTH OF THE FIRST CHINESE REPUBLIC

The Boxer Rebellion, and the repression of the Hundred Days' Reform by Empress Dowager Cixi, ignited a more far-reaching, radical, and revolutionary approach to modernizing China. One prominent leader who emerged calling for revolution was Sun Yat-sen. Sun's early years followed the path of many Chinese who escaped the country's poverty and sought a better life by living abroad. In 1879, at the age of 13, Sun was sent by his father to live with his older brother, Sun Mei, in the Kingdom of Hawaii. Sun Mei was a successful rancher and entrepreneur, and Sun Yat-sen worked on his brother's farms while receiving his first formal education at an Anglican missionary school called Iolani.

Coming of age in Hawaii gave Sun Yat-sen access to a Western education. He learned about the English and American ideals of a constitutional government, the history of political struggles elsewhere, and Christianity at Iolani.[33] Sun Yat-sen's exposure to this education left an impression on him, setting the stage for his worldview and his later revolutionary activities. He returned to China in 1894 and with the support of several other reformers, established the Revive China Society (Xingzhonghui).This organization would later become the Revolutionary Alliance and would lay the foundation for China's Nationalist Party.

Even today Sun Yat-sen is considered the father of the Chinese nation on both sides of the Taiwan Strait.[34] Sun became increasingly convinced that gradual change and constitutional reform wouldn't be quick enough; the Chinese imperial dynasty needed to be overthrown and replaced by a modern constitutional republican structure.

Sun presented his revolutionary ideals in the Three Principles of the People. Its primary tenets were the *minzu* (the ethnic nation and freedom from imperial rule), *minquan* (the people's rights), and *minsheng* (well-being of the people).[35] First presented in 1905 at a speech in Brussels, the Three Principles were the values of his larger political plan to overthrow and end Qing rule. His appeal and popularity swelled in the first decade of the century, with active membership in the Revolutionary Alliance growing from 400 in 1905 to more than 10,000 by 1911.[36] In those six years, Sun Yat-sen and the Revolutionary Alliance directed or instigated at least seven different uprisings against the Qing.

Sun's Three Principles of the People were inspired by President Abraham Lincoln's 1863 Gettysburg Address—that government should be "of the people, by the people, and for the people." Sun also had definitive ideas, informed by pseudo-scientific notions of race and blood, about who was included and excluded in the Chinese nation:[37]

> Considering the law of survival of ancient and modern races, if we want to save China and to preserve the Chinese race, we must certainly promote Nationalism. To make this principle luminous for China's salvation, we must first understand it clearly. The Chinese race totals four hundred million people; of mingled races there are only a few million Mongolians, a million or so Manchus, a few million Tibetans, and over a million Mohammedan Turks. These alien races do not number altogether more than ten million, so that, for the most part, the Chinese people are of the Han or Chinese race with common blood, common language, common religion, and common customs. . . .
>
> The greatest force is common blood. Chinese belong to the yellow race because they come from the blood stock of the yellow race. The blood for ancestors is transmitted by heredity down through the race, making blood kinship a powerful force.[38]

Sun was not China's only revolutionary figure. Another was Zou Rong. Educated in Japan, Zou wrote one of the most widely circulated pamphlets on revolution of the time, *The Revolutionary Army* (1903). The pamphlet was the first clear call for a Chinese revolution:

> Revolution is a universal rule of evolution. Revolution is a universal principle of the world. Revolution is the essence of a transitional period of struggle for survival. Revolution follows nature and man. Revolution eliminates what is corrupt and holds on to what is good. Revolution is to advance from savagery to civilization. Revolution is to eradicate slavery and become the master. . . .
> I have heard that the English Revolution of 1688, the American Revolution of 1775, and the French Revolution of 1870 were all revolutions that followed nature and corresponded to the nature of man. They were all revolutions designed to eliminate what was

corrupt and hold on to what is good and to advance from savagery to civilization. . . .

I am a young person with little learning or refinement. I cannot really discuss the great significance of revolutionary independence but, timidly and with trepidation, I have conscientiously tried to copy the meaning of American revolutionary independence. Prostrating myself before my most respected and beloved four hundred million exalted Han Chinese countrymen, I list the following proposals for your consideration and action.[39] *(See Source 3: Pamphlet, The Revolutionary Army [excerpt].)*

---

33 Sun was baptized in 1886.
34 This reference to the Taiwan Strait refers to the political divisions that exist between mainland China and the island of Taiwan, which has been separated politically from China since 1949 and the Communist Revolution.
35 The term *minzoku* was coined in Japan in the nineteenth century and the Chinese adopted the term.
36 Jonathan D. Spence, *The Search for Modern China* (New York: W. W. Norton & Company, 1990), 262.
37 Milestone Documents; "Sun Yat-sen: 'The Three Principles of the People' (1921)," commentary by Torsten Weber, accessed March 19, 2014, https://www.milestonedocuments.com/documents/view/sun-yat-sensthe-three-principles-of-the-people.
38 Sun Yat-sen, *Sanminzhuyi* [The Three Principles], (Shanghai: Shangwu yinshuguan, 1927), 4–5, quoted in Frank Dikötter, *The Discourse of Race in Modern China* (Stanford: Stanford University Press, 1992), 124–25.
39 Pei-kai Cheng, Michael Lestz, and Jonathan D. Spence, eds., (New York: W. W. Norton & Company, 1999), 198-202.

READING 9

AN END OF TWO MILLENNIA

Revolutionary writings and efforts by leaders such as Sun Yat-sen and Zou Rong played a key role in the end of Qing rule in China. By the early twentieth century, feudalism was on the verge of collapse. Years of humiliation and defeat at the hands of Western colonial powers and the Japanese, and a series of failed uprisings, set the stage for the end of the Qing dynasty. Two key events were seminal in this process.

In November 1908, Emperor Guangxu died of a mysterious ailment at age 37. A day later, Empress Dowager Cixi fell ill and died. Upon her deathbed, the empress chose her successor, the two-year-old Puyi, the nephew of Guangxu. From 1908 until Qing rule finally ended in 1912, Puyi ruled while surrounded by Qing officials who largely insulated him from the unrest and revolts that were occurring throughout China. In the absence of an effective ruler, revolutionary activity was able to grow and spread.

The second turning point was a bomb explosion on October 9, 1911. Revolutionary cells had spread throughout China and were largely comprised of radical young Chinese who had been educated in Japan and elsewhere. Their call "to avenge the national disgrace" (as they called it) and "to restore the Chinese" resonated throughout the land.[40]

The bomb that exploded was being assembled by one such cell in the city of Wuchang. Qing authorities loyal to the empire moved in and tried to stop the spread of their revolutionary activities, executing those they could capture and hunting down others on the membership registries. Unless the alliance of revolutionary groups acted quickly against Qing authorities, their entire network and goal to overthrow the empire would be dismantled. When the bomb went off, the revolutionaries gained the upper hand.

The Manchu rulers were incapable of handling the crisis. The imperial government offered an appointment to Beiyang Army leader Yuan Shikai, the leader of one of the big regional armies in northern China, in the hope of stabilizing the unrest. As these events unfolded, Nationalist Party leader Sun Yat-sen was actually not in China but was fund-raising in the United States during the late months of 1911. In fact, he learned of the sequence of revolutionary events while on a train en route from Denver, Colorado, to Kansas City, Missouri. With three key provinces in China (Jiangsu, Sichuan, and Shandong) showing support for the revolution and the city of Nanjing falling to the rebels in early December, the Qing court began to see the end of their rule on the horizon.

Rather than continue to adhere to Qing orders of continuing to fight, several senior military officials from the north issued 12 demands to the Qing court in order to curb any further violence.[41] These included:

> Deny the emperor all rights of summary execution of criminals.

> Elect a premier ratified by the emperor.

> Declare amnesty for all current political offenders held by the court.

Prevent members of the Manchu imperial clan from serving as future cabinet members.

Parliament will henceforth review all treaties before the emperor approves.

Within days of being issued, the Qing accepted these demands and the provisional national assembly elected Yuan Shikai premier of China on November 11, 1911.[42]

This artwork represents President Sun Yat-sen at the Shanghai train station on his way to Nanjing, where he would proclaim the foundation of the Republic of China.

By Christmas 1911, Nationalist leader Sun Yat-sen had returned to China. The Revolutionary Alliance's widespread popularity had grown, as had support for Sun to become the leader of the new Chinese republic. Out of respect for his leadership, the Revolutionary Alliance elected Sun provisional president of the Chinese republic and he assumed office on January 1, 1912. Understanding that he lacked the full support of the military, Sun sent a telegram to Yuan Shikai on the same day stating that even though he accepted the presidency the office is waiting for you and I hope you accept the offer.[43]

In January 1912, several assassination attempts had been made against high ranking Manchu princes and generals, as well as Yuan Shikai, and four senior commanders of the Beiyang Army had sent a telegram urging the formation of a republic in China. With these final blows, Yuan was able to reach a settlement with Emperor Puyi and his family to abdicate in February

1912 in exchange for their financial security and safety Yuan also negotiated an accompanying edict that he would be granted full powers to organize a provisional republican government, establish national unity with Sun's Revolutionary Alliance and be recognized him as the first official president of the new republic.

The Edict of Abdication was issued on February 12, 1912, and the provisional government in Nanjing agreed to The Articles of Favorable Treatment of the Great Qing Emperor after his Abdication. Yuan was sworn in as the first president of the Republic of China on March 10, 1912. Two hundred sixty-seven years of Qing rule had come to an end. *(See Source 4: Newspaper Article Reporting on the Proclamation of the First Chinese Republic.)* As historian Jonathan Spence notes:

> So, with a few simple words, the more than two millennia of China's imperial history were brought to a close. And with almost no experience whatsoever in the arts and institutions of self-government, the Chinese people were presented with the option of devising their own future in a watchful and dangerous world.[44]

After the abdication Sun Yat-sen tasked fellow revolutionary Song Jiaroen to help organize for the upcoming elections for a national parliament that were to be held in February 1913. Song had helped Sun Yat-sen establish the Chinese Nationalist Party, drafted one of the provisional constitutions for the new republic, and was an outspoken critic of what he saw as Yuan Shikai's increasing authoritarian rule. While the Nationalists Party did not win the overall majority, it had become the majority in the new parliament.

Then one of the first tragedies in a long period of tragic Chinese political change happened. On March 20, 1913 Song Jiaoren, was shot by an assassin in the Shanghai train station and died very soon afterward.[45] The assassination was a strong blow to the Nationalist Party and their hopes of the for attaining constitutional government in China.

By mid-summer 1913, Yuan Shikai, the militarist leader based in Beijing abolished parliament. By mid-fall Yuan declared martial law and instituted a military dictatorship dismantling the remaining republican institutions and became sole dictator. Recognizing his vulnerability, Sun Yat-sen fled to Japan in November 1913, one of the countries that had had an imperial presence in China, but also proved a safe haven for many Chinese nationalists at the time.

For the next several years, Yuan Shikai continued to assert his presidential authority by reorganizing provincial governments, increasing his control over military spending and foreign policy and attempting to revive many of the Qing religious observances and rituals. By the time of his death on June 5, 1916 Yuan Shikai's power had eroded. China was now left without a recognized central authority and soon descended into a period where competing warlords in the provinces vied for political and military power.

(See Source 5: Edict of Abdication and Source 6: The Articles of Favorable Treatment of the Great Qing Emperor After His Abdication.)

---

40 Edmund Fung, *The Military Dimension of the Chinese Revolution* (Vancouver: University of British Columbia Press, 1980), quoted in Spence, The Search for Modern China, 263.
41 The New Army was the modernized Chinese army corps established in December 1895 under the Hundred Days' Reform. This was renamed the Beiyang Army in 1902 when Yuan Shikai was promoted to Minister of Beiyang.
42 Spence, The Search for Modern China, 265.
43 Ibid, p. 267.
44 Jonathan Spence, *The Search for Modern China* (New York: W. W. Norton, 1990), 268. For another perspective on the abdication see the reporting of the event by the *New York Times*: http://query.nytimes.com/mem/archive-free/pdf?res=FA0E11F83C5813738DDDAA0994 DA405B828DF1D3.
45 A later investigation found circumstantial links to the president's office and Chinese historians conclude that Yuan engineered the assassination. Jonathan Lipman, Barbara Molony, Michael Robinson, eds., *Modern East Asia: An Integrated History* (London: Laurence King Publishing, 2011), 258.

PRIMARY SOURCES

SOURCE 1

THE TREATY OF NANKING (SUMMARY)

Article 1: Stipulated peace and friendship between Britain and China and "full security and protection for their persons and property within the dominions of the other."

Article 2: Allowed British subjects and their families to live in five cities (Canton, Fuzhou, Xiamen, Ningbo, and Shanghai) for "purposes of carrying on their mercantile pursuits without molestation or restraint." It also allowed for the establishment of consulates.

Article 3: Ordered "the Island of Hong Kong to be possessed in perpetuity" by Queen Victoria and her successors, who could rule as they see fit.

Article 4: Required payment of $6 million by the emperor of China to Britain "as the value of the opium which was delivered in Canton" and as ransom for holding two British officials in China.

Article 5: Abolished the Canton cohong monopoly system in China. Permitted British merchants "to carry on their mercantile transactions with whatever persons they please" at the ports of Canton, Fuzhou, Xiamen, Ningbo, and Shanghai.[46] The Qing were to also pay $3 million in settlement for outstanding cohong debts.

Article 6: Ordered payment to the British for a further $12 million "on account of the expenses incurred" in the recent fighting minus any sums already received "as ransom for cities and towns in China" since August 1, 1841.

Article 7: Stipulated that the $21 million in Articles 4 through 6 were to be paid in four installments before the end of 1845, with 5% annual interest charged on late payments.

Article 8: Demanded immediate release of any prisoners who were British subjects, whether Indian or European.

Article 9: Provided unconditional amnesty for all Chinese subjects who had lived with or dealt with the British.

Article 10: Required all merchants at the five treaty ports listed in Article 2 to pay "a fair and regular Tariff of Export and Import Customs and other Dues." Once those fees were paid, only fair and stipulated transit dues would be paid on goods shipped to the interior of China.

Article 11: Ended the use of terminology such as petition or beg in official correspondence between Britain and China, replacing them with nonderogatory and nonsubordinate terms of address such as communication, statement, and declaration.

Article 12: Established agreement that British forces would leave Nanjing and the Grand Canal after receiving the first installment of the indemnity money, and "no longer molest or stop the trade of China."[47]

---

46 The *cohong* was a guild of 13 *hong* merchants authorized by the Chinese central government to handle trade, particularly rights to trade tea and silk, with the West. They were the only group at the time authorized to do this, making them the main controllers of all foreign trade in the nation.

47 Quoted in Jonathan D. Spence, *The Search for Modern China* (New York: W. W. Norton & Company, 1990), 159–60.

SOURCE 2

THE BOXER PROTOCOL (SUMMARY)

The Boxer Protocol was signed on September 7, 1901, in Beijing. The following foreign powers were signatories along with the Chinese Empire:

Kingdom of Spain

United Kingdom

Russian Empire

Empire of Japan

French Republic

United States

German Empire

Austria-Hungary

Kingdom of Italy

Kingdom of Belgium

Kingdom of Netherlands

1. China was to pay a large sum of money (450 taels of silver equal to US $335 million gold dollars at the time) to the foreign powers for the losses incurred by their armies in halting the Boxers. This indemnity was to be distributed over 39 years and paid in gold.

2. Foreign countries could now base their troops in Beijing. The Legation Quarters were under the exclusive power of the occupying foreign government and could be guarded accordingly. No Chinese would have the right to reside in the Legation.

3. Boxers and government officials involved in the rebellion would be punished for crimes or attempted crimes against foreign government or their nationals.

4. The Taku Forts were destroyed.

5. Membership in any anti-foreign society was abolished.

6. Civil service examinations were suspended for five years in all areas where foreigners were massacred by Boxers.

7. The emperor of China was to convey his regrets to the German emperor for the assassination of Baron von Ketteler and a commemorative arch was to be erected on the spot of his death in his memory.

8. The envoy extraordinary of China would convey his regrets to the government of Japan for the assassination of Mr. Sugiyama.[48]

---

48 "Boxer Protocol, Peking 7. September 1901 Peace Agreement between the Great Powers and China," accessed January 1, 2014, http://www.100jia.net/china1900/ereignisse/boxerprotokoll.htm.

PAMPHLET, THE REVOLUTIONARY ARMY (1903) (EXCERPT)

Revolution is a universal rule of evolution. Revolution is a universal principle of the world. Revolution is the essence of a transitional period of struggle for survival. Revolution follows nature and man. Revolution eliminates what is corrupt and holds on to what is good. Revolution is to advance from savagery to civilization. Revolution is to eradicate slavery and become the master. . . . I have heard that the English Revolution of 1688, the American Revolution of 1775, and the French Revolution of 1870 were all revolutions that followed nature and corresponded to the nature of man. They were all revolutions designed to eliminate what was corrupt and hold on to what is good and to advance from savagery to civilization. . . .

I am a young person with little learning or refinement. I cannot really discuss the great significance of revolutionary independence but, timidly and with trepidation, I have conscientiously tried to copy the meaning of American revolutionary independence. Prostrating myself before my most respected and beloved four hundred million exalted Han Chinese countrymen, I list the following proposals for your consideration and action.

1. China belongs to the Chinese. Our countrymen should all recognize that this is the China of the Han race.

2. We will not permit any alien race to tamper with the slightest right of our China.

3. All responsibility to obey the Manchus is abolished. . . .

4. Let us overthrow the barbaric government established by the Manchu people in Beijing. . . .

7. Oppose foreigners and Chinese who interfere with our Chinese revolutionary independence.

8. Set up a central government as the central mechanism for the entire country. . . .

10. Everyone in the country, male or female, will be a citizen.

11. All men in the country will have the obligation to provide military service.

12. Everyone will have the responsibility to pay national taxes. . . .

14. All citizens of the nation, male or female, will be equal and there will be no distinction between high and low, noble and base. . . .

16. Life, liberty, and the pursuit of happiness are all heaven-bestowed rights.

17. Such freedoms as the freedom of speech, thought, and publication cannot be violated.

18. Everyone's individual rights should be protected. The establishment of the government should occur through public agreement and the government will fully employ its power to protect the rights of the people.

19. Whenever the government violates the rights of the people, the people should be able to make a revolution to overthrow the old government in order to satisfy their hopes for peace and happiness. When the people have attained peace and happiness, they should be able through public discussion to rearrange rights and set up a new government. . . .

When revolutionary independence is accomplished, people will not be satisfied if there is still the bitterness of a despotic system. This is the reason we must change the national polity of the past.

1. The government will be named the Republic of China.

2. The Republic of China will be a free and independent nation.

3. This free and independent nation should enjoy equal rights with other great nations in international affairs like the declaration of war, peace negotiations, signing treaties, commercial agreements, and all necessary affairs of state.

4. The constitution will be modeled on the American constitution and will conform to China's situation.

5. Laws for self-governance should all follow American laws for self-governance.

6. Any matter involving the whole populace or an individual, diplomatic negotiations, and the domestic division of government should all follow the American model.[49]

---

49 Pei-kai Cheng, Michael Lestz, and Jonathan D. Spence, eds., *The Search for Modern China: A Documentary Collection* (New York: W. W. Norton & Company, 1999), 198–202.

SOURCE 4

NEWSPAPER ARTICLE REPORTING ON THE PROCLAMATION OF THE FIRST CHINESE REPUBLIC

This article is excerpted from The Hankow Daily News, a local English newspaper, and was a proclamation issued by an anonymous military leader.

I have the honor of the Military Government to let you, my dear country men, know that our[s] is a righteous cause. Don't be suspicious of our army as wherever they march there will be a true reason. I raise the National Army against the Manchus not for the good or merit of myself, but for us as a whole. To rescue you out from the hot fires and deep waters. To deliver you from the sufferings of Manchus just as to heal your ulcers and sores. Why have the Manchus put you under such sufferings? Because they are a different tribe, and naturally cast you away just like a bit of straw.

So far as to-day, you must have known that the Manchu are not the sons of Han. Although you have been so loyal and righteous to them, yet they pay nothing for your service.

Now I can bear it no longer so that we suddenly gather ourselves together under the righteous flag and the foremost thing we want to do is to demolish what is harmful or injurious to you, and we are perfectly willing to exert as much effort as we can only for the welfare of you. We will not allow those who are treacherous to the sons of Han and those who are the thieves of our countrymen to breathe any longer. . . .[50]

---

50 Pei-kai Cheng, Michael Lestz, and Jonathan D. Spence, eds., *The Search for Modern China: A Documentary Collection* (New York: W. W. Norton & Company, 1999), 208.

SOURCE 5
_____

EDICT OF ABDICATION

By Associated Press to Gazette Times.

Peking, Feb. 12—After occupying the throne of China for nearly three centuries, the Manchu dynasty, represented by the child emperor, abdicated today. Three edicts were issues, the first proclaiming the abdication, the second dealing with the establishment of the republic, and the third urging the maintenance of peace and approving the conditions agreed upon by the imperial premier, Yuan Shi-Kai, and the republicans. The text of the first imperial edict is as follows:

We (the Emperor) have respectfully received the following Imperial Edict from the hands of her majesty the dowager empress:

In consequence of the uprising of the Republican army, to which the people of the provinces have responded, the empire is seething like a boiling cauldron and the people are plunged into misery.

Yuan Shi-Kai was therefore commanded to dispatch commissioners in order to confer with the Republicans with a view to the calling of a national assembly to decide on the future form of government. Months have elapsed and no settlement is now evident.

The majority of the people are in favor of a republic. From the preference of the people's hearts the will of heave is discernible. How could we oppose the desires of millions for the glory of one family?

Therefore, we, the dowager empress and the emperor, hereby vest the sovereignty of the Chinese empire in the people.

Let Yuan Shi-Kai organize to the full powers of the provisional republican government and confer with the Republicans as to the methods of union assuring peace in the empire and forming a great republic with the union of Manchus, Chinese, Mongols, Mohammedans and Tibetans.

We, the empress dowager and the emperor, will thus be enabled to live in retirement, free of responsibilities and cares and enjoying without interruption the nation's courteous treatment. . . .[51]

---

51 Associated Press, "Edict Accepting Established Fact Follows Abdication of Dynasty,"
    The Gazette Times, February 13, 1912, accessed May 27, 2013, http://news.google.com
    /newspapers?nid=1126&dat=19120213&id=PQFRAAAAIBAJ&sjid
    =MWYDAAAAIBAJ&pg=1615,3663287.

SOURCE 6

THE ARTICLES OF FAVORABLE TREATMENT [OF THE GREAT QING EMPEROR AFTER HIS ABDICATION]

1. After the abdication of the TaQing emperor, his title of dignity is to be retained by the Republic of China with the courtesies which it is customary to accord to foreign monarchs.

2. After the abdication of the TaQing emperor, he will receive from the Republic of China an annual subsidy of Tls.4,000,000. [four million silver taels approximately four million dollars] . . .

3. After the abdication of the TaQing emperor, he may, as a temporary measure, continue to reside in the Palace (in the Forbidden City), but afterwards he will remove himself to the Yi- Ho Park (the Summer Palace). He may retain his bodyguard.

4. After the abdication of the TaQing emperor, the temples and mausoleums of the imperial family with their appropriate sacrificial rites shall be maintained in perpetuity. The Republic of China will be responsible for the provision of military guards for their adequate protection.

5. As the Ch'ung mausoleum of the late emperor Te Tsung has not yet been completed, the work will be carried out according to the proper regulations (relating to imperial tombs). The last ceremonies of sepulture will also be observed in accordance with the ancient rites. The actual expenses will all be borne by the Republic of China.

6. The services of all the persons of various grades hitherto employed in the Palace may be retained; but in future no eunuchs are to be added to the staff.

7. After the abdication of the TaQing emperor, his private property will be safeguarded and protected by the Republic of China.

8. The imperial guard corps as constituted at the time of the abdication will be placed under the military control of the War Office of the Republic of China. It will be maintained at its original strength and will receive the same emoluments as heretofore.[52]

---

52 Reginald Fleming Johnston, *Twilight In The Forbidden City* (London: Victor Gollancz Ltd., 1934), 96-98, quoted in "The Articles of Favorable Treatment," Exploring Chinese History website, accessed January 1, 2014, http://www.ibiblio.org/chinesehistory/contents/03pol/c02sb01.html.

SPHERES OF INFLUENCE (1850–1914)

From the mid-1850s to the beginning of World War I, many Western nations were expanding into Asia. The "Age of Imperialism" was fueled by the Industrial Revolution in Europe and the United States, and it profoundly influenced nation building efforts in Japan and China. As the desire to exert regional strength grew, Japan also began to expand its colonial influence across East Asia.

PRELUDE TO WAR: 1911–1931

The readings in Chapter Three expand upon the experiences and challenges of nation building in China and Japan. The readings begin prior to the outbreak of World War I and set the stage for World War II in China by examining the evolution of nationalism in Asia including important military, economic, political, and cultural turning points in both nations. By the turn of the twentieth century, both nations increasingly navigated a more connected world. Institutional reforms in each nation continued to play a critical role in their growth and prosperity, but changes in one country increasingly affected another. No longer did China and Japan live in isolation. As the infrastructure of a modern nation-state became firmly grounded in each nation in the first decades of the twentieth century, first in Japan followed by China, each contended with a range of opportunities and critical decisions that would play decisive roles once war became a reality in the late 1930s.

The following questions may be helpful to consider as you deepen your study of nation building leading up to war.

- Under what conditions does nationalism lead to war?
- What are the conditions that make a country vulnerable to war?
- What were the critical steps leading up to the outbreak of World War II in East Asia?
- Was war avoidable?

For media and classroom materials such as discussion questions and additional primary sources, visit www.facinghistory.org/nanjing-atrocities.

INTRODUCTION

If Japan had been a champion of Asian nationalism, had really desired independence and progress from its neighbor, and had joined with China to liberate Asia from Western imperialism, the subsequent history of the region would have been vastly different. Japan would have identified with Chinese nationalism, helped to end foreign domination, and made a real effort to create enduring good relations with new China. Unfortunately, Japanese leaders chose the opposite course of action. They competed with the West for a place at the imperialist table and a slice of the Chinese melon.[1]

—JAPANESE HISTORIAN IENAGA SABURO

Around the world change, upheaval, growth, and creativity marked the first decades of the twentieth century. As industrialization continued to expand at a rapid pace, colonialism spread into Africa and Asia and was fueled by beliefs of racial and cultural superiority. In some ways, the relationships between foreign powers and their colonial holdings facilitated a global exchange that broke down traditional ideas of national sovereignty and, paradoxically, inspired local nationalist and pan-nationalist responses. Amidst this climate, both China and Japan continued to forge their own paths toward becoming modern nations. By the turn of the century China's Qing dynasty had not modernized at the same pace as Meiji Japan. As a result, China lacked the infrastructure, military power, and political leadership to challenge Japan's regional status. After the first Chinese republic was formed in 1911, China began the process of building an industrialized and modernized nation-state, but it was a path fraught with internal strife, violence, and corruption.

Across the Sea of Japan (the East Sea), nation building in Japan took quite a different form.[2] After less than four decades of industrialization and modernization, Japan was a nation more unified and nationalistic than ever. Military, education, industrial, and governing reforms all contributed to Japan's rapid rise. Japan's victory in the Sino-Japanese War of 1894–1895, followed by victory in the Russo-Japanese War of 1904–1905, were key

In this French political cartoon from 1898, the Qing official observes powerlessly as a pastry representing China is divided up by Queen Victoria of the United Kingdom, William II of Germany, Nicholas II of Russia, the French Marianne, and a samurai of Japan. The cartoon is intended to portray the imperialist tendencies towards China at the time.

turning points in Japan's emergence as the superior imperial power in the region. A year after the end of the Sino-Japanese War, writer Lafcadio Hearn recounted:

> The real birthday of the new Japan . . . began with the conquest of China. The war is ended; the future, though clouded, seems big with promise; and, however grim the obstacles to loftier and more enduring achievements, Japan has neither fears nor doubts.
>
> Perhaps the future danger is just in this immense self-confidence. It is not a new feeling created by victory. It is a race feeling, which repeated triumphs have served only to strengthen.[3]

Yet Japan's territorial expansion across East Asia unfolded gradually. Korea became a Japanese colony in 1910 and with the death of Emperor Meiji in 1912 and the ascension to power of his first son, Yoshihito, Japan's Taisho era (1912–1926) began. For many within Japan the transition of power was quite unsettling, but for very different reasons. Emperor Meiji afforded some a level of stability, while his young son was unknown, untested, and physically frail. Although the Taisho era was brief in comparison to other

Japanese eras, it covered important historical events such as the span of World War I, the devastating Great Kanto earthquake of 1923, and a period of unforeseen cultural and artistic experimentation. Despite these challenges and shifts in the status quo, the Taisho years remained relatively stable during the critical interwar years of the 1920s.

China, on the other hand, continued on a path of political and economic turmoil and upheaval during the first decades of the century. General Yuan Shikai was appointed as the first provisional president of China in 1911, but power also remained rooted in a handful of powerful provincial warlords. Many controlled important areas of the countryside, such as the resource-rich north, and most strongly resisted any challenge to their power. Sun Yat-sen attempted to unite all of China's far-flung regions under a government led by the Nationalist Party while Yuan Shikai and the republican provisional government, attempted to reestablish monarchic rule. By 1921 the Chinese Communist Party was established, quickly growing in strength and popularity and seeking to consolidate their own power base. These political struggles escalated into a civil war between the Nationalists and the Communists lasting from 1927 through World War II with Japan.[4] The resulting domestic upheaval constricted many of the modernization efforts and attempts at national unity.

Amidst these domestic and regional conflicts, World War I broke out in Europe during the summer of 1914. Japan declared war in August 1914 and immediately sent troops to fight German forces in German colonial territories in China including Qingdao (Tsingtao), points in Shandong, and German-held islands in the Pacific. Japan also sent naval ships to assist the Allies in the Mediterranean. With European powers' focus on the war effort, Japan in 1915 presented China a diplomatic ultimatum known today as the Twenty-One Demands.[5] Japanese leadership outlined a series of economic and political provisions placing China under further colonial rule by Japan. Failing to agree to them, Japanese threatened, would result in more war. With the political support and negotiating muscle of Great Britain and the United States, most of the demands were ultimately rejected by Chinese leaders yet they still took a toll in further fracturing an already fragile republican government.

Despite this setback, Japan's demands marked a new chapter in their growing militarism and expansionism. With the outbreak of World War I, Japanese manufacturing and trade experienced a tremendous boom as many domestic industries filled a large gap left by Europe's devastated markets. As Japan's economic prosperity grew, so did its population. In 1900 Japan's population was 45 million. By 1925 it had reached 60 million with the ma-

~~jority residing in cities rather than in the countryside.~~ This rapid population growth stretched Japan's natural resources and food supplies, propelling the country's leaders to look beyond the nation's shores to meet domestic needs including raw materials and space to settle the expanding populous.

Ultranationalist groups within Japan's government, military, and civilian population also advocated for the expansion of Japan's territory to meet resource needs and to fulfill their imperial and ideological ambitions.[7] Unlike Hitler in Nazi Germany or Mussolini in Italy, Japanese ultranationalists did not strive to build large-scale organizations or amass large followings to achieve their goal. Instead they believed that a few violent and uncoordinated acts would force major changes in the social and political order of the nation.

China's experience during World War I was quite different from Japan's. China had one crucial resource that many European countries lacked: manpower. Even before China declared war on Germany in 1917, men worked in China's processing plants in Shandong Province or agreed to go to France and Belgium to provide industrial support for the Allied war effort. Given the poverty of the times, many eager Chinese men came forward to work with upward of 140,000 laborers traveling to France and Belgium.[8]

Attracted to Europe by higher wages, sometimes as high as four times more than laborers in China earned, many of these workers were peasants who had never experienced life outside their village. They worked in unsavory and unsanitary conditions in a variety of manufacturing plants and confronted discrimination throughout their time.[9] Initially working in munitions factories and promised they would be nowhere near the front lines, by 1918 some 100,000 Chinese worked in areas of heavy fighting. Many of the infamous trenches of World War I in Flanders and France were actually dug by Chinese workers. In fact, around 3,000 Chinese are buried alongside fallen soldiers in the cemeteries in this part of Europe.

After World War I ended in 1918, both China and Japan had great hopes for what would result since they both fought with the victorious Allied side. Both Japan and China were present at the Paris Peace Conference where the Treaty of Versailles, outlining Germany's conditions of surrender was signed. But Japan was the only Asian nation part of the "Big Five" powers—England, France, Italy, and the United States—negotiating the terms of the treaty. With Germany's defeat, China believed it would reclaim German territorial possessions, imperial-held possessions in the Shandong Province, even though Japan had conquered the territory.[10] This did not happen.

Through a combination of dealings by Chinese warlords, arrangements made by the Japanese government, and a certain amount of unscrupulous behavior by the Western powers, the same territories had essentially been promised to both the Chinese and the Japanese at the same time.[11] As a result the territories were, in the end, handed over to the Japanese, the more powerful and the more technologically advanced of the two countries.

When this news reached Beijing, the Chinese capital at the time, many of the nation's nationalistic and patriotic youth were outraged. In their minds China had made a significant contribution to World War I, they had fought on the Allied side, and they had been denied the right to reconstitute themselves as a free and sovereign nation-state. On May 4, 1919, some 3,000 students from some of the capital's finest institutions in China, gathered in front of the Gate of Heavenly Peace (Tiananmen), made speeches, and then made their way to the house of a Chinese government minister who they felt had been responsible for what they saw as the betrayal at the Paris Peace Conference.[12] Professor Rana Mitter speaks of May 4, 1919, as a defining event in modern China:

> This patriotic demonstration and the raiding of the minister's house quickly became enshrined in legend as a sign that China's nationalistic youth, in particular, would no longer tolerate what they saw as the two perils that were facing China . . . warlordism from within China—the idea that China was split between rival military factions instead of being a genuine democratic republic, and imperialism from without—the idea that the foreign powers, Britain, France, the United States could just push China around, could make it do whatever it wanted.
>
> They came up with a two part slogan for what China needed instead, and again it's a slogan that still is heard in China today . . . Mr. Science and Mr. Democracy, two kinds of characters thought up to express what China needed. These two ideas, Mr. Science and Mr. Democracy, sit at the heart of what these young thinkers and many of their older counterparts thought had to happen in China. In other words, Mr. Science was a way of saying China needed to modernize, it needed to develop its own technology, it needed to do what Japan had done and increase its educational level so that it could learn to defend itself, to educate itself, and create a strong and prosperous society, economy, and culture.

At the same time [Mr. Democracy] was a reminder that technology had to change along with politics. China needed to move away
from the kind of world where having the biggest army would
get you into power and instead move back to the promise of the
republic that had been founded in 1911 when the last Emperor
had to abdicate the throne, and instead go back to the idea of
constitution, perhaps of elections, but certainly of mass popular
participation in politics.[13]

By the early 1920s, fearing China's political consolidation as a possible
regional rival, Japanese militarists and ultranationalists pursued an even
more aggressive policy toward China. The ultranationalists and militarists
demanded Japan's imperial forces prevent the Chinese Nationalist government from controlling Manchuria, a Chinese territory where Japan held
substantial commercial and political interests. By 1928 Japan's militarist
prime minister, Tanaka, sent troops to China. To him and his followers,
expanding into Manchuria made sense politically, as additional territory
would help ease Japan's raw material shortage and offer a place to reside
for the growing Japanese population. With the Chinese government severely
destabilized by the growing conflict between the Chinese Communist Party
and the Nationalist Party, Japanese imperial forces capitalized on their
vulnerability and successfully occupied the Manchurian city of Mukden
(Shenyang) and the whole of Manchuria by 1931. This marks the beginning
of nearly a decade and a half of Japan's territorial expansion into the Asian
mainland and is known by some Chinese as the start of the war of resistance to Japanese invasion lasting from 1931 through 1945. For others, the
occupation of Manchuria stands as the precursor and sets the stage for the
outbreak of World War II in China.[14]

---

1 Saburo Ienaga, *The Pacific War* (New York: Random House, 1978), Kindle edition.
2 The body of water that borders Japan, North Korea, Russia, and South Korea is referenced with
   different names. For Japanese the recognized name is the Sea of Japan. For others, the preferred
   reference is "East Sea" for South Korea and "East Sea of Korea" for North Korea. Currently most
   international maps use either "Sea of Japan" by itself or include "East Sea" in parentheses.
3 John W. Dower, "Prints & Propaganda," in "Throwing off Asia II: Woodblock Prints of the Sino-
   Japanese War (1894-95)," MIT OpenCourseWare – Visualizing Cultures (Massachusetts Institute
   of Technology, 2008) accessed November 9, 2013, http://ocw.mit.edu/ans7870/21f/21f.027
   /throwing_off_asia_01/pdf/toa2_essay_01.pdf. Lafcadio Hearn arrived in Japan in 1890 as a
   journalist and later was appointed to several universities to teach English. He married a Japanese
   woman, changed his name to Koizumi Yakumo, fathered four children, renounced his British
   citizenship, and "adopted" Japan as his home country. Hearn published widely about his life in
   Japan. In 1904 he died of heart failure.
4 The struggle for power between these two groups finally ended with the Communist takeover of
   China in 1949.
5 The demands were grouped into five categories with the most contentious being Group 5, which
   would have allowed Japanese officials to serve in the Chinese central government and be on the
   police force and allow Japanese Buddhist preachers to serve as missionaries. With the rejection by

Chinese officials of Group 5's request, Japan gained very little and harmed its international stature by appearing as a diplomatic bully.

6   The 10% growth is attributed to the years between 1920 and 1930 (the first year a national census was conducted in Japan).

7   *Ultranationalism* within Japan refers to Japan-centered radical ideas that encouraged a religious belief in the mythological history of Japan and sought to preserve the unique national character of Japan and its special mission to be the dominant power in Asia.

8   Jonathan D. Spence, *The Search for Modern China* (New York: W. W. Norton & Company, 1990), 291.

9   Spence, *The Search for Modern China*, 292. A Chinese phrase book created for Chinese laborers from the time perhaps best illustrates the climate with statements such as "Why don't you eat the food?," "The inside of this tent is not very clean," and "This latrine is reserved for Europeans and is not available for Chinese."

10 Historically, Shandong has remained an important province. It was leased to Germany in 1897 and was considered part of the German sphere of influence. For Russia, Shandong was also desirable as it was their closest warm water access port for trade.

11 Worth noting, in particular, were the allowances made by Lloyd George of Britain and Clemenceau of France.

12 Initially a protest was to be held on May 7, 1919, chosen to commemorate the fourth anniversary of China's rejection of the Twenty-One Demands, but fearing official opposition, they moved the date to May 4.

13 Rana Mitter (professor, Oxford University), interview with the author, March 11, 2014.

14 The occupation of Mukden, Manchuria is also referred to as the Mukden Incident or the Manchurian Incident.

READING 1

EXPRESSIONS OF IMPERIALISM

By the turn of the twentieth century, Japan began to develop its own imperial ambitions. With its growing population and need for natural resources, it began to pursue its expansionist ambitions more aggressively. It established a military draft in 1872, forcing all able-bodied males between the ages of 17 or 18 and 35, regardless of class, to serve a mandatory term of three years in the reserves and subjecting them to the military draft at age 20. Many Japanese, including peasants and samurai, opposed mandatory military service. For the samurai it signaled the end of their social standing, as they were now sharing military service with what they called "dirt farmers." For the peasants, the expectation of military service was viewed as a "blood tax" since the idea of dying for Japan, the nation that gave them so little, was not welcomed.

Nevertheless, the militarization of Japan escalated. Japanese historian Marius Jansen explains, "After decades of weakness, it was good to be a Japanese and to humble the mighty neighbor that had dominated the horizon for so long."[15] In less than four decades Japan went from being a feudal society to a modern state, with sophisticated weaponry, a developed military bureaucracy, advancements in governing structures, and education-al institutions.[16] In fact, one of the only things that distinguished Japan from Europe at the turn of the century was its lack of engagement in any foreign

Library of Congress

In this woodcut print, Chinese troops fire at an oncoming Japanese battleship during the First Sino-Japanese War.

war. While this does not explain the motivations behind Meiji Japan's first belligerent act against China, it does highlight Japanese leaders beliefs that victory in war would elevate its global stature and position Japan as a domi-nant power in the region.

The Sino-Japanese War (1894–1895), Japan's "first foreign war," was fought between the Japanese Imperial Army and the Qing Empire. As Japan sought new resources and a position of power in the region, Japanese lead-ers viewed Czarist Russia, who already had much of Manchuria under its thumb and who was eyeing Korea for further expansion, as a serious threat. After a series of confrontations between pro-Chinese and pro-Japanese forces beginning in Korea on August 1, 1894, Japan's military advanced into China and occupied the strategically important Port Arthur as well as the Liaodong (Liaotung) Peninsula and Weihaiwei. China conceded defeat roughly one year after the war's outbreak, signaling for the first time a sig-nificant shift in regional dominance in East Asia from China to Japan.

Japanese poet Takamura Kotaro's poem captures the spirit of this moment.

FUNDS FOR BUILDING WARSHIPS

The Sino-Japanese War was over
but war consciousness rose still higher.
To be prepared for the next war
Funds for building warships had to be scraped together.
First, His Majesty gave a large sum
and government officials were to have part of their salaries
deducted
for some years to come.
Father told mother and me about it in detail
at night in the dining room.
The return of the Liaotung Peninsula
the Emperor was terribly worried,
father feared from the bottom of his heart.
"So from now on, Mitsu, don't be wasteful.
Understand?"[17]

Following its defeat, China was forced to sign the Treaty of Shimonoseki
(Treaty of Maguan), which had devastating consequences for the nation
both in land and in morale. *(See Source 1: Treaty of Shimonoseki/Treaty of
Maguan [excerpt].)* Just days after the signing of the treaty, three of the most
active Western powers in China—Russia, France, and Germany—moved in
quickly to establish their authority over certain ports and apply diplomatic
pressure on the Japanese to return Liaodong to China. The three countries—
known as the Tripartite, or Triple Intervention—were concerned about
Japan gaining a solid foothold in China. Japan, with its military already
stretched thin after 1895, could no longer defend the territory and retreated.
Within days, Russian forces occupied the area, gaining a clear path to
the Yellow Sea. Great Britain then joined the Tripartite powers, and all
occupied parts of China, continuing the carving up of the country that
began decades earlier.

The loss had devastating consequences for China. To finance the war,
China had been forced to take out large loans, mostly from Britain. To
pay the debt, Russia, France, and Germany loaned money in exchange for
the ability to lease strategic ports. These leases enabled the three imperial
powers to have exclusive rights over much of China's railroads, mines,
and harbors. Known as the "scramble for concessions" or pejoratively as

THE SCENE AT HIBIYA TO WELCOME EMPEROR AFTER THE PEACE

Emperor Meiji is welcomed back to Tokyo in 1895 after Japan's victory in the First Sino-Japanese War.

the "slicing of the Chinese melon," this national humiliation encouraged Chinese reformers to accelerate modernization in order to defend themselves against any future foreign occupation. After the Western powers intervened in China, Japan was forced to retreat from Liaodong. While they received a large payment from Russia, the Japanese lost what they perceived to be as their spoils of war.

15 Marius Jansen, *Japan and China: From War to Peace, 1894–1972* (Chicago: Rand McNally College Publishing, 1975), 71–72.
16 Henry D. Smith, "Five Myths about Early Modern Japan," in *Asia in Western and World History: A Guide for Teaching,* ed. Ainslie T. Embree and Carol Gluck (London: M. E. Sharpe Publishing, 1997), 517. Historian Henry Smith argues that Japan in the early nineteenth century was no longer as "feudal" as many may think but much closer to European states, albeit without a foreign war.
17 Takamura Kotaro's, *Chieko and Other Poems of Takamura Kotaro,* trans. Hiroaki Sato, (University of Hawaii Press, 1980), 134.

COMPETITION FOR THE REGION: THE RUSSO-JAPANESE WAR

In Japan, the splendor of victory in China was quickly followed by anger directed toward incompetent Japanese decision-makers who many felt negotiated away their spoils. An accelerated push to strengthen Japan's military to prevent interference began in earnest. Hayashi Tadasu, the first Japanese ambassador to the Court of St. James (the royal court of the United Kingdom) discussed the actions of the Tripartite powers (France, Germany, and Russia) in an internal Meiji memo:

> If new warships are considered necessary we must, at any cost build them. If the organization of our army is inadequate we must start rectifying it from now; if need be, our entire military system must be changed. . . . At present Japan must keep calm and sit tight, so as to lull suspicions nurtured against her; during this time the foundation of nautical power must be consolidated; and we must watch and wait for the opportunity in the Orient that will surely come one day. When this day arrives, Japan will decide her own fate.[18]

The efforts to continue to bolster the nation and strengthen the Japanese military became evident less than 10 years later when Japan declared war on Russia, who the Japanese viewed as the largest competitor in the region. Although the war is called the Russo-Japanese War, it took place in neither Russia nor Japan, but mostly in Manchuria. By 1904 Japan's investment in state-of-the-art military machinery was a reality as Japan quickly moved in to occupy regions of strategic importance. At the time Russia still controlled the Liaodong Peninsula and the valuable Port Arthur. For Russia this port was important as they looked to complete the monumental Trans-Siberian railway linking Moscow and Vladivostok. The significance of completing this project was twofold: it would be Russia's only warm water port to access and the rail would solidify a more stable Russian presence in the region.

The battles that followed between Russia and Japan occurred in the icy waters and the frozen landscape. The Japanese forces sank Russia's Pacific Fleet. The battles were hard fought, exacting a much higher death toll for both Russia and Japan than all their previous conflicts.[19] Japan's naval victories allowed them to capture Port Arthur and sink Russia's four major battleships from its land outposts—an unprecedented military victory at that time.[20] From this point onward, Russia was quite weak and Japan advanced with confidence into the interior of China, occupying the city of Mukden in the winter of 1905.

The Japanese defeated the Russians in many battles during the conflict and ended with a negotiated settlement known as the Portsmouth Agreement, brokered by American president Theodore Roosevelt in Portsmouth, New Hampshire.[21] Officially signed on September 5, 1905, the terms of the agreement included Japan being given Korea, Port Arthur, the Kwantung Peninsula, and all railroads in southern Manchuria.

In this woodblock print by artist Kiyochika Kobayashi, the Russian Tsar Nicholas II wakes from a nightmare in which he dreams of wounded Russian forces returning from the Russo-Japanese War.

However, Russia paid no war reparations to Japan. This development prompted the eruption of riots in many of the industrial centers of Japan. One of the most famous was the Hibiya Riot in Tokyo that lasted for three days and marked the first major social protest in Meiji Japan.

Despite what many viewed as the disappointing terms of the agreement and the domestic strife, Japan's victory over Czarist Russia was a watershed moment for Japan as a modern nation. Not only was it Japan's first victory over a Western power, it happened against a modernized foe. Japan's status as a formidable and respectable military power in the region was now firmly in place. The victory also signaled the start of Japan's territorial expansion into China. The United States and Britain had granted Japan loans to finance the war, while France provided Russia with financial support. Global relationships had shifted, and now Japan was poised to taking a leading role in the region and across the globe.

---

18 Richard Story, *A History of Modern Japan* (New York: Penguin Books, 1991), 118.
19 John W. Dower, "Spoils of War," in "Throwing off Asia III: Woodblock Prints of the Russo-Japanese War (1905-05)," MIT OpenCourseWare – Visualizing Cultures (Massachusetts Institute

of Technology, 2008), accessed October 22, 2013, http://ocw.mit.edu/ans7870/21f/21f.027
/throwing_off_asia_03/toa_essay01.html. In the Battle of Mukden in early 1905, 250,000 Japanese
confronted a Russian force of 320,000. All told, around one million Japanese were mobilized for the
war.

20 John W. Dower, "Yellow Promise/Yellow Peril," MIT OpenCourseWare – Visualizing Cultures
(Massachusetts Institute of Technology, 2008), accessed October 18, 2013, http://ocw.mit.edu
/ans7870/21f/21f.027/yellow_promise_yellow_peril/yp_visnav02.html. This victory was later exploited by Allied forces in World War II as evidence of Japan's perennial ambition to control continental
Asia, yet Japan's military at the time was largely funded by loans raised in New York and London.

21 In 1906 President Roosevelt became the first American to win a Nobel Peace Prize for his
negotiations leading up to the Portsmouth Agreement. See his acceptance speech at
http://www.nobelprize.org/nobel_prizes/peace/laureates/1906/roosevelt-lecture.html.

READING 3

NEW WAYS OF THINKING: RACIAL PURITY

Ideas of difference circulate in nations for many reasons and are heightened
during different periods of time. Japan's military victory against Czarist
Russia in the beginning of the twentieth century was one such moment. With
the nation's confidence swelling and their global prestige growing, new ways
of thinking about themselves and their world soon followed.

Leading this shift were many Japanese nationalists who claimed that Japan's
rapid and successful modernization was testament to the nation's superiority
and signaled their rightful place as the Asian leader in the region. Some
believed a necessary ingredient in furthering their expanding empire was to
separate, even distinguish themselves from neighboring China despite the fact
that a great deal of Japanese culture is rooted in traditions from China. As in
many other imperial powers at the time, such differences were often framed
in language about race and ethnic superiority. As Japanese professor Kazuki
Sato argued:

> As early as the 1870s, the idea of a distinctive Japanese national
> identity was intricately linked to imagining differences from peo-
> ple in China. In order for the Japanese to form their own national
> identity, the construction of the Chinese as racially different people
> was crucial to that purpose. Even before the Sino-Japanese war,
> when the Japanese came into direct contact with the Chinese, the

first recorded discussions centered around dissimilarities in appearance and later came to address differences in genealogy and the genetic factors determining their behavior. By the twentieth century, although the debates about the presumed biological differences between Japanese and Chinese continued, the most vocal arguments were based upon culture. These debates generally stressed the purity of the Japanese "race" and subsequently gave rise to a new way of thinking.[22]

This racialized way of thinking necessitated the coining of new words to reflect these beliefs. The term *minzoku* ("ethnic nation") became a popular and widely used word to describe Japan. It is believed that Nakamura Kyushiro, a Japanese scholar of Chinese history at the time, was an early publisher of the word and its definition. In the 1916 multivolume text *The Nations of the Far East,* he drew upon the English word for nation and the German concept of *volk* ("the people.)[23]

Nakamura believed that humanity was divided into five races (yellow, white, black, dark [Malay], and red copper.) According to him and others like him, the yellow and the white were 'historical' races and the dark and red were passive races that had yet to make any significant contribution to history. They believed that while the white race had achieved greater success in the modern era, in the pre-modern [and] especially medieval period, the Asian race contributed almost everything of significance to world history, including the invention of paper, printing, gunpowder, and the magnetic needle.[24] Scholars like Nakamura were not alone in the belief that groups of people could be ranked by racial characteristics. The idea of ranking people based on race was central to the pseudo scientific ideas of eugenics that were a popular in the West during this time.[25] Scientists today, however, explain that race as determined by skin color, is not a meaningful way to understand the differences between humans.

However, as these ideas became more popular in Japan, many Japanese began to think about their country differently. For them, they were connected by a special ethnic and national purpose.

---

22 Kazuki Sato, "'Same Language, Same Race': The Dilemma of *Kanbun* in Modern Japan," in *The Construction of Racial Identities in China and Japan,* ed. Frank Dikötter (London: C. Hurst & Company, 1997), 125.

23 The concept of *volk* ,which German intellectuals had established to unite the German people against the invading French during the Napoleonic era, grew more potent over time. Chancellor Otto von Bismarck used volk to urge Germans to "think with your blood" and united most German-speaking people into a single state in 1871.

24 Nakamura Kyushiro, Kyokuto no minzoku, in Gendai sosho, ed. Tokutomi Iichiro, (1916), 6-7, quoted in Kevin M. Doak, "Culture, Ethnicity, and the State in Early Twentietch-Century Japan,"

in *Japan's Competing Modernities: Issues in Culture and Democracy,* 1900-1930, ed. Sharon A. Minichiello, (Honolulu: University of Hawaii Press, 1998), 18-28.

25 For more on these ideas see Facing History and Ourselves' publication *Race and Membership in American History: The Eugenics Movement.*

READING 4

TAISHO DEMOCRACY IN JAPAN: 1912-1926

With the death of Emperor Meiji in 1912 a great deal of uncertainty about Japan's future followed. Many believed that Meiji Japan had flourished under the steadfast rule of the emperor who reigned for more than 40 years. Now his first son, Yoshihito, ascended to the throne and took the name Taisho, ushering in the next era. Those deeply loyal to Emperor Meiji and resistant to modernization efforts were particularly vulnerable. Some would hold fast to the centuries of Japanese tradition, rejecting any shifts in gender roles or education and military reforms, while other reformers embraced change.

The young Taisho emperor was born in 1879 and at an early age contracted cerebral meningitis. The ill effects of the disease, including physical weakness and episodes of mental instability, plagued him throughout his reign. Because of his sickness there was a shift in the structure of political power from the old oligarchic advisors under Meiji to the members of the Diet of Japan—the elected representative officials increasingly gaining influence and power. By 1919 Emperor Taisho's illness prevented him from performing any official duties altogether. By 1921 Hirohito, his first son, was named *sesho,* or prince regent of Japan. From this point forward, Emperor Taisho no longer appeared in public.

Despite the lack of political stability, modernization efforts during Taisho continued. A greater openness and desire for representative democracy took hold. Literary societies, mass-audience magazines, and new publications flourished. University cities like Tokyo witnessed a burgeoning culture of European-style cafés, with young people donning Western clothing. A thriving music, film, and theater culture grew, with some calling this period "Japan's roaring 20s."

For these reasons the Taisho era has also been called Taisho democracy as Japan enjoyed a climate of political liberalism unforeseen after decades of Meiji authoritarianism.[26] One of the leading political figures, and the man who coined the term *Taisho democracy,* was professor of law and political theory Dr. Yoshino Sakuzo. After observing and traveling extensively in the West, he returned to Japan and wrote a series of articles promoting the development of a liberal and social democratic tradition in Japan. In the preface to his 1916 essay "On the Meaning of Constitutional Government," Yoshino wrote:

> [T]he fundamental prerequisite for perfecting constitutional government, especially in politically backwards nations, is the cultivation of knowledge and virtue among the general population. This is not the task that can be accomplished in a day. Think of the situation in our own country [Japan]. We instituted constitutional government before the people were prepared for it. As a result there have been many failures. . . . Still, it is impossible to reverse course and return to the old absolutism, so there is nothing for us to do but cheerfully take the road of reform and progress. Consequently, it is extremely important not to rely on politicians alone but to use the cooperative efforts of educators, religious leaders, and thinkers in all areas of society.[27]

With such ideas openly circulating, Japan also saw the rise of mass movements advocating political change. Labor unions started large-scale strikes to protest labor inequities, political injustices, treaty negotiations, and Japanese involvement in World War I. The number of strikes rose from 108 in 1914 to 417 strikes in 1918. At the outset of World War I, there were 49 labor organizations and 187 at the end, with a membership total of 100,000.[28] A movement for women's suffrage soon followed. While the right of women to vote was not recognized until 1946, these early feminists were instrumental in overturning Article 5 of the Police Security Act, which had prevented women from joining political groups and actively participating in politics. They also challenged cultural and family traditions by entering the workforce in greater numbers and asserting their financial independence.

One of the most widespread political protests occurred in 1918 with Japan's rice riots. Like the rest of the world, Japan was experiencing wartime inflation and low wages. The dramatic increase in the price of rice, a staple of the Japanese diet, had an impact on the entire country. In August 1918 in the fishing village of Uotsu, fishermen's wives attempted to stop the export of grain from their village in protest against high prices. By October more than

30 separate riots were documented, the vast majority organized by women workers. They refused to load grain, attacked rice merchants, and protested the continued high prices. They inspired other protests, such as the demand by coal miners for higher wages and humane work conditions.

Much of this social unrest, political uprising, and cultural experimentation came to a halt on September 1, 1923. On this day a powerful earthquake struck Japan measuring 7.8 on the Richter scale. This natural disaster is referred to today as the Great Kanto Earthquake. The force of the quake was so strong that a 93-ton Buddha statue 37 miles from the epicenter moved almost two feet. The disaster devastated the entire city of Tokyo, the third largest city in the world at that time, destroyed the port city of Yokohama, and caused large-scale destruction in the surrounding area. The earthquake and subsequent fires killed more than 150,000 people and left over 600,000 homeless. Martial law was immediately instituted, but it couldn't prevent mob violence and the targeting of ethnic minorities. Koreans living in Tokyo were targeted, as rumors spread that they were poisoning the water and sabotaging businesses. Newspapers reported these rumors as fact. According to standard accounts over 2,600 Koreans and 160–170 Chinese were killed, with about 24,000 detained by police. The numbers include political opponents such as the anarchist Osugi Sakai, his wife, and their six-year-old nephew, who were tortured to death in military police custody. The officer responsible for this crime later became a high-ranking official in Manchuria.[29]

Using the social unrest as an excuse, the Japanese Imperial Army moved in to detain and arrest political activists they believed were radicals. After events surrounding the earthquake, the relationship between the military and the emperor began to shift. According to the Meiji Constitution, the emperor led the army and navy. However, all military decisions were actually made by the prime minister or high-level cabinet ministers. As political activists became more vocal, many were abducted and were never seen again. Local police and army officials who were responsible claimed these so-called radicals used the earthquake crisis as an excuse to overthrow the government. More repression and violence soon followed. Prime Minister Hara (1918–1921) was assassinated, and a Japanese anarchist attempted to assassinate Taisho's first son, Hirohito.

Order was firmly restored when a more conservative arm of the government gained influence and passed the Peace Preservation Law of 1925. Besides threatening up to 10 years imprisonment for anyone attempting to alter the *kokutai* (rule by the emperor and imperial government, as opposed to popular sovereignty), this law severely curtailed individual freedom in Japan

and attempted to eliminate any public dissent.[30] The transition in the emperor's role to one of greater power began with the death of Emperor Taisho on December 18, 1926. Following tradition, his son Hirohito ascended to the throne and chose the name Showa, meaning "peace and enlightenment." Hirohito neither suffered from physical or mental ailments like his father nor held the commanding presence of his grandfather. Rather, Hirohito began his reign by performing all the ceremonial duties flawlessly but appearing in public only for highly orchestrated formal state occasions. Over time as the political climate within Japan shift-

Hirohito at his coronation in 1928.

ed to a more militaristic stance, so did the role of the emperor. One specific gesture is emblematic of the changes occurring in the role and power of the emperor. When Hirohito first appeared in public in the early years of his reign, commoners would always remain dutifully seated to avoid appearing above the emperor, but they were permitted to look at him. By 1936 it was illegal for any ordinary Japanese citizen to even look at the emperor.

---

26 Professor Kevin M. Doak also argues that it is important to recognize that "nationalism, especially the popular ethnic version, were the central ingredient in what has come to be known as Taisho democracy." Doak, "Culture, Ethnicity, and the State in Early Twentieth-Century Japan," 19.

27 Wm. Theodore de Bary, Carol Gluck, and Arthur E. Tiedemann, eds., *Sources of Japanese Tradition,* 2nd edition, vol. 2, (New York: Columbia University Press, 2005), 838.

28 In 1914 over 5,700 workers were involved in strikes and by 1918 over 66,000 were involved. See http://libcom.org/library/1918-rice-riots-strikes-japan.

29 Bob Tadashi Wakabayashi (professor, York University), private correspondence with the author, January 22, 2014.

30 Ironically, this conservative faction passed the 1925 Universal Manhood Suffrage Act, increasing the number of males eligible to vote from 3.3 million to 12.5 million. It also transformed the most devastated areas of earthquake-ravaged cities by building parks and erecting modern concrete buildings that would withstand future quakes with funds that came from cutting military spending in half. Nevertheless, the early stages of repression and militarism during the final years of the Taisho era foreshadowed the extreme rise in nationalism and militarism that followed in the coming decades.

STRENGTHENING THE JAPANESE NATION

The spirit of the Japanese nation is, by its nature, a thing that must be propagated over the seven seas and extended over the five continents. Anything that may hinder it must be abolished, even by force.[31]

—ARMY MINISTER SADAO ARAKI, JANUARY 23, 1933

The post–World War I economy wreaked havoc on many nations, Japan included. Due to the postwar production slowdown, increased trade barriers and tariffs imposed by the West, and economic strains caused by the Great Kanto Earthquake, Japan fell into an economic depression two years before the global Great Depression began in 1930.[32] Thirty-seven banks were forced to close after Japanese citizens tried to cash in government-issued earthquake bonds that had been sold to raise funds for reconstruction. The economic crisis brought down the civilian government and brought to power the *zaibatsu*, family-controlled businesses that held monopolies within the Japanese Empire and kept close ties, and influence, with the civilian government.[33] When the Great Depression began, Japan was economically and politically vulnerable and increasingly unstable. Like other nations during such fragile times, Japan saw a rise in political groups promising to fix the problems of the nation.

The Cherry Blossom Society, or Sakurakai, was one such group. The cherry blossom carries significant symbolic meaning in Japan. In Buddhist cultural tradition, the flower, with its short blooming period, expresses the fleeting nature of life. Sakurakai adopted this as a name not only to connect its nationalist ideology to the symbol of the nation but also to give its activities spiritual meaning. Founded by Hashimoto Kingoro, a leader in the Japanese Imperial Army, Sakurakai advocated military insurrection and "Showa Restoration," which would free Emperor Hirohito from all political party affiliations. The Cherry Blossom Society believed the political parties established during Taisho were to blame for Japan's current economic struggles, and their elimination was the first step in strengthening the nation.

~~Sakurakai began with only a few members in September 1930.~~ It quickly grew in size and attracted several hundred ultranationalist officers from the army's general staff headquarters in Tokyo. In October 1931 Sakurakai attempted their first of two coup d'états, or overthrows of the government. Both efforts ultimately failed. Those involved in the first insurrection suffered few consequences, but those conspirators involved in the second insurrection were arrested and transferred to other posts. Hashimoto was forced to retire, and the group had to disband. Despite these setbacks, other like-minded nationalist factions arose, and the military continued to play a dominant role in the political affairs of the nation.

The ideology of the radicalized factions of the *Sakurakai* found a receptive audience with Japanese military leaders. While the emperor was the country's leader, actual power was divided among his advisers, the police, and the military. By the 1930s many military officers held legislative and

MHJ Collection, Belgium

This child's printed silk kimono from the1930s shows how some Japanese clothing was designed to celebrate military ambitions.

executive power and formed an independent body that was answerable to only the emperor. A formative figure in this shift was General Araki Sadao, appointed as Army Minister in 1931. He was a staunch, outspoken proponent of a policy known as Kōdōha, or the "Imperial Way," which advocated expansionism, totalitarianism, and greater militarism. General Araki retired from this post in 1936 and one year later was appointed minister of education where he used propaganda to promote patriotism and loyalty. Throughout the 1920s and early 1930s Japanese students were taught about their nation's new status as a world power and the responsibility they held in sustaining this status.

Each school day began with a procession to a courtyard where the Japanese flag was run up a poll while the national anthem played, further reinforcing the strength and connection to Japan's imperial past with its current status. *(See Source 2: National Anthem Kimagayo—Japan's National Anthem.)* At other educational institutions, such as one private Jesuit institution in Tokyo, the Fathers and the students were forced to undergo military training. Scholarships for higher education were granted not solely for good grades or hard work but to students who personified the Japanese military ideal of discipline, tradition, strength, and loyalty to the emperor. In the early 1930s the Japanese government established the Board of Information, which censored the media and outlawed "dangerous thoughts," ideas that originated in the West and conflicted with the goals of the Japanese Imperial Army. History books were revised and history classes were transformed into courses on Japanese ethics and morals. Books about the divinity of the emperor and the duty of every citizen to worship at the imperial altar become compulsory reading in all high schools and colleges.

One Japanese soldier, who served in World War II and was interviewed for the book *Evil Men*, recounted the impact of his schooling during this period:

> You know, public education, they drove loyalty and patriotism,
> that sort of ideology home. In other words, what does that mean?
> It means that the country of Japan is, well, the country of God. It is
> the absolute best country in the world—that idea was thoroughly
> planted into us. . . . If you turn it over, it means to despise other
> races. That is the sort of ideology it is. And from the time we
> were small, we called Chinese people *dirty chinks*—made fun of
> them. We called Russians *Russkie pigs.* We called Westerners *hairy
> barbarians,* you know? And so this meant that when the people of
> Japan joined the army and went to the front, no matter how many

Chinese they killed, they didn't think of it as being much different than killing a dog or a cat.

Another reason is, like I said before, to give your life to the leader, His Majesty the Emperor, of what is absolutely the greatest country in the world, Japan, is a sacred duty and the highest honor. There's that ideology, you know. And this ideology, when you go into the military, is strengthened more and more, and your personality is taken away. . . . When it's time to go to battle—at those times, when you were ordered by a superior, you couldn't resist. So the humanitarian ideology I learned about in college just couldn't win out over the ideology of "loyalty and patriotism" that had been drilled into me from the time I was small.[34]

---

31 To see a photograph of Araki from January 23, 1933, see
    http://www.time.com/time/covers/0,16641,19330123,00.html.
32 The Smoot-Hawley Tariff Act in America and other trade barriers in Britain
    highly restricted the export sector of Japan's economy.
33 At this time there were at least four large zaibatsus that controlled a great deal
    of the Japanese Empire's business holdings. These companies were Sumitomo,
    Mitsui, Mitsubishi, and Yasuda, all performing a variety of business endeavors
    including tax collection, foreign trade, and military procurement.
    See http://en.wikipedia.org/wiki/Zaibatsu.
34 James Dawes, *Evil Men* (Cambridge: Harvard University Press, 2013), 49.

READING 6

FIRST DECADES OF THE CHINESE REPUBLIC: 1911–1931

From the 1911 revolution to Japan's occupation of Manchuria in 1931, the Chinese experienced a flurry of competing political allegiances and unrest. The provisional government and the Nationalist Party competed for power while corrupt warlords continued ruling the rural areas of the country. Warlords, or military cliques, were military men who seized the opportunity during politically vulnerable times following the 1911 revolution to gain and hold onto local power bases.

Political power struggles weren't the only cause of China's instability and chaos. Rather, it resulted from a combination of many factors: geographic, economic, political, and cultural. China's population at this time was approximately 330 million.[35] The land mass was vast, with many ethnicities speaking multiple languages. Seventy-five percent of its estimated population lived in small villages and had little, if any, access to new technologies, transportation, education, or information at the turn of the century. Foreign companies, with Japan included, conducted trade, businesses, and investment in China under extraterritoriality agreements. Primarily in Shanghai and Manchuria, these agreements created enormous economic advantages for the foreign powers in the region.

In response, a group of young reformers emerged. They hoped to modernize education and institute democratic values and institutions for everyone in China, including those previously excluded, such as women. As in Europe, America, or Meiji Japan, these young reformers looked to discard traditional practices and replace them with modern practices and institutions, strengthening and creating a stronger China at the beginning of the twentieth century.

One of the most visible groups to emerge was the New Culture Movement. Based at Peking University, the New Culture Movement encouraged young students to join intellectuals and publically challenge traditional Chinese values and policies. Among the changes they advocated for was language reform—the abandonment of classical writing with its tens of thousands of ideographs to be memorized in favor of a standardized national language. Their flagship journal promoting this practice and other reforms was *New Youth,* or *La Jeunesse,* established in 1915. The magazine became an outlet for youth to express their political and social ideas. The magazine's founder, Chen Duxiu, believed strongly in the power of youth to transform society and participate in social revolution. *New Youth* influenced many Chinese student leaders, some of whom would later become leaders of the Chinese Communist Party after its founding in 1921. They believed old-fashioned social and cultural beliefs were at the heart of Chinese "weakness" and China could only survive if, like a human body, she were to shed old vital cells for new.[36]

A seminal moment in the New Culture Movement occurred once the provisions of the Treaty of Versailles negotiated at the Paris Peace Conference became publically known. On May 4, 1919, over 3,000 students assembled at the Gate of Heavenly Peace Square (Tiananmen Square) to protest the treaty. Luo Jialun, who established the literary magazine *New Tide,* was asked to pen a manifesto expressing the movement's frustrations:

At the Paris Peace Conference, Japan's request to occupy and control (the Chinese province of) Shandong, is about to be granted! Their diplomacy has triumphed completely while ours has failed utterly! The loss of Shandong means the destruction of China's territorial integrity. Once territorial integrity is destroyed, China will soon be annihilated. Therefore today, we, the students, form a procession and demonstrate in front of every embassy of every country, and demand that they defend justice. We hope people in industry, business and every walk of life all over the country will hold citizens' meetings to fight; internationally for China's sovereignty and domestically to rid the country of traitors. China's survival depends on this next move! Today we swear two solemn oaths with all our countrymen: (1) China's territory may be conquered, but it cannot be given away; (2) the Chinese people may be massacred, but they will not surrender.[37]

Calling the members of the government who negotiated these terms "traitors to China," the students marched to the legation quarter in Beijing, carrying signs with messages written in English, Chinese, and French and chanting slogans such as "Protect our Sovereignty." The students found their way to the home of pro-Japan foreign minister Cao Rulin, burned it down, and violently attacked a guest staying in the house, a former ambassador to Japan. Eventually 32 students were arrested and the May Fourth Movement, as it is referred to today, was born.[38]

---

35 W. W. Rockhill, "The 1910 Census of the Population of China," *Bulletin of the American Geographical Society* 44, no. 9 (1912): 668–73.

36 Jonathan Lipman, Barbara Molony, and Michael Robinson, eds., *Modern East Asia: An Integrated History* (London: Laurence King Publishing, 2011), 260.

37 Ibid., 261.

38 About two years after these protests, an international disarmament conference convened in Washington, DC. Organized initially as an attempt by the United States to minimize its naval expenditures, the Washington Naval Conference resulted in agreements including the Nine Power Treaty, which returned Japanese-held territories to China, but did not expel foreign companies as some protested had demanded.

INTERNAL STRIFE IN CHINA

China in the 1920s was a new republic confronting great challenges—economic, political, and social. One of the most devastating was the early 1920s North China famine. Because this region of China was densely populated, the effects of this crisis affected millions. Triggered by a severe drought, the famine killed crops and devastated the livelihood of farmers in the northern plains of China. But dying crops was only one consequence. Thousands fled the area; others sold children into slavery, and upward of half a million people died. The areas decimated were largely governed by warlords, which further aggravated the situation since they used the crisis for their own political and economic gain.

Famine, warlord power, and a largely ineffective government were the backdrop for revolutionary activity in China to foment. By 1921 the Chinese Communist Party (CCP) was formally established. The emergence of the CCP not only challenged the current hold of power by the Nationalists but also reflected the worldwide emergence of political ideologies and movements with direct anti-imperialist platforms. Several years earlier, in 1917, the Russian Revolution had occurred. Communist revolutionaries in Russia and China argued that imperialism was the root cause of the economic exploitation and political domination of their country by another people. As political discontent in China continued, Russian Communist leader Vladimir Lenin looked to China, its direct southern neighbor, as a country ripe for the spread of communism.

On July 21, 1921, the first meeting of the Chinese Communist Party was held in Shanghai. Chen Duxiu, a leader in China's 1911 revolution, founder of *New Youth,* and a leader in the May Fourth Movement, was cofounder of the CCP along with Li Dazhao. Chen became the first general secretary and argued that a complete overhaul of the "feudal" system was necessary for China's survival. In order to remove the powerful northern warlords and further solidify their power base, the Chinese Communist Party formed an alliance with Sun Yat-sen and the Nationalist Party, the First United Front. The Soviets lent financial and political support to this alliance to ensure their future involvement in Chinese affairs. Some of this money was used to establish the Whampoa (Huangpu) Military Academy in the spring of 1924. In exchange for their financial support, the Soviets expected graduates of Whampoa to provide China with a cadre of highly trained and motivated young officers who would promote their revolutionary cause while establishing a pipeline for future military leaders. Chiang Kai-shek, a favored leader of Nationalist leader Sun Yat-sen, was named the first commandant of the academy. In this role, Chiang was able to cultivate soldiers loyal to the Nationalists and also to himself. These goals were articulated by Sun Yat-sen in the opening ceremonies of the academy:

> Honored guests, faculty and students, today marks the opening of
> our academy. Why do we need this school? Why must we definite-
> ly open such a school? You all know that the Chinese Revolution
> has gone on for thirteen years; although these years have been
> counted as years of the Republic there has been in reality, no
> Republic. After thirteen years of revolution, the Republic is just an
> empty name and, even today, the revolution is a complete failure.
> . . .
>
> What is our hope in starting this school today? Our hope is that
> from today on we will be able to remake our revolutionary enter-
> prise and use the students of this school as the foundation of a
> revolutionary army. You students will be the basic cadres of the
> revolutionary army of the future. . . . Without a good revolution-
> ary army, the Chinese revolution is doomed to failure. Therefore,
> in opening this military academy here today, our sole hope is to
> create a revolutionary army to save China from extinction![39]

When Nationalist leader Sun Yat-sen died of cancer in 1925, a period of political instability followed as to who was to lead. One year later, Chiang Kai-shek emerged as party leader and despite differing politically, both the Chinese Communist Party and the Nationalists advocated for the reunification of China at this time. As a result, the First United Front Alliance was formed as a means to end warlordism, a consistent obstacle in forging a unified country, and as a means to forge a central government and ultimately put an end to foreign domination.

Despite this attempt of solidarity, China's future continued to be uncertain. By April 1927, the Chinese Communist Party had more than 60,000 members and continued to grow. When Chiang Kai-shek was named director of the state council, equivalent to president of the nation in October 1928, he used his authority to enlist civilian and military troops, police, and mafia groups to "purge" (kill) thousands of Communist party members, leftists, workers, and labor union leaders in Shanghai, China's most populous city and its economic engine. A year later, still more Communist organizers were hunted down by Nationalists and killed across China in a campaign of anti-communist suppression.

In response, the weakened Chinese Communist Party attempted two subsequent but unsuccessful coups against the Nationalists. Within a year of the purges, fewer than 10,000 remained. The core of China's Communist power was decimated. Communists fled to the rural countryside and the Nationalists emerged as the power stronghold in the country initiating the first phase of the Chinese Civil War. With the Communist threat temporarily diminished, Chiang Kai-shek led his troops toward Beijing riding upon a high tide of nationalism and public support. By the beginning 1929, the Nationalists had unified many of the urban areas, approved a provisional constitution, garnered the support of three key warlords, and set up its government in its new capital, Nanjing.

But in the rural areas, many peasants remained under the control of a weakened warlord system or were aligned with the Communist Party. Mao Zedong, one of the CCP's early regional leaders, had relocated his base to the Jiangxi borderland establishing the Chinese Soviet Republic.[40] After enduring five campaigns lead by Chiang meant to wipe out the Communist rivals, Mao and his Communist followers fled and sought out a new base for their political organizing. This retreat, referred to by Communist leaders as the Long March, lasted from October 1934 to October 1935, led to misery, starvation, and death. By the time their new base was set up in Shaanxi, Chinese Communist members had marched over 6,200 miles. And of the 80,000 troops that began with Mao, roughly 8,000 to 9,000 survived. Because of his organizing efforts during the Long March, Mao ascended to the top ranks of the CCP leadership. In December 1935, Mao wrote the following:

The leadership of the CCP included, from right, Mao Zedong, Zhu De, Zhou Enlai and Qin Bangxian, seen here after the Long March in 1936.

Wikimedia

~~The Long March is the first of its kind in the annals of history. It~~
is a manifesto, a propaganda force, a seeding-machine. . . . It has
proclaimed to the world that the Red Army is an army of heroes,
while the imperialists and their running dogs, Chiang Kai-shek and
his like, are impotent.[41]

The ongoing political discord between China's two main political parties
throughout the early 1930s undermined the stability of the country. These
vulnerabilities appeared increasingly attractive to ultranationalists, particularly in Japan, who desired parts of China to fall under their spheres of
influence.

---

39 Pei-kai Cheng, Michael Lestz, and Jonathan D. Spence, eds., *The Search for Modern China: A
Documentary Collection* (New York: W. W. Norton & Company, 1999), 253.
40 Mao Zedong was born in 1893 in Hunan Province in central China. His father was a reasonably
rich peasant farmer and he and the young Mao Zedong did not get on well at all. Mao left home
at an early age and ended up first in the provincial capital, Changsha, where he started to study
and also to write. He wrote about a variety of issues from women's rights to the need for China to
develop a stronger and more vibrant culture.
41 Jonathan D. Spence, *The Search for Modern China*, (New York: W. W. Norton & Company,
1990), 409.

READING 8

EXCLUSION AND HUMILIATION

Chinese and Japanese encountered strife abroad that directly affected life at
home. In late nineteenth- and early twentieth-century America, immigration
quotas limiting Chinese and Japanese from entering the United States
reflected widespread prejudices directed toward individuals of Asian descent.
The Chinese Exclusion Act of 1882 restricted the numbers of Chinese
laborers from entering the United States based upon their nationality and
denied any Chinese laborer from becoming a citizen. The discriminatory
practices directed toward Chinese also affected Japanese laborers. While
over time the United States and Japan accepted agreements such as the
Gentleman's Agreement allowing small numbers of Japanese to enter the
country, the existence of such policies led to ongoing diplomatic tensions
with Western nations.[42]

Such strains were evident in 1919 when China and Japan attended the Paris Peace Conference to help negotiate the post–World War I Treaty of Versailles. Japan's feelings of self-confidence soon grew to animosity. Japanese leaders participating in the negotiations believed their status around the table came about as a result of their declaration of war against Germany on August 23, 1914. Japan's motivations for declaring war were to secure German-held territory in China so as to further elevate their global stature.

But the Japanese delegation arrived in Paris with another goal as well—to get a clause on racial equality written into the covenant of the League of Nations. The establishment of the League of Nations was recommended by United States president Woodrow Wilson in the last point of the 1918 "Fourteen Points" speech. It called for a "league of nations," an international institution whereby future conflicts would be resolved around a table rather than on a battlefield. Japanese leaders believed the inclusion of a racial equality clause in such a document could be used to outlaw racial discrimination in all future international dealings. Makino Nobuaki, a leader of the Japanese delegation, introduced his proposal by saying:

> [P]rejudices had been a source of troubles and wars throughout history and they may become more acute in the future. The problem possessed a very delicate and complicated nature involving the play of human passions, but equality could not be denied simply because of one's race. Shared struggles during the war demonstrated that different races worked with each other, saving lives irrespective of racial differences, and a common bond of sympathy and gratitude had been established to an extent never before experienced. I think it only just that after this common suffering and deliverance the principle of equality among men should be admitted. . . . For these several reasons, political and moral integrity required the delegates to go on record supporting the following amendment:
>
>> The equality of nations being a basic principle of the League of Nations, the High Contracting Parties agree to accord as soon as possible to all alien nationals of States, members of the League, equal and just treatment in every respect making no distinction, either in law or in fact, on account of their race or nationality.[43]

While Japan was one of five Allied nations officially at the table with the "Big Four" (France, Italy, Great Britain, and the United States), its influence was ultimately undermined by its allies, who wanted to keep Japan's regional power at bay. For Japanese nationalists, this was yet another piece of evidence that the Japanese were disrespected by Western nations. On April 11, 1919, Makino made his final plea in support of the racial equality clause:

> The whole purpose of the League was to regulate the conduct of nations and peoples toward one another, according to a higher moral standard than has reigned in the past, and to administer justice throughout the world. In this regard, the wrongs of racial discrimination have been and continue to be, the source of profound resentment on the part of large numbers of the human race, directly affecting their rights and their pride. Many nations had fought in the recent war to create a new international order, and the hopes of their nationals now have risen to new heights with victory. Given the noble objectives of the League, the heavy burden of the past, and the great aspirations of the future, the leaders of the world should openly declare their support for at least the principle of equality of nations and just treatment of their nationals.[44]

At the insistence of the Japanese delegation, a vote was held. The modified amendment asked for nothing more than a formal recognition of the principle of equality of nations and just treatment of their nationals. Eleven of the 17 delegates voted for the amendment and despite the vote the racial equality clause was not adopted.

Historian Margaret MacMillan writes that the loudest opposition came from the British Empire delegation, specifically Billy Hughes who believed approval of the clause would be the first breach "in the dike protecting Australia." She goes on to quote one of Hughes' subordinates as saying, "No Govt. could live for a day in Australia if it tampered with White Australia."[45] President Wilson, who was chairing the meeting, knew that any reference to racial equality would alienate key politicians on the West Coast of the United States, and he needed their support to get the League of Nations ultimately through the US Congress.[46] With this in mind and because there were strong objections from many of the members of the delegation, Wilson announced the amendment could not carry.[47]

Many in the international and Japanese press were highly critical of this decision. A headline in the *Sacramento Union* announced "Peace Delegates Beat Japan's Proposal for Racial Equality" and a Japanese newspaper said the decision would be a "medium for provoking racial hatred and jealousy that will lead to friction and hostilities throughout the world."[48] After the Japanese delegation returned home, they did not retreat from their call for racial equality, but they were dismayed at the league's decision. Makino noted: "Such a frame of mind, I am afraid, would be detrimental to that harmony and co-operation, upon which foundation alone can the League now contemplated be scarcely built."[49]

In the following years, Japan turned away from international cooperation and became a more insular and militaristic nation. Japanese statesmen Ishii Kikujiro, implementing discriminatory policies despite their position at the Paris Peace Conference, later reflected:

> The problems of population and race will in the future form the hardest and most important issues between nations. These problems have failed of solution by the old methods of aggression and diplomatic intrigue and the world is expecting a new style of diplomacy to solve them. . . . It must be remembered that these problems do not concern Japan and the United States alone, but are common to most countries of the world. The satisfactory solution to these baffling problems is the responsibility of twentieth century diplomacy.[50]

42 The Gentlemen's Agreement of 1907 was an informal agreement made between the United States and Meiji Japan stating that the United States would neither impose nor enforce restrictions on Japanese immigration and Japan would not allow further emigration to the United States. For more information on Chinese and Japanese immigration policy, see Facing History's *Becoming American: The Chinese Experience*.

43 Paul Gordon Lauren, "Human Rights in History: Diplomacy and Racial Equality at the Paris Peace Conference," *Diplomatic History* 2, no. 3 (1978): 257-58. The first draft of the proposed clause was presented to the League of Nations on February 13, 1919, as an amendment to Article 21 of the league's charter.

44 Michael L Krenn, ed., *The Impact of Race on U.S. Foreign Policy: A Reader* (New York: Routledge, 1999), 270.

45 Margaret MacMillan, *Paris 1919: Six Months That Changed the World* (New York: Random House, 2003), 319.

46 Ibid, 320.

47 Ibid.

48 "Anglo-Saxons Want to Dominate the World," Japan Times, April 26, 1919, quoted in Lauren, "Human Rights in History." The original Japanese quote was in the Japanese-language *Tokyo Nichi Nichi Shimbun* newspaper, and translated in the contemporary English-language *Japan Times* newspaper.

49 MacMillan, *Paris 1919*, 321.

50 Ishii Kikujiro, *Diplomatic Commentaries*, trans. W. R. Langdon (Baltimore: Johns Hopkins University Press, 1936), 270–71, quoted in Lauren, "Human Rights in History," 107.

RESTORING THE STATUS OF ASIA

Japanese imperialism was not simply about increasing its territory. It was also fueled by a strong ideological sense of mission. These ideas were captured in a word widely used at the time but rarely heard today: *Pan-Asianism*.

Advocates of Pan-Asianism in Japan believed they were expanding their empire in order to liberate Asian territories from Western imperialism.[51] In the mind of many Japanese, expanding their empire into other Asian regions was somehow different. They thought of their ambitions as bringing their Asian brethren together.

Outside of Japan, Pan-Asianism found other audiences and other meanings. Many Chinese nationalists in the 1920s and 1930s wanted Asian nations to work together against further Western colonization, but without Japanese expansion into China. While Chinese exclusion and discrimination abroad was one motivating element, so was the ongoing political and social disorder in the new Chinese republic. Chinese nationalists supporting Pan-Asianism believed a unified China working in concert with other Asian nations would ultimately be a stronger nation.

On November 28, 1924, Nationalist leader Sun Yat-sen delivered a speech in Kobe, Japan, translated as "Greater Asianism" (Da Yaxiyazhuyi). An excerpt of the speech follows:

> Gentlemen: I highly appreciate this cordial reception with which you are honoring me today. The topic of the day is "Pan-Asianism," but before we touch upon the subject, we must first have a clear conception of Asia's place in the world. Asia, in my opinion, is the cradle of the world's oldest civilization. Several thousand years ago, its peoples had already attained an advanced civilization; even the ancient civilizations of the West, of Greece and Rome, had their origins on Asiatic soil. In Ancient Asia we had a philosophic, religious, logical and industrial civilization. The origins of the various civilizations of the modern world can be traced back to Asia's ancient civilization. It is only during the last few centuries that the countries and races of Asia have gradually degenerated and become weak, while the European countries

have gradually developed their resources and become powerful. After the latter had fully developed their strength, they turned their attention to, and penetrated into, East Asia, where they either destroyed or pressed hard upon each and every one of the Asiatic nations, so that thirty years ago there existed, so to speak, no independent country in the whole of Asia. With this, we may say, the low water mark had been reached. . . .

If we want to realize Pan-Asianism in this new world, what should be its foundation if not our ancient civilization and culture? Benevolence and virtue must be the foundations of Pan-Asianism. With this as a sound foundation we must then learn science from Europe for our industrial development and the improvement of our armaments, not, however, with a view to oppressing or destroying other countries and peoples as the Europeans have done, but purely for our self-defense.

Japan is the first nation in Asia to completely master the military civilization of Europe. Japan's military and naval forces are her own creation, independent of European aid or assistance. Therefore, Japan is the only completely independent country in East Asia. . . . At present Asia has only two independent countries, Japan in the East and Turkey in the West. In other words, Japan and Turkey are the Eastern and Western barricades of Asia. Now Persia, Afghanistan, and Arabia are also following the European example in arming themselves, with the result that the Western peoples dare not look down on them. China at present also possesses considerable armaments, and when her unification is accomplished she too will become a great Power. We advocate Pan-Asianism in order to restore the status of Asia. Only by the unification of all the peoples in Asia on the foundation of benevolence and virtue can they become strong and powerful.

But to rely on benevolence alone to influence the Europeans in Asia to relinquish the privileges they have acquired in China would be an impossible dream. If we want to regain our rights we must resort to force. In the matter of armaments, Japan has already accomplished her aims, while Turkey has recently also completely armed herself. The other Asiatic races, such as the peoples of

Persia, Afghanistan, and Arabia are all war-like peoples. China has a population of four hundred millions, and although she needs to modernize her armament and other equipment, and her people are a peace-loving people, yet when the destiny of their country is at stake the Chinese people will also fight with courage and determination. Should all Asiatic peoples thus unite together and present a united front against the Occidentals, they will win the final victory. Compare the populations of Europe and Asia: China has a population of four hundred millions, India three hundred and fifty millions, Japan several scores of millions, totaling, together with other peoples, no less than nine hundred millions. The population in Europe is somewhere around four hundred millions. For the four hundred millions to oppress the nine hundred millions is an intolerable injustice, and in the long run the latter will be defeated. . . .

What problem does Pan-Asianism attempt to solve? The problem is how to terminate the sufferings of the Asiatic peoples and how to resist the aggression of the powerful European countries. In a word, Pan-Asianism represents the cause of the oppressed Asiatic peoples. Oppressed peoples are found not only in Asia, but in Europe as well. Those countries that practice the rule of Might do not only oppress the weaker people outside their continent, but also those within their own continent. . . . Japan today has become acquainted with the Western civilization of the rule of Might, but retains the characteristics of the Oriental civilization of the rule of Right. Now the question remains whether Japan will be the hawk of the Western civilization of the rule of Might, or the tower of strength of the Orient. This is the choice which lies before the people of Japan.[52]

---

51 These included territories held by the British, French, Dutch, and Americans.
52 Sun Yat-sen, "Greater Asianism," quoted in Sun Yat-sen, Tang Liang-li, and Wang Jingwei, *China and Japan: Natural Friends, Unnatural Enemies* (Shanghai: China United Press, 1941). This is a translation of the speech delivered in Kobe, Japan, on November 28, 1924, a copy of which may be found on the internet at https://en.wikisource.org/wiki /Sun_Yat-sen%27s_speech_on_Pan-Asianism.

JAPAN'S EXPANSION INTO MANCHURIA

Despite Japan's disappointing territorial gains following World War I, Japanese nationalists and militarists within the country continued their efforts to expand their empire. On the night of September 18, 1931, near the southern Manchurian city of Mukden (Shenyang), a section of railroad owned by the Southern Manchurian Railroad (SMR) was destroyed in a dynamite-fueled explosion. The Japanese expansion into Manchuria had begun.

Manchuria is situated in the northeast region of China and is bordered by Russia, Mongolia, and Korea.[53] The Qing emperors of China's last dynasty were of Manchu descent, meaning their ancestors came from Manchuria. In addition to Manchuria's cultural and historical importance, the region was strategically critical. Russia's Chinese Eastern Railway (CER) passed through Manchuria to link the country with the Far East. And Japan's Guandong Army, which had been posted there in 1905 to "protect" their nation's interests after the establishment of the SMR, remained stationed in Manchuria.

After 1911, Manchuria, like elsewhere in China, was beset by a confusing variety of political, military, and warlord actors. As alliances shifted, the region became politically and economically unstable. In 1916 the warlord Zhang Zuolin, "The Old Marshal," emerged as Manchuria's dominant leader. In 1928 he was assassinated by a Japanese Guandong Army officer who thought that Zhang's son would be an easier warlord to manipulate. As it turned out, he was very wrong. Known as "The Young Marshal," Zhang Xueliang emerged as the new leader in the region. His Northeastern Border Defense Army grew to 400,000 men and in 1930 he was named deputy commander in chief of the Chinese Armed Forces.[54]

Because of Manchuria's vulnerability, Japanese leaders became concerned that their commercial and ideological interests might become jeopardized. For some Japanese their incursion into Manchuria was an expression of national self-determination. They claimed the five ethnicities in Manchuria, Japanese, Manchus, Koreans, Chinese, and Mongols, sought an effectively ruled state rather than the corrupt Nationalists. Others believed in a more traditional East Asian element, meaning that it didn't matter who ruled as long as it did so in a benevolent Confucian fashion. Still others had commercial interests in mind. The SMR and other Japanese commercial holdings in the area, such as lumber, manufacturing, mining, and banking, had become the backbone of their expansionist plans. *(See Source 3: Newspaper Article "Rich Land is Goal for Japanese Army.")* The SMR is especially illustrative of the importance of this region to Japan. Between 1908 and 1930, the assets in this railway rose from 163 million yen to over 1 billion yen, making it both the largest Japanese company and the most profitable at the time.[55] Many in Japan wanted to exploit their interests in the region, especially the army minister, General Araki.

The choice to explode this section of the railway was strategic—the tracks were closer to the Chinese troops than any other railroad in the region. Skirmishes immediately broke out between the Japanese and Chinese troops over who was responsible for initiating the explosion. The Japanese accused Chinese dissidents of the act and attacked a nearby Chinese barrack. Many members of Hirohito's cabinet in Tokyo urged restraint. They had little, if any, ability to control their forces in the Mukden region. Others, such as Army Minister General Araki, supported increasing military expansion and saw this "incident" as an opportunity.

In China, Chiang Kai-shek did not have a political incentive to confront Japan's advancing forces. Whether the decision not to send troops to defend China's interests came from Chiang himself, or from Zhang Xueliang, the Nationalist troops did move to defend the region south of the Great Wall.[56] At the time he was intent on launching campaigns to eliminate his Communist opposition by murdering them, and the Communists were more intent on deposing Chiang than fighting the Japanese. By the end of the year, Manchuria was fully under Japanese control and became the new puppet state of Manchukuo, the kingdom of the Manchus. Both a Japanese military and domestic objective had been fulfilled: imperialist expansion into the resource-rich and strategically important Manchuria and emigration of some of Japan's growing population to Manchukuo.[57] Chiang Kai-shek had to play a very different hand once Japan's imperialist pursuits were real and growing.

A few days after Japan's military actions, the Chinese government made an official appeal to the League of Nations against Japanese aggression and specifically in violation of Articles 10 and 11 of the covenant. *(See Source 4: Excerpts of the Covenant of the League of Nations.)* This made the conflict an international affair and a task for the league's system of collective security to address. The next day, the United States minister to China sent a telegram to the United States secretary of state, stating that Japan's actions constituted "an aggressive act . . . long planned and systematically put into place" and strongly expressing that such acts "must fall within any definition of war." By December the league created a commission that would enlist a handful of international diplomats to travel to the region, collect information, observe the situation, and report back to the league. The commission, led by British statesman Lord Lytton, returned in October 1932.

Before the Lytton mission completed their report, the Japanese sought to justify, and legitimize, their takeover by installing the last Qing emperor, Puyi, as the leader of the new country of Manchukuo. Japanese officials assured Puyi that the Japanese military acted in self-defense against Zhang Xueliang and his troops and promised to fully support Manchukuo as an independent state. *(See Source 5: A Case for Japanese Expansion [close reading].)* When the Lytton report became public, the direct cause of the Mukden incident was not identified, nor did it single out either China or Japan as the aggressor. Instead, with a conciliatory tone, the report stated that Japan did not act in self-defense and that Manchukuo could not exist without the presence of the Japanese Imperial Army. The report then recommended the evacuation of the Japanese troops from the region and the appointment of a committee of negotiators to resolve future conflicts. Before the vote on adopting the recommendations was held, Japan's delegation leader, Matsuoka Yosuke, spoke up: "I beg you not to adopt the report of the sake of peace in the Far East and the peace of the world."[58] The vote was 42-1. Japan was the lone dissenter.

In response, Japan formally withdrew from the League of Nations on February 24, 1933. Matsuoka said in response to the vote, "Would the American people agree to such control of the Panama Canal Zone; would the British permit it over Egypt?"[59] Only two other countries had withdrawn from the league: Costa Rica in 1925 and Brazil in 1926. However, Germany would follow suit only months later, and Italy would leave in 1935. Japan's occupation of Manchuria and their withdrawal from the League of Nations positioned Japan as a pariah nation among the league's members and further alienated their relations with the Western imperial powers. The world was once again poised on the brink of war.

Daniel K. E. Ching collection, Box 22, Hoover Institution Archives

This postcard from 1934 depicts Puyi, the last emperor of China and the puppet emperor of Japanese-occupied Manchukuo.

In China the occupation of Manchuria did not go unnoticed, nor did resentment abate over time. Opponents of Nationalist leader Chiang Kai-shek never missed an opportunity to remind him that a huge portion of China was under Japanese occupation. Two men, Tian Han and Nie Er, responded by writing a song, "The March of the Volunteers" (1934). This anthem was sung throughout the Japanese occupation of China during World War II and today is the national anthem of the People's Republic of China:

Arise! All who refuse to be slaves!

Let our flesh and blood become our new Great Wall

As the Chinese nation faces its greatest period,

All forcefully expand their last cries.

Arise! Arise! Arise!

Our million hearts beat as one,

Brave the enemy's fire, March on!

Brave the enemy's fire, March on!

March on! March on!

---

53 Until quite recently, Chinese historians both in the People's Republic of China and Taiwan opposed the use of Manchuria, even as a historical term, or they insisted on prefacing it with "the pseudo-state of." The politically correct term was, and for many still remains, the Three Provinces of Northeast China, which contained the five ethnicities (Japanese, Manchus, Koreans, Chinese, and Mongols). Bob Tadashi Wakabayashi (professor, York University), personal communication with the author.

54 For more information about Zhang Xueliang, see Nicholas D. Kristof, "Zhang Xueliang, 100, Dies; Warlord and hero of China," *New York Times*, October 19, 2001, accessed January 1, 2014, http://www.nytimes.com/2001/10/19/world /zhang-xueliang-100-dies-warlord-and-hero-of-china.html.

55 Alvin Coox, *Nomonhan: Japan Against Russia, 1939* (Stanford: Stanford University Press, 1939), 21.

56 While it was long believed that Chiang was the one to give the order not to defend Mukden, recent historical studeies suggest that it was Zhang Xueliang's personal decision to withdraw troops all the while keeping in concert with Chiang's policy not to resist. Fan Ho (professor, Nanjing University), email correspondence with the author.

57 In August 1932 Tokyo began funding the annual emigration of 500–1,100 Japanese households.

58 "Japanese Leave the League of Nations Assembly," *Barrier Miner* (Broken Hill, New South Wales), 1, February 25, 1933, accessed July 1, 2103, http://trove.nla.gov.au/ndp/del/printArticlePdf/48422271/3.

59 The US controlled the territory from 1903 to 1979 under the compliance of the Isthmian Canal Commission, and British rule in Egypt spanned from 1882 to 1922. From 1935 to 1938 Matsuoka served as president of the SMR, cabinet adviser and in the 1940s as Japan's minister and in this capacity brought about the Tokyo-Rome-Berlin Axis. At the end of the war he was brought to trial as a class A war criminal.

PREPARING FOR WAR: ALLIANCES WITH GERMANY

Political and military alliances between countries occur for a variety of reasons. At times they can serve to benefit both nations mutually, such as with trade agreements. But alliances can also support ideological aims of both nations.

By the early 1930s both Japan and Germany had adopted a militaristic approach to nation building. With this shared aim they found themselves forging a new political alliance that would continue to the end of World War II. Japan had set up a puppet government in Manchukuo and expanded its control in north China. Isolated diplomatically because of this expansion and condemned at the League of Nations, Japan turned to Nazi Germany. On November 25, 1936, Imperial Japan and Nazi Germany signed the Anti-Comintern Pact. Forged by German ambassador Joachim von Ribbentrop, the pact was an effort to unite Japan and Nazi Germany under a united front against the Comintern, or the Communist International. The pact clearly stated the alliance opposed the Comintern, not Soviet Russia. One year later, Italy joined the pact, thus creating the alliance that became known as the Axis during World War II.

Across the Sea of Japan, China began developing a close relationship with Nazi Germany as well. Beginning in 1934, China, like Nazi Germany, was attempting to unify its country under one party and a single leader. Given their instability many in China viewed Nazism as an attractive model and sought to develop closer diplomatic ties. Some in the Nationalist Party, including Chiang Kai-shek, admired German education and military discipline and sent their sons to Germany for military and police training. German advisers also trained Chinese forces in the 1930s and provided sizable quantities of military armaments. Like many other nations around the world at this time, China did not feel that the antisemitic policies of Nazi Germany impinged upon the desire for diplomatic ties.

German General von Falkenhausen was interested in seeing Chiang Kai-shek emerge as a president with powers similar to those of Mussolini and Hitler. His interests were communicated in the following letter he sent to Chiang in 1936:

Office of the General Advisor

Tbg. No. 5972

Top Secret!

Nanjing, September 6, 1936

. . . The history of all times has taught us that leaders are needed by states and nations in times of distress, when only the concerted application of *all* state and national power can provide the necessary control over their destiny. Absolute power made possible the great deeds of such historical figures, from Julius Caesar to Genghis Khan, such as Cromwell, Frederick the Great, and Napoleon I. Though history has examples of leadership shared by several persons, *one* person always was clearly in the leadership, and the others subordinate; . . .

The recent period has everywhere shown tendencies to return to practical absolutism. For example in Italy and Germany, but also in Russia, all power is concentrated in one hand, while in some instances no constitutions even exist, and no control organ such as, legally, in Italy the King and in Germany Hindenburg until his death.

Therein lies the natural striving to have a personality at the head of the state endowed with ultimate responsibility, a person independent from election, party politics, and public mood, and capable to provide a stability immune to the turnover of individual personalities. But this is the essence of monarchy.

[But] we must distinguish leaders [Führer] from dictators. Leaders are those who command the allegiance of the masses of the people and who provide for some check through occasional plebiscites. Dictators derive power from material power, supported by a minority. Dictators can nevertheless be historically justifiable at a time when no consensus is possible among the people and the state is in need of firm guidance in order to survive.[60]

By September 1940 imperial Japan, fascist Italy, and Nazi Germany signed the Tripartite Pact, formally establishing a military alliance and relationship as the Axis Powers. In signing the pact each nation agreed to support and defend economic, political, and military interests and advances—and, if necessary, mutually protect one another if attacked by a country that was not already at war. One year later in 1941, Adolf Hitler began to record a series of private conversations. In the entry almost one month after Japanese imperial forces attacked Pearl Harbor, Hawaii, Hitler said:

> Night of 4th–5th January 1942
>
> Just as there has always been two Germany's, so there have always been two Japans: the one, capitalist and therefore Anglophile [admirer of everything English]—the other, the Japan of the Rising Sun, the land of the samurai. The Japanese Navy is the expression of this second world. It's amongst the sailors that we've found the men nearest to ourselves. . . .
>
> Throughout a period of two thousand six hundred years, Japan never had war on her own soil. One thing for which one must be grateful to Ribbentrop is having understood the full significance of our pact with Japan, and drawn the conclusions from it with great lucidity. Our Navy was inspired by the same state of mind, but the Army would have preferred an alliance with China.[61]

Getty Images

Adolf Hitler meets with Japanese Ambassador Viscount Mushanokoji Kintomo (Mushakoje Kintomo) at the Anniversary of the signing of the German-Japanese Anti-Comintern Pact at the Japanese embassy in Berlin.

tinued to shift and strengthen. In 1943 the Nazi Party's publishing house circulated a 128-page booklet. In the excerpt below, the pamphlet's author, Albrecht Fürst von Urach, expressed the growing alliance among Germany, Japan, and the Axis powers:

The Strength of the Axis

National Socialist Germany is in the best position to understand Japan. We and the other nations of the Axis are fighting for the same goals that Japan is fighting for in East Asia, and understand the reasons that forced it to take action. We can also understand the driving force behind Japan's miraculous rise, for we National Socialists also put the spirit over the material. The Axis Pact that ties us to Japan is not a treaty of political convenience like so many in the past, made only to reach a political goal. The Berlin-Rome-Tokyo alliance is a world-wide spiritual program of the young peoples of the world. It is defeating the international alliance of convenience of Anglo-Saxon imperialist monopolists and unlimited Bolshevist internationalism. It is showing the world the way to a better future. In joining the Axis alliance of the young peoples of the world, Japan is using its power not only to establish a common sphere of economic prosperity in East Asia. It is also fighting for a new world order. New and powerful ideas rooted in the knowledge of the present and the historical necessities of the future that are fought for with fanatical devotion have always defeated systems that have outlived their time and lost their meaning.[62]

60- Pei-kai Cheng, Michael Lestz, and Jonathan D. Spence, eds., *The Search for Modern China: A Documentary Collection* (New York: W. W. Norton & Company, 1999), 286-88.

61 Adolf Hitler, *Hitler's Table Talk, 1941-1944: His Private Conversations*, trans. Norman Cameron and R. H. Stevens (New York: Enigma Books, 2000), 178-79.

62 Albrecht Fürst von Urach, *Das Geheimnis japanischer Kraft* [The Secret of Japan's Strength] trans. Randall L. Bytwerk (Berlin: Zentralverlag der NSDAP, 1943; 1998), accessed October 9, 2013, http://www.calvin.edu/academic/cas /gpa/japan.htm.

POLITICAL CONFLICTS WITHIN CHINA

When asked why he didn't fight Japan's encroachment into Manchuria, Chiang Kai-shek replied, "the Japanese constituted a disease of the limbs, but the Communist affliction lay close to China's heart."[63] Although this wasn't what some Chinese wanted to hear, the priority of the Nationalist Party in the early 1930s was not only the Japanese, but the Chinese Communist Party (CCP), who Chiang saw as a significant threat.[64]

Following their expulsion to the northern province of Shaanxi after the Long March, many within the Chinese Communist Party wanted to build a Second United Front to defend their country against Japanese expansion. Some leaders favored this tactic while others continued to view Chiang Kai-shek as the greater threat to the party's survival; foremost among the critics was Mao Zedong. The CCP settled on prioritizing the unification of the nation, even as Japan continued to expand into China making strong inroads into portions of inner Mongolia and northern China between 1932 and 1936. Because the Nationalist policy was "internal consolidation first, expulsion of foreign encroachment later" the Japanese army was able to continue its encroachment into China with little opposition.

Chiang Kai-shek's dislike for the CCP was so entrenched that he remained unwilling to negotiate with them despite the Japanese advances. Tensions came to a climax on December 12, 1936, in the city of Xi'an, the provincial capital of Shaanxi. Chiang dispatched the Manchurian warlord Zhang Xueliang and his army, along with Yang Hucheng, the Nationalist commander in the region, to finally "eliminate" the CCP's leadership. Chiang did not foresee, however, that Zhang and Yang would attempt to forge an alliance with the CCP, whose military prowess they found impressive. Incensed at their insubordination, Chiang flew to Xi'an himself. At this point, Zhang took matters into his own hands. With his personal bodyguards in tow, Zhang surrounded the guest house where Chiang was staying and kidnapped him, demanding that he agree to end the civil war and negotiate with the Communists. After being held hostage for two weeks and under intense international media coverage, Chiang verbally agreed to negotiate with the Communists and establish a Second United Front. He was released on Christmas Day, 1936, and he flew back to Nanjing. Negotiations ensued and the two parties reached an agreement in April 1937 stipulating that Mao Zedong would retain independent command of his Red Army in the countryside.

~~Even though the merger was supposed to improve China's chances of fend-~~ing off the Japanese, the Japanese army saw an opportunity to capitalize on an ongoing politically fractured nation.

---

63 Jonathan Lipman, Barbara Molony, and Michael Robinson, eds., *Modern East Asia: An Integrated History* (London: Laurence King Publishing, 2011), 295.

64 Bob Tadashi Wakabayashi states "that it is best to see Japan (the invader) as intervening in the Chinese civil war lasting from 1927 to 1949, which itself capped earlier warlord struggles from 1916. This invasion from 1931 or 1937 to 1945 was part of a three-way war in China, and the two Chinese sides fought each other as much as they fought Japan. Especially early on the Communists talked bravely from the bleachers, but they were geographically beyond the reach of Japanese armies. Their patriotic egging on of Chiang was to lure him into engaging with Japan and getting defeated." Bob Tadashi Wakabayashi (professor, York University), private correspondence with the author, January 22, 2014.

READING 13

THE ROAD TO WAR

The historic Marco Polo Bridge crosses the Yongding River, about 10 miles southwest of Beijing. For centuries, this bridge has stood strong and has welcomed many travelers, including the Venetian Marco Polo, who praised its beauty in his book *Travels of Marco Polo.*

Centuries later, the bridge became the site of another historic moment, the beginning of the Sino-Japanese War, or World War II in East Asia. By the 1930s a strategic railway link at the junction town of Wanping had been constructed adjacent to the bridge. Whoever controlled Wanping would have greater access to most of the railroad lines in resource-rich northern China.

For decades China endured the presence of military troops on her soil in accordance with the provisions of Article IX of the Boxer Protocol of 1901 allowing military guards to be posted and military maneuvers to be conducted at 12 specific points along this rail line. Chinese authorities were not required to be notified when such maneuvers took place. However, in the summer of 1937 Japan's military presence had grown exceedingly large, causing alarm by the Chinese government.

On the night of July 7, 1937, the Japanese Guandong Army, stationed on China's South Manchurian Railroad, staged military night maneuvers. After several months of witnessing the growing presence of Japanese soldiers in the area (upward of 5,000), Chinese troops feared an attack was under way. Both sides fired blank shots at each other, and when the fighting stopped, a Japanese soldier was feared missing. In response, the Japanese commander ordered an attack on Wanping the next day. The Chinese were able to win this battle, but it is considered the beginning of World War II in East Asia.

Although the two sides negotiated a cease-fire, both nations violated it and continued to send more troops into the area. Japanese Prince Konoe insisted at a press conference that "the incident was entirely the result of an anti-Japanese military action on the part of China and that Chinese authorities must apologize to us for the illegal anti-Japanese actions," while Chiang Kai-shek announced, "If we allow one more inch of our territory to be lost, we shall be guilty of an unpardonable crime against our race."[65]

With this impasse, other nations took notice and communicated accordingly. Two memos between the Japanese ambassador to the United States, Saito, and Secretary of State Cordell Hull illustrate the increasing concern in the international community:

> Memorandum by the Secretary of State Regarding a Conversation with the Japanese Ambassador Saito, Washington D.C.
>
> July 12, 1937.
>
> The [Japanese] Ambassador . . . handed me a manuscript containing six paragraphs or points relative to the Japanese-Chinese military trouble which commenced on July 7th. . . .
>
> At the conclusion of the reading, I specially emphasized with approval the remarks of the Ambassador about the efforts of his government to work out a friendly settlement without war. I elaborated upon the futility of any other course and the awful consequences of war. I said that a great civilized first-class power like Japan not only could afford to exercise general self-restraint in such circumstances but that in the long run it was far better that this should characterize the attitude and policy of his government; . . . that no two great countries have rarely had such an opportunity in these respects as seems to be ahead for our two countries and that of course it means everything from this viewpoint, as

well as others, that serious military operations should not be
allowed to get under way; . . . that of course this country is greatly
interested and greatly concerned in conditions of peace in every
part of the world, and that I would welcome anything further in
the way of information from time to time, and would be glad to
treat in very strictest confidence any confidential information
he might care to give me on the subject. I again emphasized the
great injury to the victor as well as the vanquished in case of any
important war in this day and time, of the great concern of this
government for peace everywhere.[66] . . .

Two weeks later another exchange followed between the two officials:

The Ambassador of Japan called this morning at my request. After
brief preliminaries, I very seriously addressed the Ambassador
and said that, of course, he must be fully aware that when two
nations comprising 500 million people are engaged in a controversy in which danger of general hostilities appear imminent, this
country cannot help but be greatly interested and concerned;
that it is in the light of this situation and of the intense desire of
this country for peace everywhere that I have been undertaking
to confer with the ambassadors from both Japan and China from
time to time regarding developments, present and prospective,
in the danger zone; that I have approached each government,
in a spirit of genuine friendliness and impartiality in an earnest
effort to contribute something to the cause of peace and to the
avoidance of hostilities in the Far East that, . . . a war would result
in irreparable harm to all governments involved and would prove
utterly disastrous, in the present chaotic state of world affairs, to
all phases of human welfare and human progress.[67] . . .

Despite the diplomatic pressure and intervention, on August 9, 1937, a
Japanese Lieutenant by the name of Oyama Isao was shot in Shanghai by
a member of the Chinese Peace Preservation Corps.[68] Whether the incident
was staged by forces aligned with Mao Zedong and the Communists as
a way to undermine Chiang Kai-shek and the Chinese Nationalists is still
debated by historians today. Nevertheless, this final clash escalated tensions
further, with the Japanese demanding the final withdrawal of the Peace
Preservation Corps surrounding the city. The Japanese Imperial forces also
made clear it believed the shooting of a Japanese soldier was considered

an act of humiliation that necessitated a response. More Japanese Imperial troops and Chinese Nationalist troops were deployed to Shanghai. War in China was imminent.

The escalation of tensions occurred outside of diplomatic relations as well. Ienaga Saburo, one of Japan's most prominent historians of the twentieth century, recalls how the climate in Japan during this time impacted his life:

> I graduated [university] in March 1937, shortly before the outbreak of the Marco Polo bridge incident that became the beginning of the all-out war between Japan and China. One of the constant topics [among my classmates] was how to avoid military service. The weaklings like me who could predict that they would be classified as 4-F listened almost as bystanders to the anguish of friends who had no hope of avoiding 1-A. Once one of us egged them on: "Is being conscripted as horrible as all that?" They responded with real anger: "You don't have to worry. Try putting yourselves in our shoes."

Abe Gosei/Hyogo Prefectural Museum of Art

A painting by Abe Gosei titled "Seeing People Off, 1938" depicts Japanese people sending off the troops headed to war.

I was classified 4-F.[69] But as the war got fiercer, those subject to conscription were called to periodic musters [periodic gathering of troops], and to prepare for those, we had to take part in Reservists' Association training. With illness as my excuse, I sought to avoid this training as much as I could, but even I couldn't get by without ever showing my face. The following incident took place while I was employed at Niigata Higher School. . . . It was the night before muster, and drill went on until about 10:30. One person couldn't take it any longer. He went to the section chief and asked: 'Tomorrow's muster is a formal affair. I want to take a bath and be clean for muster, so please can't we call it quits for tonight?' It was a really brave speech. But there was one scatterbrained fellow, and he raised his voice: 'Right on!' Immediately, the top brass of the branch association shouted, 'This is the army! What's this 'Right On' stuff? Fall Out!' They dragged the fellow out and punched and kicked him for a long time. It was so brutal that finally the branch chief shouted, 'Enough!' I felt I was getting a peek at . . . life in an army unit.[70]

By the outbreak of World War II, Japanese soldiers were sometimes referred to as "Issen Gorin," loosely translated as a penny postcard. Because Japanese soldiers received notice of their draft status vis-à-vis a penny postcard, for some the term became associated with the value placed upon Japanese draftees.

---

65 James Crowley, *Japan's Quest for Autonomy: National Security and Foreign Policy, 1930–1938* (Princeton: Princeton University Press, 1966), 331, 335, quoted in Jonathan D. Spence, *The Search for Modern China* (New York: W. W. Norton & Company, 1990), 445.

66 US Department of State, *Peace and War: United States Foreign Policy, 1931-1941* (Washington, DC: US Government Printing Office, 1943), 367-68, accessed June 11, 2014, http://www.ibiblio .org/pha/paw/.

67 Ibid., 367-368.

68 The Chinese Peace Preservation Corps was established as part of the cease-fire following the occupation of Manchuria by Japanese imperial forces. The corps would maintain public order within the confines of an established demilitarized zone that buffered the occupation zone around Manchukuo.

69 The use of "4-F" is most likely a mistake in translation as this refers to a US military classification for being unfit to serve.

70 Ienaga Saburo, *Japan's Past, Japan's Future* (Lanham: Maryland, Rowman and Littlefield, 2001), 101–02.

PRIMARY SOURCES

SOURCE 1

TREATY OF SHIMONOSEKI/ TREATY OF MAGUAN (EXCERPT)

The Treaty of Shimonoseki (Japanese), also known as the Treaty of Maguan (Chinese), was signed between the Empire of Japan and the Qing Empire of China, ending the First Sino-Japanese War.

Treaty of Shimonoseki

Signed April 17, 1895

His Majesty the Emperor of Japan and His Majesty the Emperor of China, desiring to restore the lessings of peace to their countries and subjects and to remove all cause for future complications . . . have agreed to the following:

Article 1

China recognizes definitively the full and complete independence and autonomy of Korea, and, in consequence, the payment of tribute and the performance of ceremonies and formalities by Korea to China, in derogation of such independence and autonomy, shall wholly cease for the future.

Articles 2 and 3

China cedes to Japan in perpetuity and full sovereignty the Penghu group, Taiwan and the eastern portion of the bay of Liaodong Peninsula together with all fortifications, arsenals and public property.

Article 4

China agrees to pay Japan as a war indemnity the sum of 200,000,000 Kuping taels of silver. [1 Kuping tael = 578.84 grains of pure silver]

Article 6

The following cities, towns, and ports, in addition to those already opened, shall be opened to the trade, residence, industries, and manufactures of Japanese subjects, under the same conditions and with the same privileges and facilities as exist at the present open cities, towns, and ports of China:

1. Shashih, in the province of Hubei.

2. Chungking, in the province of Sichuan.

3. Suzhou, in the province of Jiangsu.

4. Hangchow, in the province of Zhejiang.

The Japanese Government shall have the right to station consuls at any or all of the above named places.

Second.—Steam navigation for vessels under the Japanese flag, for the conveyance of passengers and cargo, shall be extended to the following places:

1. On the Upper Yangtze River, from Yichang to Chungking.

2. On the Wusong River and the Canal, from Shanghai to Suzhou and Hangchow.

Third.—Japanese subjects purchasing goods or produce in the interior of China, or transporting imported merchandise into the interior of China, shall have the right temporarily to rent or hire warehouses for the storage of the articles so purchased or transported without the payment of any taxes or extractions whatever.

Fourth.—Japanese subjects shall be free to engage in all kinds of manufacturing industries in all the open cities, towns, and ports of China, and shall be at liberty to import into China all kinds of machinery, paying only the stipulated import duties thereon.

Article 10

All offensive military operations shall cease upon the exchange of the ratifications of this Act. . . .[71]

---

71 Treaty of Shimonoseki, Japan-China, April 17, 1895, accessed January 1, 2014, http://www.taiwandocuments.org/shimonoseki01.htm.

NATIONAL ANTHEM KIMAGAYO— JAPAN'S NATIONAL ANTHEM

君が代は	May your reign
千代に八千代に	Continue for a thousand,
	eight thousand generations,
さざれ（細）石の	Until the pebbles
いわお（巌）となりて	Grow into boulders
こけ（苔）の生すまで	Lush with moss

SOURCE 3

NEWSPAPER ARTICLE
"RICH LAND IS GOAL FOR JAPANESE ARMY"

Journalist, author, and economic adviser to President Franklin Roosevelt, Eliot Janeway, warned in an August 15, 1937, *New York Times* piece of Japan's impending assault on China and the motivations underlying this decision.

Rich Land is Goal of Japanese Army: Raw Materials of North China Are of Vast Importance to Both Tokyo and Nanking

Japan's new offensive in the [Beijing] region is her answer to the question upon which the future of Asia apparently hinges: Who is to use the abundant raw materials of the Chinese provinces which lie west of [Beijing]? Both China and Japan greatly desire these materials.

Disappointed and unsatisfied with her Manchurian possessions, Japan is bent upon pushing her empire south to richer lands. Her success here will mean far more than the shrinking of China's boundaries. The industrialization of China's central and southern provinces must be fatally hampered by the loss of this principal source of raw materials. Japan requires the products of this district for its own uses, but even if she did not she would have had to strike here in order to prevent China's industrialization and the unification which she fears would result from it.

The most generously endowed northern provinces are [Shaanxi] and [Hebei.] . . .

Japan's Ore Needs

There are the very commodities that Japan needs most desperately. If her steel industry is ever to become self-sufficient she must secure for herself the 300,000,000 tons of ore which lie in Shansi and its vicinity.

Japan's coal shortage is for the first time becoming dangerous. While her coal reserves are not as significant, they are of a low grade. The coal her smelting industries use must be imported, and again Shansi is the nearest source.

Japan's difficulties in securing adequate supplies of raw cotton are as well known. Embarrassed by the growing strain of her raw cotton import bill, Japan last Spring demanded that China supply her with fully half of the cotton for which she now spends 900,000,000 yen a year in India and the United States.

Now for the first time China's cotton crop has become large enough to make this feasible and more than half of the expected 1937 crop of about 4,000,000 bales will come from these northern provinces. . . .

Tokyo Wool Shortage

The wool shortage has been even more troublesome; lack of the raw material has forced Japan's wool mills to run on part time for a protracted period. Much is being spent to establish a satisfactory wool supply in Manchuria. But in the district back of Tientsin one of the world's largest sources of carpet wool already exists.

It was to obtain command of the wealth of the [Shanxi] region, that Japan recently asked Nanking for permission to build a railroad link between Shihkiachwang [capital of Hebei Province] and Tsangchow [city in Hebei Province] that is, between already existent roads blanketing the Northern provinces and the one which leads to the port of Tsingtao, a Japanese concession. Such a concession, if granted, would have given the Japanese a thorough route from the coast to their military base in Chahar [Province.]

Moreover, this line would have intercepted the two railroads which connect [Beijing] with the Chinese centers to the south. It would have enabled Japan to ship [Shaanxi] wealth north to Manchuria or east to the mother country. . . .

Steel Plant

Large modern steel works are to be constructed at Canton, and the Ministry of Railways is planning a central railway equipment plant. But these ambitious works will not be able to produce the materials the new China requires unless this new China is able to exercise sovereignty rights over the iron ore and coking coal lands of the north.

While one of the new roads is to run from Canton to the inland tin mines of Yunan Province, and while antimony, wolfram, and molybdenum are available in the central industrial region, they can be of no use in the absence of iron ore and coking coal. Both are necessary for the projected growth of electrification—the one for utility equipment, the other for fuel. And without the cotton of the north, China's determination to challenge Japan's dominance of the Chinese cotton goods market must fail. Thus, if the raw materials of the northern provinces are vital to Japan's empire, they are as vital to China's existence.[72]

---

72 Eliot Janeway, "Rich Land is Goal of Japanese Army: Raw Materials of North China Are of Vast Importance to Both Tokyo and Nanking" *New York Times*, August 15, 1937, accessed January 1, 2014, http://proquest.umi.com/?login.

SOURCE 4

EXCERPTS OF THE COVENANT
OF THE LEAGUE OF NATIONS

ARTICLE 10.

The Members of the League undertake to respect and preserve as against external aggression the territorial integrity and existing political independence of all Members of the League. In case of any such aggression or in case of any threat or danger of such aggression the Council shall advise upon the means by which this obligation shall be fulfilled.

ARTICLE 11.

Any war or threat of war, whether immediately affecting any of the Members of the League or not, is hereby declared a matter of concern to the whole League, and the League shall take any action that may be deemed wise and effectual to safeguard the peace of nations. In case any such emergency should arise the Secretary General shall on the request of any Member of the League forthwith summon a meeting of the Council.

It is also declared to be the friendly right of each Member of the League to bring to the attention of the Assembly or of the Council any circumstance whatever affecting international relations which threatens to disturb international peace or the good understanding between nations upon which peace depends.[73]

---

73 League of Nations, *The Covenant of the League of Nations*, (Montreal: A. T. Chapman, April 28, 1919), accessed January 1, 2014, http://avalon.law.yale.edu/20th_century/leagcov.asp.

SOURCE 5

A CASE FOR JAPANESE EXPANSION
(CLOSE READING)

In 1939 Hashimoto Kingoro gave a speech that gave insights into Japan's expansion into Manchuria. Hashimoto had been involved in right-wing politics within the military in the 1930s and by the time of this speech, he had been promoted to colonel in the Japanese Imperial Army.[74] His words were later used as evidence at the Tokyo Trials to convict him as a war criminal.

Addresses to Young Men

We have already said that there are only three ways left to Japan to escape from the pressure of surplus population. We are like a great crowd of people packed into a small and narrow room, and there are only three doors through which we might escape, namely, emigration, advance into world markets, and expansion of territory. The first door, emigration, has been barred to us by the anti-Japanese immigration policies in other countries. The second door, advance into world markets, is being pushed shut by tariff barriers and the abrogation [end] of commercial treaties. What should Japan do when two of the three doors have been closed against her? It is quite natural that Japan should rush upon the last remaining door.

It may sound dangerous when we speak of territorial expansion, but the territorial expansion of which we speak does not in any sense of the word involve the occupation of the possessions of other countries, the planting of the Japanese flag thereon, and the declaration of annexation to Japan. It is just that since the Powers have suppressed the circulation of Japanese materials and merchandise abroad, we are looking for some place overseas where Japanese capital, Japanese skills, and Japanese labor can have free play, free from the oppression of the white race.

We would be satisfied with just this much. What moral right do the world powers who have themselves closed to us the two doors of emigration and advance into world markets have to criticize Japan's attempt to rush out of the third and last door? If they do not approve of this, they should open the doors which they have closed against us and permit the free movement overseas of Japanese emigrants and merchandise.

At the time of the Manchurian incident, the entire world joined in criticism of Japan. They said that Japan was an untrustworthy nation. They said that she had recklessly brought cannon and machine guns into Manchuria, which was the territory of another country, flown airplanes over it, and finally occupied it. But the military action taken by Japan was not in the least a selfish one. Moreover, we do not recall ever having taken so much as an inch of territory belonging to another nation. The result of this incident was the establishment of the splendid new nation of [Manchukuo]. The Power[s] are still discussing whether or not to recognize this new nation, but regardless of whether or not other nations recognize her, the Manchurian empire has already been established, and now, seven years after its creation, the empire is further consolidating its foundations with the aid of its friend, Japan.

And if it is still protested that our actions in Manchuria were excessively violent, we may wish to ask the white race just which country it was that sent warships and troops to India, South Africa, and Australia and slaughtered innocent natives, bound their hands and feet with iron chains, lashed their backs with iron whips, proclaimed these territories as their own, and still continues to hold them to this very day?

They will invariably reply, these were all lands inhabited by untamed savages. These people did not know how to develop the abundant resources of their land for the benefit of mankind. Therefore it was the wish of God, who created heaven and earth for mankind for us to develop these undeveloped lands and to promote the happiness of mankind in their stead. God wills it.

This is quite a convenient argument for them. Let us take it at face value. Then there is another question we must ask them. Suppose that there is still on this earth land endowed with abundant natural resources that have not been developed at all by the white race. Would it not then be God's will and the will of Providence that Japan go there and develop those resources for the benefit of mankind?

And there still remain many such lands on earth.[75]

---

74 Hashimoto actively participated in several coups in Japan in the early 1930s under the pretense of eliminating of what he perceived as corrupt party government. During World War II he continued to advocate for a single party dictatorship. At the time of the sinking of the USS Panay on the Yangtze River outside of Nanjing on December 12, 1937, Hashimoto was the senior Japanese officer in the region.
75 IMTFE, document 487B, exhibit 1290, quoted in Wm. Theodore de Bary, Carol Gluck, and Arthur Tiedemann, eds., *Sources of Japanese Tradition,* 2nd edition, vol. 2 (New York: Columbia University Press, 2005), 989–90.

JAPANESE EMPIRE BUILDING (1870-1942)

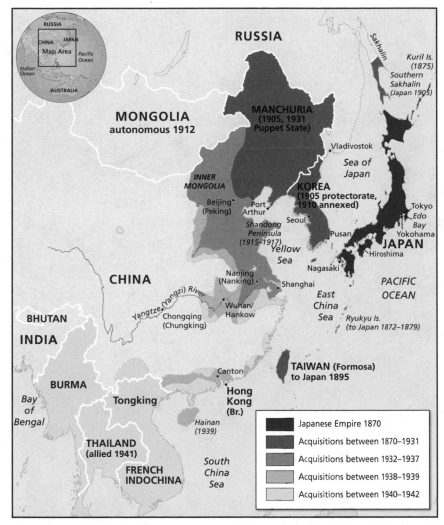

RUSSIA

Kuril Is. (1875)
Southern Sakhalin (Japan 1905)

MONGOLIA
autonomous 1912

MANCHURIA
(1905, 1931
Puppet State)

Vladivostok

Sea of Japan

INNER MONGOLIA

KOREA
(1905 protectorate, 1910 annexed)

Tokyo
Edo Bay
Yokohama

Beijing (Peking)

Port Arthur

Seoul

Pusan

JAPAN

Shandong Peninsula (1915–1917)

Hiroshima

Yellow Sea

Nagasaki

CHINA

Nanjing (Nanking)

Shanghai

East China Sea

PACIFIC OCEAN

Yangtze (Yangzi) River

Wuhan/ Hankow

Ryukyu Is. (to Japan 1872–1879)

BHUTAN

Chongqing (Chungking)

INDIA

BURMA

Canton

TAIWAN (Formosa) to Japan 1895

Bay of Bengal

Tongking

Hong Kong (Br.)

Hainan (1939)

THAILAND
(allied 1941)

South China Sea

FRENCH INDOCHINA

	Japanese Empire 1870
	Acquisitions between 1870–1931
	Acquisitions between 1932–1937
	Acquisitions between 1938–1939
	Acquisitions between 1940–1942

While China dealt with internal economic and political upheaval after the formation of the First Chinese Republic in 1911, Japan was emerging as a formidable imperial power. Following their victories in the Sino-Japanese War (1894–1895) and the Russo-Japanese War (1904–1905), Japanese leaders sought for more territories in the region. Gradually, Japan grew a vast empire.

CHAPTER 4

THE NANJING ATROCITIES

The readings in Chapter Four focus on the Nanjing Atrocities which occurred from December 13, 1937 through the end of March 1938. During this time soldiers from the Japanese Imperial Army ran riot in the captured Chinese capital, unleashing a spree of violence, murder, and rape on the population. The mass violence that took place marked the opening phase of World War II in China and was one of the greatest war crimes committed during the entire war.[1]

In framing this chapter it may be helpful to keep the following questions in mind:

- Are atrocities committed during war inevitable?
- What are the conditions in wartime that lead to atrocities?
- How do you discriminate between wartime violence, war crimes, and crimes against humanity?

For media and classroom materials such as discussion questions and additional primary sources, visit www.facinghistory.org/nanjing-atrocities.

INTRODUCTION

When Purple Mountain burns, Nanjing is lost.

—OLD CHINESE ADAGE

As a city, Nanjing (Nanking) did not hold the strategic importance of Shanghai with its central port and economic activity. But it did hold tremendous symbolic power. The establishment of the city can be traced as far back to the Spring and Autumn Period in China (722–481 BCE). Historians conventionally date the city's origin from the start of the Ming dynasty (1368–1644) when the city was explicitly named Nanjing, meaning "southern capital," and was the dynasty's secondary capital, in contrast to Beijing (Peking), or "northern capital," which was the main capital. Most of the towering city walls, built by the first Ming emperor in the fourteenth century, remain standing today. To date they are the largest and longest city walls in the world and continue to be a reminder of China's imperial past.

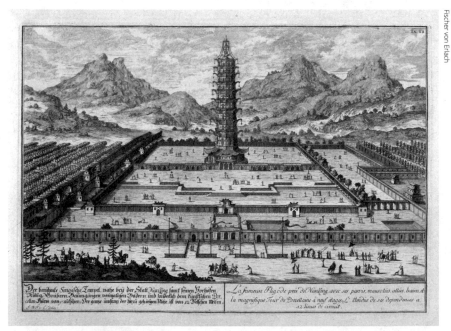

Fischer von Erlach

This 1721 illustration by Fisher von Erlach from *Plan of Civil and Historical Architecture* shows the Nanjing pagoda and the surrounding city.

When fighting initially broke out between China's Nationalist (Guomindang) Revolutionary Forces and Japanese Imperial forces in July 1937 at the Marco Polo Bridge nine miles southwest of Beijing, the military skirmish set the pretext for Tokyo to launch a full-scale invasion of Shanghai. Emperor Hirohito stated on September 4, 1937 at the 72nd session of the Imperial Diet, "China does not really understand our empire's true intention. To our deep regret they have constantly caused difficulties and problems that have finally resulted in the present incident. Our troops, displaying loyalty and bravery, are suffering hardships solely to make China self-reflect and to quickly establish peace in East Asia."[2] On the same day Japan's Army Minister Sugiyama issued a directive to his commanders stating, "Our present situation is completely different from any the empire has experienced before. We must bear in mind that this war has become total war."[3]

Chiang Kai-shek and his government knew war against Japan was coming, but they didn't know when. Many measures were set in motion prior to the Imperial Army's invasion such as moving a national economy council and many Chinese factories and resources into the interior of the country. These premeditated steps were in place so if and when China was invaded and occupied, it would still be possible to carry on the war from within China. Ultimately, this is in fact what occurred.[4]

Once full combat commenced with the Battle of Shanghai on August 13, 1937, Chiang Kai-shek threw his best divisions into service, fiercely fighting and resisting Japanese advances during the first battle of the war, the 90-day defense of Shanghai (August–November 1937). The Chinese losses, killed or wounded, amounted to upward of 250,000 Chinese troops, the nucleus of the Nationalists' finest forces. Japan, too, suffered tremendously, with as many as 30% of its troops killed or wounded in this battle. This included the defense of the Sihang Warehouse in which Nationalist forces held off the Japanese army for an entire week despite being greatly outnumbered.[5] *(See Source 1: Song, "Eight Hundred Heroes.")*

Following the Battle of Shanghai, the Japanese Imperial Army's march toward China's capital city by November 1937 was both to occupy strategic locations and to demonstrate their victory over the Chinese Nationalists, "[a] force they considered pernicious and alien to their vision of East Asia's future."[6] Japanese General Iwane Matsui, the commander-in-chief of the Central China Area Army (CCAA) leading the invasion said, "Unless the Nanking Government reconsiders its attitude and ceases its resistance, Japanese troops will continue to advance to Nanking, Hankow, and even Chungking, China's new capital."[7]

In the end, Nationalist troops could not withstand Japan's superior military armaments and forces and began their retreat westward. Chiang directed his troops to practice a "scorched earth policy" along the way. This entailed burning the homes and fields of their own countrymen in order to wipe out any traces of supplies, food, shelter, roads, and transportation that the invading Japanese forces could use. As Japanese troops advanced, Chinese peasants were forced to flee to Nanjing in order to survive.[8] The retreat from Shanghai signaled both a defeat in manpower and arms for China and a loss in credibility for Chiang Kai-shek.

When the Chinese capital city fell on December 13, 1937, Japanese soldiers unleashed an assault of wanton destruction, burning, rape, robbery, and murder of thousands of civilians and noncombatants. Some Japanese leaders were known to cite Chinese resistance in Shanghai and the loss of so many soldiers as a possible explanation for the brutality of their troops. Others believed the lack of supplies was the trigger unleashing the violence. With no rational explanation available, the Nanjing Atrocities stand as one of the greatest war crimes of World War II.[9] Lasting at its height into March 1938 when the Japanese Imperial Army continued their northern offensive, the carnage in Nanjing did not occur without notice. Journalists and Westerners living in the city documented the violence, captured photographs and film, and publicized the atrocities for the world to know. And within China, stories of the brutality of the Japanese Imperial troops before, during, and after Nanjing spread far and wide.

Despite being outgunned and massacred in Nanjing, Nationalist forces did mount several successful resistance efforts. For example, in April 1938 in the town of Taierzhuang in southern Shandong, Nationalist forces trapped and inflicted heavy casualties on Japanese troops. The Battle of Taierzhuang became a celebrated effort among Chinese resistance forces and was enormously significant for the Chinese overall as it shattered the myth of Japanese invincibility during the first years of the war. But this triumph was short-lived. In May 1938 the Japanese took Taierzhuang, the nearby key railway junction of Xuzhou. By October 1938 the city of Wuhan had fallen. Until the end of the war in 1945, this region of China remained in the clutches of Japanese occupation as China's foreign allies were consumed with war in Europe and elsewhere. By late 1938 Japanese Imperial forces controlled the main coastal cities and major railway lines in China—effectively 10% of the territory in north and central China.

Aware of the escalation of war elsewhere in Europe, the Japanese turned to consolidate their hold over eastern and northern China. As the Japanese soon realized, occupation was only the first step in securing control of a region; the second was its administration. In some cases the Japanese strengthened their power by establishing various puppet regimes. In Nanjing Wang Jingwei (1883–1944) was named the executive and chairman of the new national government in 1940. Wang was an early supporter of Sun Yat-sen and the Nationalist Party. However, after Sun's death Wang and Chiang Kai-shek both vied for control of the party, with Chiang prevailing. Wang initially continued to support the Nationalists, but eventually his disagreements on the party's direction led him to accept an "invitation" to lead the Japanese-supported Nanjing Special Municipality and serve in the puppet regime until the end of the war. From 1940 through 1945 Nanjing remained under Wang's leadership as the fighting elsewhere in China settled into a long and costly stalemate.

With Japanese firmly occupying the coastal region of China, large numbers of urban Chinese migrated to the interior of China. Some followed Chiang Kai-shek to new places like the Nationalist capital, Chongqing (Chungking)—a city a thousand miles from Nanjing. Chongqing was located upriver in Sichuan Province and was consistently flattened by Japanese bombers throughout the war. These assaults did not diminish Chinese resistance fighters around the country. They consistently engaged in guerilla activities, including sabotaging rail lines and intercepting intelligence. One key turning point occurred in July 1941 when the United States put a freeze on all Japanese funds in the United States and terminated all trade with Japan, including its lifeline of oil. At the time four-fifths of Japan's oil supply was imported from the United States and without this resource, the military and the country were strangled.[10] Up to this point China had suffered four years of war and demoralization and had been largely left alone to fight the Imperial Army without international support. While the United States' sanctions were welcomed in 1941, four years of

The Granger Collection

Chinese troops marching on The Great Wall during the Second Sino-Japanese War, October 28, 1937.

war had left the Chinese civilian and military population largely dislocated from their homes and suffering from rampant hunger and malnutrition.

Another turning point, the attack of Pearl Harbor, Hawaii, by Japanese Imperial forces on December 7, 1941, shifted the war effort even further. The bombing of Pearl Harbor extended the scope of Japan's efforts for empire building and expanded the war from mainland China into the Pacific theater. Up to this point, China had not technically declared the existence of the state of war with Japan. But on December 9, 1941, president of the Chinese republic, Lin Sen, officially declared war on Japan.[11]

The readings in Chapter Four focus our attention on the experiences of individuals who perpetrated and survived the period of time we refer to today as the Nanjing Atrocities. The stories of violence highlight the vulnerability of civilians and women in times of war and raise profound questions about the relationship between war, war crimes, and leadership during such periods. What can be done to protect civilians in times of war, or are such crimes, as some would argue, inevitable? In learning about the varied experiences of military leaders, soldiers, and survivors and attempting to understand their perspectives, we hope to explore the choices made by individuals, groups, and nations throughout the brutal assault on Nanjing.

Historian Rana Mitter offers one way to think about the atrocities in Nanjing:

> Why did the atrocities happen? Few believe that there was a pre-planned conspiracy to massacre the population of Nanjing. What made it shocking was the violent manner in which the looting and killing took place, not its cold calculation. In fact, Nanjing was just one, albeit the most prominent, of a series of atrocities carried out by the Japanese during their invasion of eastern China. The Japanese Army was deeply angry. It had assumed that it would conquer China fast, and that the lack of resistance that it had met on earlier incursions between 1931 and 1937 would be repeated. The strength of the opposition, and the length of time it took to secure Shanghai, had enraged troops who were already whipped up by propaganda about the rightness of their cause, and who had themselves been brutalized by their military training in Japan. . . .
>
> Even if there was no meticulous plan for the massacre in Nanjing, the wider ideological clash between Japan and China was a central cause of the tragedy. Japanese Pan-Asianism had meta-

morphosed in the decades between 1900 and the 1930s, and the
Japanese were seized with a sincere, if deluded, belief that they
had a duty to lead their Asian neighbors, including China, in a
journey of liberation from Western imperialism.[12]

---

1   Rana Mitter (professor, Oxford University), interview with the author, March
    11, 2014.
2   Herbert Bix, *Hirohito and the Making of Modern Japan* (New York:
    HarperCollins, 2009), 325–26, Kindle edition.
3   Ibid.
4   Rana Mitter (professor, Oxford University), interview with the author, March
    11, 2014.
5   The defense of the Sihang Warehouse became the last assault before the
    Chinese began to retreat from Shanghai.
6   Rana Mitter, *Forgotten Ally: China's World War II, 1937–1945* (Boston:
    Houghton Mifflin Harcourt, 2013), 126.
7   Ibid., 127. The Japanese Central China Area Army (CCAA) was organized as
    a reinforcement expeditionary army by combining the Shanghai Expeditionary
    Force and the Japanese Imperial Army Tenth Army. General Matsui Iwane
    was appointed as its commander in chief. Matsui reported directly to Imperial
    general headquarters. After the Battle of Nanjing, the CCAA was disbanded
    on February 14, 1938, and its component units were reassigned to the Central
    China Expeditionary Army.
8   The scorched earth policy was not unique to the Nationalist forces. By 1942
    the Japanese Imperial Army had designed a policy referred to as the Three All's
    (kill all, loot all, destroy all) as a method of retaliation against the Nationalist
    and Chinese Communist Party troops. The devastation and brutality of this
    policy throughout China cost millions of lives and an untold amount of de
    struction throughout the country.
9   Rana Mitter (professor, Oxford University), interview with the author, March
    11, 2014.
10 Irvine H. Anderson Jr., "The 1941 *De Facto* Embargo on Oil to Japan: A
    Bureaucratic Reflex," *Pacific Historical Review*, 2 (May 1975): 201, accessed
    January 1, 2014, http://www.jstor.org/discover/10.2307/3638003. In 1939 the
    last year that comparative data could be located, Japan produced 2.3 million
    barrels of crude while 27.2 million barrels were imported from the US, 4.8
    million barrels were imported from the Indies and Borneo, and 1.5 million
    were imported from other sources.
11 Japanese forces also attacked Thailand, Malaya, the Philippines, the Pacific
    Islands of Guam, Wake Island, and Midway. In weeks following they invaded
    Burma, British Borneo, and Hong Kong.
12 Mitter, *Forgotten Ally*, 142–43.

THE COMING OF WAR AND TERROR TO NANJING

By the late fall of 1937, the Chinese newspaper *Hankow Ta-Kung-pao* reported that Japanese Imperial troops were approaching the capital city of Nanjing from three directions. Chinese troops had thus far thwarted their efforts and mounted a strong defense of the city, killing many Japanese troops. This was soon to change. By early December Shanghai had fallen and Nationalist leader Chiang Kai-shek made a last-ditch effort to defend Nanjing by appealing to the Soviet leader Stalin to send in reinforcements. Stalin had no plans to launch a land assault in China so refused Chiang's plea. On December 6 Chiang assessed his chances: Japanese troops were far superior, Chinese forces had been depleted, and morale within Nanjing was destroyed.[13] By December 7, 1937, Chiang Kai-shek fled the city.

Chinese general Tang Shengzhi (Tang Sheng-chih) was left in charge of the Nanjing garrison to defend the city.[14] While not always loyal to Chiang Kai-shek and the Nationalist Party forces, Tang did follow Chiang's statement made in a press release to foreign reporters that he would never surrender the capital city. Unfortunately, the roughly 100,000 troops he commanded were not well trained and many had recently endured the brutal battle in Shanghai. They had been deprived of sufficient provisions for months and in reaching Nanjing many attacked their follow countrymen simply to obtain civilian clothing.

Japan's belligerent actions around Nanjing continued to escalate. On December 12 the Japanese sunk the American gunboat the USS *Panay* anchored in the Yangtze (Yangzi) River outside of Nanjing. This deliberate attack sent a clear message of military aggression to the international community. While the Japanese claimed they did not see the US flags on the gunboat and quickly issued an apology and compensation, the Japanese actions shifted US opinion away from Japan and further tested its neutrality. As Japanese troops surrounded Nanjing, Chinese troops burned homes outside the city walls in an effort of defiance and resistance. Despite fighting the approaching Imperial forces with vigor, General Tang reversed his stance of fighting at all costs and issued a retreat order.[15] Boarding a launch himself on December 12, Tang travelled up the Yangtze, leaving many of his troops to engage in an unwinnable battle.[16]

Once the Japanese Imperial forces flanked the ancient city walls of Nanjing, the thousands of remaining Chinese troops abandoned their posts. While an order was passed on from Tang to his troops to shoot any fleeing soldier, thousands attempted to run from the city, stripping off their uniforms and looting shops and civilians to obtain nonmilitary clothing in order to escape the oncoming Japanese troops.

Several foreign journalists reported on the Chinese retreat and subsequent looting. Archibald Steele of the *Chicago Daily News* called the siege and capture of Nanjing "Four Days of Hell." On December 15, 1937, he wrote, "I saw Chinese troops looting shop windows, but later I saw the Japanese troops outdo them in a campaign of pillage which the Japanese carried out not only in the shops but in homes, hospitals and refugee camps."[17]

New York Times journalist F. Tillman Durdin reported about the Chinese retreat and defeat in the following account dated December 18, 1937:

> The capture of Nanking was the most overwhelming defeat suffered by the Chinese and one of the most tragic military debacles in the history of modern warfare. In attempting to defend Nanking the Chinese allowed themselves to be surrounded and then systematically slaughtered.
>
> The defeat caused the loss of tens of thousands of trained soldiers and millions of dollars worth of equipment and the demoralization of the Chinese forces in the Yangtze Valley whose courage and spirit in the early phases of the warfare enabled the Chinese troops to hold up the Japanese advance around Shanghai nearly two months. Generalissimo Chiang Kai-shek was responsible to a great degree because against the unanimous counsel of his German military advisers and the opinions of his chief of staff, General Pai Chung-hsi, he permitted the futile defense of the city.
>
> More immediately responsible was General Tang Sheng-chih [Tang Shengzhi] and associated division commanders who deserted their troops and fled, not even attempting to make the most of a desperate situation following the entry of the first Japanese troops inside the city's walls.
>
> The flight of the many Chinese soldiers was possible by only a few exits. Instead of sticking by their men to hold the invaders at bay with a few strategically placed units while the others withdrew,

many army leaders deserted, causing panic among the rank and file.

Those who failed to escape through the gate leading to Hsiakwan [Xiaguan] and from there across the Yangtze were caught and executed.

The fall of Nanking was predicted in most details two weeks before the Japanese entered. Overwhelming the ill-equipped Chinese troops pitted against them around Kwang-teh and north-ward, the Japanese broke through and captured Wuhu and other points above Nanking on the Yangtze some days before entering the capital. They thus blocked the Chinese Army's chance to retire upriver.[18]

13 Mitter, *Forgotten Ally*, 128.
14 Garrison is used to refer to a body of troops stationed in a particular location.
15 Masato Kajimoto, "The Reign of Terror: I . What Japanese Journalists Witnessed," in "Online Documentary: The Nanking Atrocities" (University of Missouri-Columbia, 2000).
16 Mitter, *Forgotten Ally*, 133. Despite the retreat order, some 70,000 Chinese troops died defending Nanjing.
17 A. T. Steele, "Nanking Massacre Story: Japanese Troops Kill Thousands," *Chicago Daily News*, Red Streak edition, December 15, 1937.
18 F. Tillman Durdin, "All Captives Slain; Civilians Also Killed as the Japanese Spread Terror in Nanking," *New York Times*, December 18, 1937, accessed January 1, 2014, http://query.nytimes.com/mem/archive/pdf ?res=FB0A12FD3A59177A93CAA81789D95F438385F9.

READING 2

DECEMBER 13, 1937

On the morning of December 13, 1937, four divisions of the Japanese army and two navy fleets on the Yangtze River invaded Nanjing. The capital city now became one of the largest cities under the Japanese Central China Area Army (CCAA). The prewar population of over one million had shrunk considerably by November as the Japanese army advanced. On the morning of

A procession of Japanese troops enters the city of Nanjing on December 17, 1937.

the 13th approximately 500,000 Chinese still remained. These were largely the poor who had little alternative while those able to leave had either financial resources or a place to go west of Nanjing.

The actual orders to occupy the city were carried out by the commander-in-chief of the CCAA, Iwane Matsui, and were handed down from Tokyo on December 1, 1937.[19] *(See Source 2: Secondary Source from Scholar— Dissenting Opinion of Radhabinod Pal.)* There were two known objectives from the Japanese Supreme Command at this juncture: to establish a political regime in Beijing and to capture and occupy Nanjing. Matsui understood the importance of decisively capturing the capital, and before advancing on the actual campaign he issued the following order to his officer corps and to the Japanese forces sometime after December 7:

> That Nanjing was the capital of China and the capture thereof was an international affair; that therefore, careful study should be made so as to exhibit the honor and glory of Japan and augment the trust of the Chinese people, and that the battle in the vicinity of Shanghai is aimed at the subjugation of the Chinese Army, therefore protect and patronize Chinese officials and people, as far as possible; that the Army should always bear in mind not to involve foreign residents and armies in trouble and maintain close liaison with foreign authorities in order to avoid misunderstandings.[20]

When the Japanese army entered the capital, Matsui himself was not physically present due to illness, but Prince Asaka, his temporary commanding officer, was in charge of the final assault.[21] By this time the city was in disarray. The retreating Chinese soldiers had left behind their uniforms and their weapons. Homes had been burned and some looting had already occurred. Three days after the city was taken, Matsui arrived triumphantly. A day later a religious service was held for the many soldiers and civilians who had perished. After the gathering Matsui issued the following statement:

> I extend much sympathy to millions of innocent people in the
> Kiangpei [Jiangbei] and Chekiang [Zhejiang] districts, who suffered
> the evils of war.[22] Now the flag of the Rising Sun is floating high
> over Nanking, and the Imperial Way is shining in the southern
> parts of the Yangzi River. The dawn of the renaissance of the East
> is on the verge of offering itself. On this occasion I hope for recon-
> sideration of the situation by the 400 million people of China.[23]

Until the Japanese Imperial Army began its assault further into the interior of China at the end of February 1938, soldiers of the Imperial Japanese Army ran riot in the capital city. Unlike other places under Japanese occupation like Shanghai, Beijing, or Tianjin (Tientsin), something very different occurred in Nanjing. Soldiers of the Japanese Imperial Army directed their vitriol against the center of the civilian population, embarking on an uninterrupted spree of rape, murder, and pillage. The violence was thorough and particularly brutal. Thousands of women and girls were raped, many of whom died after repeated assaults, and thousands of Chinese civilians and POWs (prisoners of war) were murdered in astonishingly brutal and torturous ways. Businesses and homes were looted and burned and the capital city of China was left in ruins.

Historian Jonathan Spence describes this important moment in twentieth-century Chinese history in the following:

> Over the centuries, Nanjing had endured its share of armed
> attacks and the sustained propaganda campaigns that accompa-
> nied them: the Manchus in 1645, the Taiping rebels in 1853, the
> Qing regional armies in 1864, the republican forces in 1912. Now,
> in 1937, Chiang Kai-shek pledged that Nanjing would never fall,
> but he entrusted its defense to a Nationalist party politician and
> former warlord, Tang Shengzhi, who had never shown him any
> particular loyalty. Tang's distinguishing feature was the abiding
> faith he held in his Buddhist spiritual advisor, whom he had used

in the past to indoctrinate his troops in the ways of loyalty, and as a source of advice on career decisions. This Buddhist now advised Tang to accept the task of directing the city's defense, and Tang did so after the flight from Shanghai was in full swing. As the Japanese bombarded the city with leaflets promising decent treatment of all civilians remaining there, skeptical Chinese troops—fugitives from the Shanghai fighting—killed and robbed the people of Nanjing to obtain civilian clothing and make good their escape. On December 12, Tang himself abandoned the city; since he had vowed publicly to defend Nanjing to the last breath, he made no plans for the orderly evacuation of the garrison troops there, and his departure worsened the military confusion.

There followed in Nanjing a period of terror and destruction that must rank among the worst in the history of modern warfare. For almost seven weeks the Japanese troops, who first entered the city on December 13, unleashed on the defeated Chinese troops and on the helpless Chinese civilian population a storm of violence and cruelty that has few parallels. . . . Robbery, wanton destruction, and arson left much of the city in ruins. There is no obvious explanation for this grim event nor perhaps can one be found. The Japanese soldiers, who had expected easy victory, instead had been fighting hard for months and had taken infinitely more casualties than anticipated. They were bored, angry, frustrated, tired. The Chinese women were undefended, their men folk powerless or absent. The war, still undeclared, had no clear-cut goal or purpose. Perhaps all Chinese regardless of sex or age seemed marked out as victims.[24]

---

19 Timothy Brook, *Documents on the Rape of Nanking* (Ann Arbor: University of Michigan, 1999), 289.
20 Ibid., 289.
21 Prince Asaka Yasuhiko was a member of the Japanese imperial family, son-in-law of Emperor Meiji and uncle by marriage to Emperor Hirohito.
22 Both Kiangpei and Chekiang are areas surrounding the city of Nanjing.
23 Brook, *Rape of Nanking*, 262.
24 Jonathan D. Spence, *The Search for Modern China* (New York: W. W. Norton & Company, 1990), 448. It is also important to note the Chinese were not to declare war on Japan until December 9, 1941, after the Imperial Army's attack on Pearl Harbor, Hawaii.

A FAILURE OF LEADERSHIP

The victorious army must have its rewards and those rewards are to plunder, murder and rape at will, to commit acts of unbelievable brutality and savagery. . . . In all modern history surely there is no page that will stand so black as that of the rape of Nanking.[25]

—GEORGE FITCH, HEAD OF THE YMCA IN NANJING
AND MEMBER OF THE NANJING SAFETY ZONE COMMITTEE,
CHRISTMAS EVE, NANJING, CHINA, 1937

The Japanese consul general in Nanjing, Hidaka Shunrokuro, entered the city in the wake of the Japanese troops and immediately cabled back to his foreign ministry a vivid and graphic description of what he witnessed. Hidaka recounts General Matsui stating that those under him seemed to have behaved outrageously and when pressed about the men who were leading these troops, Matsui admitted that in fact some of the superiors themselves were sometimes to blame.[26]

Hidaka found that Matsui's orders calling for restraint and discipline had been disobeyed. Originally ordering only a few handpicked units to enter the city, handfuls of units entered; the most infamous troops were from the Sixteenth Division. The troops disregarded the December 1 order making "military discipline and morality very strict" and proceeded to commit unrestrained atrocities.[27]

Excerpts taken from the post-war judgment against Colonel Muto Akira, vice chief of staff of the Japanese Central China Area Army, reveal that several high-ranking Japanese leaders had full knowledge of the atrocities being committed in and around Shanghai and Nanjing. A summary, written by one of the members of the prosecution team and presented at the International Military Tribunal for the Far East (IMTFE) in Tokyo at the end of the war, revealed the full extent of their knowledge:

> Muto, then a colonel, had joined Matsui's staff on 10 November
> 1937 and was with Matsui during the drive on Nanking and partic-

ipated in the triumphal entry and occupation of the city. Both he and Matsui admit that they heard of the atrocities being committed in the city during their stay at rear headquarters after the fall of the city. Matsui admits that he heard that foreign governments were protesting against the commission of these atrocities. No effective action was taken to remedy the situation. Evidence was given before the Tribunal by an eyewitness that Matsui was in Nanking on the 19th of December when the business section of the city was in flames. On that day the witness counted fourteen fires in the principal business district alone. After the entry of Matsui and Muto into the city, the situation did not improve for weeks.

Members of the diplomatic corps and press and the Japanese embassy in Nanking sent out reports detailing the atrocities being committed in and around Nanking. The Japanese Minister-at-Large to China, Ito Nobufumi, was in Shanghai from September 1937 to February 1938. He received reports from the Japanese embassy in Nanking and members of the diplomatic corps and press regarding the conduct of the Japanese troops and sent a resume of the reports to the Japanese Foreign Minister, Hirota [Kōki]. These reports as well as many others giving information of the atrocities committed in Nanking . . . were forwarded by Hirota to the War Ministry of which Umezu was Vice-Minister. They were discussed at Liaison Conferences which were normally attended by the Prime Minister, War and Navy Ministers, Foreign Ministers Hirota, Finance Minister Kaya [Okinori], and the Chiefs of Army and Navy General Staff.

News reports of the atrocities were widespread. Minami [Jirō], who was serving as Governor-General of Korea at the time, admits that he read these reports in the press. Following these unfavorable reports and the pressure of public opinion aroused in nations all over the world, the Japanese Government recalled Matsui and approximately 80 of his officers but took no action to punish any of them. Matsui, after his return to Japan on 5 March 1938, was appointed a Cabinet Councilor and on 29 April 1940 was decorated by the Japanese Government for "meritorious services" in the China war. Matsui, in explaining his recall, says that he was not replaced by Hata [Shunroku] because of the atrocities committed by his troops at Nanking, but because he considered his work ended in Nanking and wished to retire from the Army.[28]

Muto Akira was later charged with war crimes committed in China and the Philippines and was found guilty of Count 55—"failing to act in such a way as to prevent their occurrence"—at the International Military Tribunal for the Far East. He was executed by hanging on December 23, 1948. While no explanation will ever be sufficient to explain Japanese leaders' tacit acceptance of military misconduct, historian Rana Mitter offers one perspective to consider:

> Over and over again, Japanese Embassy officials and senior officials declared that they would calm the situation down. But in the streets the rape and murder went on. Japan was at the time a very hierarchical society. Still, over the previous two decades, it had become clear that lower-level actors in Japan were quite capable of defying their supposed superiors, and that as long as they acted quickly, those superiors would not question their acts, at least not in public.[29]

---

25 Martha Lund Smalley, ed., *American Missonary Eyewitnesses to the Nanking Massacre, 1937–1938* (New Haven: Yale Divinity School Library, 1997), 81–82.
26 Edward Behr, *Hirohito: Behind the Myth* (New York: Villard Books, 1989), 162.
27 Timothy Brook, *Documents on the Rape of Nanking* (Ann Arbor: University of Michigan, 1999,) 289-90.
28 "General Akira Muto," The Tokyo War Crimes Trial: A Digital Exhibition website, accessed January 1, 2014, http://lib.law.virginia.edu/imtfe/person/156.
29 Mitter, *Forgotten Ally,* 139.

FRONTLINE HEADLINES

Once the Imperial Japanese troops occupied the city, reporting of the violence was widespread in the international press. One journalist was Frank Tillman Durdin, a longtime foreign correspondent for the *New York Times* in Asia, Africa, and Europe between the years 1937 and 1961. Born in Texas in 1907, he was assigned to report on the Sino-Japanese War beginning in August

1937. He spent the next four years reporting on the war, first in Nanjing, then later in the wartime capital of Chungking. Three days after the city fell to Japanese Imperial forces, Durdin reported:

All Captives Slain: Civilians Also Killed as the Japanese Spread Terror in Nanking. U.S. Embassy is Raided

Capital's Fall Laid to Poor Tactics of Chiang Kai-shek and Leaders' Flight

The *New York Times,* Special cable, pg. 1

December 18, 1937

Aboard the U.S.S. Oahu at Shanghai, Dec. 17 [1937]

Through wholesale atrocities and vandalism at Nanking the Japanese Army has thrown away a rare opportunity to gain the respect and confidence of the Chinese inhabitants and of foreign opinion there.

The collapse of Chinese authority and the break-up of the Chinese Army left many Chinese in Nanking ready to respond to order and organization, which seemed in prospect with the entry of the Japanese troops. A tremendous sense of relief over the outlook for a cessation of the fearful bombardment and the elimination of the threat of serious disorders by the Chinese troops pervaded the Chinese populace when the Japanese took over control within the walls.

It was felt Japanese rule might be severe, at least until war conditions were over. Two days of Japanese occupation changed the whole outlook. Wholesale looting, the violation of women, the murder of civilians, the eviction of Chinese from their homes, mass executions of war prisoners and the impressing of able-bodied men turned Nanking into a city of terror.

Many Civilians Slain

The killing of civilians was widespread. Foreigners who traveled widely through the city Wednesday found civilians dead on every street. Some of the victims were aged men, women and children.

Policemen and firemen were special objects of attack. Many victims were bayoneted and some of the wounds were barbarously cruel.

Any person who ran because of fear or excitement was likely to be killed on the spot as was anyone caught by roving patrols in streets or alleys after dark. Many slayings were witnessed by foreigners.

The Japanese looting amounted almost to plundering of the entire city. Nearly every building was entered by Japanese soldiers, often under the eyes of their officers, and the men took whatever they wanted. The Japanese soldiers often impressed Chinese to carry their loot.

Food apparently was in first demand. Everything else that was useful or valuable had its turn. Peculiarly disgraceful was the robbing of refugees by soldiers who conducted mass searches in the refugee centers and took money and valuables, often the entire possessions of the unfortunates.

The staff of the American Mission University Hospital was stripped of cash and watches. Other possessions were taken from the nurses' dormitory. The faculty houses of American Ginling College were invaded by soldiers who took food and valuables.

The hospital and the Ginling College buildings were flying American flags and bore on the doors official proclamations in Chinese from the United States Embassy denoting American ownership. . . .

Many Chinese men reported to foreigners the abduction and rape of wives and daughters. These Chinese appeared for aid, which the foreigners usually were powerless to give.

The mass executions of war prisoners added to the horrors the Japanese brought to Nanking. After killing the Chinese soldiers who threw down their arms and surrendered, the Japanese combed the city for men in civilian garb who were suspected of being former soldiers.

In one building in the refugee zone 400 men were seized. They were marched off, tied in batches of fifty, between lines of riflemen and machine gunners, to the execution ground.

just before boarding the ship for Shanghai the writer watched the execution of 200 men on the Bund. The killings took ten minutes. The men were lined against a wall and shot. Then a number of Japanese, armed with pistols, trod nonchalantly around the crumpled bodies, pumping bullets into any that were still kicking.

The army men performing the gruesome job had invited navy men from the warship anchored off the Bund to view the scene. A large group of military spectators apparently greatly enjoyed the spectacle.

When the first column of Japanese troops marched from the South Gate up Chungshan Road toward the city's Big Circle, small knots of Chinese civilians broke into scattering cheers, so great was their relief that the siege was over and so high were their hopes that the Japanese would restore peace and order. There are no cheers in Nanking now for the Japanese.

By despoiling the city and population the Japanese have driven deeper into the Chinese a repressed hatred that will smolder through years as a form of the anti-Japanism that Tokyo professes to be fighting to eradicate from China. . . .

Civilian Casualties Heavy

Civilian casualties also were heavy, amounting to thousands. The only hospital open was the American managed University Hospital and its facilities were inadequate for even a fraction of those hurt.

Nanking's streets were littered with dead. Sometimes bodies had to be moved before automobiles could pass.

The capture of Hsiakwan (Xiaguan) Gate by the Japanese was accompanied by the mass killing of the defenders, who were piled up among the sandbags, forming a mound six feet high. Late Wednesday the Japanese had not removed the dead, and two days of heavy military traffic had been passing through, grinding over the remains of men, dogs, and horses.

The Japanese appear to want the horrors to remain as long as possible, to impress on the Chinese the terrible results of resisting Japan.

Two brothers stand outside of the remains of their house and shop in the southern section of Nanjing, which was badly damaged during the fighting.

Chungshan Road was a long avenue of filth and discarded uniforms, rifles, pistols, machine guns, fieldpieces, knives and knapsacks. In some places the Japanese had to hitch tanks to debris to clear the road.

The Chinese burned nearly all suburbs, including fine buildings and homes in Mausoleum Park. Hsiakwan is a mass of charred ruins. The Japanese seemingly avoided wrecking good buildings. The scarcity of air bombardments in the capture indicated their intention to avoid the destruction of buildings.

The Japanese even avoided bombing Chinese troop concentrations in built-up areas, apparently to preserve the buildings. The fine Ministry of Communications building was the only big government structure destroyed inside the city. It was fired by Chinese.

Nanking today is housing a terrorized population who, under alien domination, live in fear of death, torture, and robbery. The graveyard of tens of thousands of Chinese soldiers may also be the graveyard of all Chinese hopes of resisting conquest by Japan.[30]

---

30 Durdin, "All Captives Slain," New York Times, December 18, 1937.

WARTIME STORIES

The Japanese press also reported on the movement and activities of the Imperial soldiers as they approached the capital city. One incident, published in December 1937 in both Japanese and English language press, became known as "the 100-man killing contest." The story of the contest involved two Japanese sublieutenants, Toshiaki Mukai and Tsuyoshi Noda. Allegedly the two soldiers were engaged in a contest to be the first to kill 100 Chinese men with their military swords as they approached Nanjing.[31] By the end of November, and just two kilometers from the city, it was reported that neither had reached 100 so with the permission of their superior officer, the contest continued.

The Chinese public may have first learned of this contest from English-language articles in the December 7 and 14 articles in the *Japan Advertiser* that read:

> [7 December 1937.] Sublieutenant Toshiaki Mukai and Sublieutenant Takeshi [*recte:* Tsuyoshi] Noda, both of the Katagiri unit at Kuyung, in a friendly contest to see which of them will first fell 100 Chinese in individual sword combat before the Japanese forces completely occupy Nanking, are well in the final phase of their race, running almost neck to neck. On Sunday when their unit was fighting outside Kuyung, the "score," according to the Ashai, was Mukai 89, Noda 78.

> [14 December 1937.] The winner of the competition between Sublieutenants Toshiaki Mukai and Iwao [*recte:* Tsuyoshi] oda to see who would be the first to kill 100 Chinese with his Yamato sword has not been decided, the Nichinichi reports from the slopes of Purple Mountain, outside Nanking.[32] Mukai has a score of 106 and his rival has dispatched 105 men, but the two have found it impossible to determine which passed the 100 mark first. Instead of settling it with a discussion, they are going to extend the goal by fifty. Mukai's blade was slightly damaged in the competition. He explained that this was the result of cutting a Chinese in half, helmet and all. The contest was "fun," he declared, and he thought it a good thing that both men had gone over the 100

mark without knowing that the other had done so. Early Saturday morning, when the Nichinichi man interviewed the sublieutenant at a point overlooking Dr. Sun Yat-sen's tomb, another Japanese unit set fire to the slopes of Purple Mountain in an attempt to drive out the Chinese troops. The action also smoked out Mukai and his unit, and the men stood idly by while bullets passed overhead. "Not a shot hits me while I am holding this sword on my shoulder," he explained confidently.[33]

After the end of the war, Mukai and Noda did not stand trial at the International Military Tribunal for the Far East, better known as the Tokyo War Crimes Trials. Both were released from Sugamo Prison, where other Japanese war criminals were being held, and were extradited to stand trial at the Nanjing Military Tribunal (NMT) in China.[34] During their trial Noda claimed the contest never took place. He suggested that the press fabricated the entire story after hearing the other defendant, Mukai, boasting of his military exploits. While both men pleaded not guilty, records from the NMT state both were found guilty of participating in a recreational killing contest held entirely on Purple Mountain on the outskirts of Nanjing. This was considered a Class B war crime and both men were executed.[35]

Historians continue to debate the veracity of the actual contest and the culpability of the two soldiers based upon the evidence collected.[36] However, questioning evidence surrounding the contest does not dismiss the fact that the story of the contest heightened popular awareness in Japan and, according to Bob Tadashi Wakabayashi, "forced postwar Japanese to confront their collective past as butchers, not just as victims, in a war of aggression that began a decade before Pearl Harbor. For such reasons, the debate warrants close examination."[37] During their trial neither Mukai nor Noda publically denied participating in the contest, nor did the journalists recant their story or claim their facts were fabricated. In fact, Mukai was known to brag about his exploits upon his return to Japan in order to get "a better wife."[38]

Currently, Mukai's surviving family still believes he participated in this killing contest. To them he valiantly killed 106 Chinese soldiers in battle for the honor of the empire and died defending the honor of the emperor.[39] *(See Source 3: Photograph, 100-Man Killing Contest.)*

---

31 Bob Tadashi Wakabayashi, "The Nanking 100-Man Killing Contest Debate, 1971–1975," in *The Nanking Atrocity 1937–38: Complicating the Picture* (New York: Berghahn Books, 2007), 117.
32 The *Nichinichi* (or *Tokyo Nichi Nichi Shimbun*) was a newspaper printed in Tokyo from 1872 to 1943.
33 Harold J. Timperly, *What War Means: The Japanese Terror in China* (London: Victor Gollancz, 1938), 284–85, quoted in Bob Tadashi Wakabayashi, "The Nanking 100-Man Killing Contest

~~Debate 1971-1975," in The Nanjing Atrocity 1937-38, Complicating the Picture (New York~~
Berghahn Books, 2007), 117–18.
34 Chiang Kai-shek's regime held the Nanjing Military Tribunal (NMT) in China. This was 1 of 10 trials.
35 The International Military Tribunal for the Far East is explored in depth in Chapter Six of this resource.
36 Wakabayashi, *Nanking Atrocity,* 142; see also Suzuki Chieko, "The Hundred Head Contest: Reassessing the Nanjing Massacre" trans. James Orr, *Shukan Kinyobi* 488 (December 12, 2003): 50-51, accessed March 1, 2014, http://www.japanfocus.org/-Suzuki-Chieko/1792.
37 Wakabayashi, *The Nanking Atrocity,* 117.
38 Ibid., 133. Wakabayashi also notes that writer Yamamoto Shichihei reminds readers should place his [Mukai's] "seemingly despicable conduct in its proper context-the abnormal state of mind produced by brutalization in the imperial army. . . . Owing to extreme physical and psychological abuse over time, all Japanese soldiers exhibited mental imbalance in varying degrees; and bragging was one way to preserve sanity. Only the infantry counted as 'real men' in the army."
39 Ibid., 148; see also Takashi Yoshida, "A Battle over History: The Nanjing Massacre in Japan," in *The Nanjing Massacre in History and Historiography,* ed. Joshua A. Fogel (Berkeley: University of California Press, 2000), 79–84.

READING 6

VOICES OF SOLDIERS

Soldiers serving in China's Nationalist forces and the Japanese Imperial Army left a trail of evidence through letters home, battlefield diaries, and other accounts. One Japanese reserve soldier, Amano Saburo, arrived in Shanghai on November 29, 1937. He was a member of the Sixty-Fifth Regiment, which, like other special units of the Imperial Army, was hastily assembled out of an acute need for soldiers following the events at the Marco Polo Bridge. These special units were largely comprised of second- and third-tier reservists. From Shanghai, Amano Saburo marched and arrived on the outskirts of Nanjing, in Mufushan, which lies north of the walled city. He wrote the following letters home to his family:

At Shanghai, Noon, 29 November [1937]

(This postcard will get to you ahead of the earlier others.) We completed landing at noon and looked about near the wharf. Total devastation! A result of bombs, artillery, and small arms fire. There is no trace of anyone, only Chink[40] patrolman, Indian traffic cops, and beyond that, the Japanese army and British automobiles.

There are shops in some places, but no customers. . . . Tomorrow we head for Chang-shu to catch up with the Morozumi Unit [Sixty-Fifth Regiment], but tonight we camp in Shanghai. The trek will take about four days on foot. This means the assault on Nanjing.[41]

Saburo, 12 December

I've completed a march right out of that poem I learned from Akiko on the way home from Higashiyama Hot Springs in Wakamatsu:

> We enter endless plains
>> That lead to nowhere,
> advancing steel helmets,
>> with the Rising Sun

We've broken past the forty ri mark [160 kilometers] since coming ashore, and entered Chen-chiang as dusk approached this evening. The Eleventh division moved in the night before. Now, there is little more than occasional machine gun fire—no real combat to speak of. . . . On the sixth, I took command of the Third Platoon in the Ninth Company (led by Sublieutenant Kinoshita), under the Third Battalion (Taira Unit), of the Sixty-fifth Regiment (Morozumi Unit). We marched four days since then, past Chiangyin city to reach Chenchiang on the tenth, today. Although I'm supposed to be a "platoon commander," this unit is down to twenty-seven men. That gives you an idea of just how awful the fighting has been. . . .

On the fourteenth [the day after the siege of Nanjing began], the Sixty-fifth Regiment, led by Battalion commander [Maj. Gen. Yamada Senji], took over the Mufushan [elevated] batteries a little over one ri [four kilometers] northeast of Nanjing. . . . Right now, the Sixty-fifth is mopping up defeated enemy stragglers in the area. Part of it left for Nanking to take part in today's triumphal entry celebrations, but most of us are charged with dealing with POWs. The Sixty-fifth by itself has taken a number approaching 20,000 to date. We hold them in the Chink army compound beneath the elevated batteries. Provisions are inadequate, so lots of Chink troops have gone without food or water for a week already.[42]

While guarding POWs at Mufushan, on the outskirts of Nanjing, Amano wrote:

> A POW from the Chink army handed me this document in the hope that I could help them out. I attach it here for your reference.
>
> **To the Commanding Officer of Great Japan:**
>
> After being cut off from our [retreating] army, we turned over our arms and surrendered to the military forces of Great Japan, imploring you to adopt appropriate measures on our behalf. Three days have passed since coming here, yet we still have no ideas of how you will deal with us. Tens of thousands of pitiable men have gone hungry for over four days. We cannot survive on this rice gruel alone; soon we will die of starvation. Oh, Great Japan! Tens of thousands [of us] lie on the verge of death, yet retain hope for life. We beg you to save our lives. If you should grant this entreaty, we will submit to you with all our hearts and repay your kind blessing by enduring fire and water to serve Great Japan henceforth. Please, please, I beseech you to bestow food on us so that we may live. We join in celebrating the Empire of Great Japan! Banzai!
>
> Most respectfully submitted,
> Fu Ho
> Ad hoc Representative of the Surrendered Army[43]

Amano Saburo also documented in writing a chronology of approaching and entering Nanjing:

> **Chen-chiang–**
>
> After departing Chiang-yin on 7 December, several days' forced march required to reach the walled city of Chen-chiang, whose batteries overlook the Yangtze River, on 4 December. . . . No defeated enemy remnants around. Saw electric lights on for the first time since landing [at Hu-p'u-chen], probably because our offensive left the Chinks with no time to destroy generating plants. An American flag flutters about the U.S. Embassy on a low-lying hill; hatred welled up inside me.

From Chen-chiang to Nanking–

Departed from Chen-chiang at 11:00 a.m. for the assault for
Nanjing. The ruins of some towns and villages en route clearly
showed that retreating Chink armies ravaged all of these to their
hearts' content. Finally established assault formations to attack
the Mufushan [elevated] batteries at 11:30 a.m., on 14 December.
Later heard that another unit captured the Wulung batteries earlier that morning. At 8:00 a.m., as the sun rose, we encountered the
enemy about one ri [four kilometers] this side of the Mufushan
batteries. Suffered slight losses; killed or wounded 15,000 of the
enemy and captured mounds of weapons.

Ch'uanchiao County–

Crossed the Yangtze from Hsiakwan outside Nanking; got here
after a two day trek. Almost no sign of the enemy. Inhabitants
seem fairly amicable toward the imperial army. Such extravagant
provisions never seen before! Chickens and pigs more plentiful
than vegetables, so we gorge on [plundered] meat everyday.
Stone mortars are available [to pound mochi]. Also, we requisi-
tioned sweet glutinous rice for making New Year's *mochi*. Will be
here on guard duty for the time being.[44]

Japanese scholar Ono Kenji examined in depth what Amano Saburo chron-
icles of the events that occurred near Mufushan in his unit, the Moruzumi
Unit. It was near Mufushan where firsthand accounts of Japanese soldiers
have largely been collected and we are able to learn, from the soldiers' perspective, of the events surrounding the large-scale atrocities at Nanjing:

> [O]n the fifteenth, came news that the local Sixty-fifth Regiment
> had taken this huge number of the enemy as prisoners of war. .
> . . on the 17th [of December] the Fukushima edition of the Tokyo
> Asahi shinbun released an exclusive "Extra" bearing the headline,
> "The Morozumi Unit Captures 15,000. What a Tremendous Feat!
> What a Grand Battlefield Achievement!" . . .
>
> [H]aving captured this huge number of prisoners, the Sixty-
> fifth Regiment went on to "slaughter them all." To the best of
> my knowledge, these massacres near Mufushan constitute the

largest incident of mass murder in the entire Nanjing Atrocity. The prisoners were detained in 22 Chinese army barracks located to the south of Mufushan where they awaited what turned out to be their execution.[45]

Ono also obtained the personal battlefield diary left by Japanese soldier Lance Corporal Meguro Fukuji, which further corroborates the executions of POWs that occurred outside the walls of Nanjing. His entry reads:

16 December: Clear. Outside the walled city of Nanjing. . . .

At 4:00 p.m. we shot to death 7,000 prisoners taken by the Yamada Unit [Detachment]. The cliff on the Yangtze looked like a mountain of corpses from a time. That was an awful site.

17 December: Clear. Outside the walled city of Nanking.

We left our encampment at 9:00 a.m. to take part in the grand historic ceremonies marking our commander's triumphant entry into the walled city of Nanking. At 5:00 p.m., we went to take up an assignment to execute about 13,000 enemy troops. Over two days, the Yamada Unit executed close to 20,000 of them. It seems that each of the units killed all the prisoners it held by gunfire.[46]

---

40 Chink is a pejorative term for someone of Chinese nationality.
41 Wakabayashi, *Nanking Atrocity,* 185–86.
42 Ibid., 186–87.
43 Ibid., 188.
44 Ibid., 194–95.
45 Ibid., 72.
46 Ono, Fujiwara, Akira and Honda, eds., *Nankin daiguakusatus o kiroku shita kogun heishi tachi,* 373–74, quoted in Wakabayashi, *Nanking Atrocity,* 72, 82.

"I WILL NEVER FORGET": VOICES OF SURVIVORS

Three testimonies from survivors of the Nanjing Atrocities are included below. They are only three of many and each has been translated from Mandarin Chinese.[47] All include memories of extreme acts of violence and trauma. Gender violence is prominent in each testimony and great care and sensitivity should be considered in any use with students.

Survivor testimonies—firsthand accounts from individuals who lived through war and atrocities—supplement what we learn from historians and other secondary sources. Their voices offer perspectives on difficult and often unimaginable situations people experienced during war and collective violence. We must remember that testimonies given decades later are voluntarily given and are based on individual experiences and personal memories. They are also self-edited and must be understood and listened to with these factors in mind.

Survivors of the 1937 Nanjing Massacre pose for a photo during a ceremony in Nanjing on July 6, 2013.

At the same time, some scholars suggest that the very thing that makes survivors' accounts so powerful can also affect their reliability. While some read survivors' stories as evidence to be weighed along with other sources, we know these accounts offer something more. They teach us not only about the past, but about memory as well. For many people they force a confrontation with the past, reminding us that behind numbers or documentary accounts are human beings.

Testimony of Wen Sunshi

My name is Wen Sunshi, this year I turn 82 years old. My house was originally in the Xiaguan district of Nanjing. I was married in 1936 of the Chinese lunar calendar. My husband's original surname was Guo, but because my family had arranged the marriage, he changed his name to Wen—my surname.

When the Japanese entered the city on the December of 1937, many retreating Chinese Nationalist troops attempted to cross the river to escape, with some even coming to my house to board. When the sky was getting dark, my entire family took refuge at the nearby [Hutchinson International].[48] En route, we saw Japanese warships rake down crossing Chinese troops with indiscriminate machine gun fire.

The refugees at the [Hutchinson International] were many. One day, six or seven Japanese troops arrived, all of them armed with guns, knives hanging by their waists. They took six or seven maidens from the crowd of refugees. I was among those taken. There was also a maiden I recognized, her name was Little Qiaozi. One Japanese soldier forced me into an empty room. I can remember him being chubby, with a beard. Once we were both in the room, he used a knife to force me to take off my pants—I would be killed if I didn't. I was thus raped in this manner.

After the rape, the Japanese soldier turned to me and said "opened path, opened path" and I was released. In order to avoid the Japanese soldiers coming again to hurt us, that night, the manager of the [Hutchinson International] ferried us—about eighteen maidens—to the cellar of the Egg Beating room. Those among us also included several maidens who had escaped from the Suzhou prefecture of Jiangsu. I hid in that cellar for several months, with the owners secretly sending me food. Only after the situation was deemed "peaceful" did I return to live with my mother and father. I had lived in the [Hutchinson International] for more than a year before I had returned home.

My husband knows that I was raped by a Japanese soldier, but empathizes with me. He passed away a couple of years ago. In my home, I can't bear to tell my sons and daughters, and I'm worried that other people will find out and look down upon me.

At that time, my cousin was only eighteen-years-old. He was taken away by the Japanese troops and never returned. I personally watched as the Japanese troops massacred many people. We had a neighbor, elderly Ms. Zhen, who was about eighty-years-old. She thought that because she was old, she could remain at home and be fine. In actuality, she was brutally murdered by the Japanese, with her stomach slashed open. There was also a tea specialist, who couldn't bear leaving his home. He was also murdered by the Japanese.[49]

Testimony of Chen Jiashou

My name is Chen Jiashou. I was born on September 16, 1918. When the Imperial Japanese Army invaded Nanjing in 1937, I was living in a small Nanjing district with my Uncle, Mother and Father, my two brothers and my sister. At that time, I was only 19 years old. I was an apprentice. After the Japanese invasion, I, along with several other people, collectively escaped to a refugee camp by Shanghai Road. At that time, since the refugee camp had run out of food, I ventured out to replenish the supply. But because of some casual remarks I made while lining up, I was taken by some nearby Japanese soldiers and brought to a pond adjacent to Shanghai Road. Having not stood there for more than two minutes, I watched as a group of armed Japanese soldiers hustled several lines of about two hundred Chinese troops toward the edge of the pond, surrounding them with weapons to prevent them from escaping.

At that time, I was also ordered to stand among the front line of Chinese soldiers. I was only 19 years old, and terribly frightened.

Thus, the instant the Japanese soldiers opened fire on us all, I immediately fell toward the ground, faking my death. Struck by the flying bullets, my Chinese comrades all piled up on my body. Right up till it got dark and the Japanese soldiers had all left, I lay under the dead bodies, not daring to move. Only then did I climb out from under the pile of bodies. It was thus how I became a fortunate survivor of the Nanjing massacre.

I was captured again by the Japanese near Sanhe Village, and sent to work at a Japanese-occupied silk factory near nowadays' Nanjing medicine factory. It was at this time that I witnessed more Japanese atrocities first-hand. One time, after I finished transporting ten barrels of gasoline to the Japanese military depot near the train station, Japanese soldiers brought me to a basement. Aside from large wooden boxes, the basement also contained a bed. The two Japanese soldiers ripped off the bedsheet covers and indiscriminately opened fire upon it. On the bed lay four women, all dead.

Another time, as I came back from transporting provisions, I walked near the main hall of the Nanjing medicine factory. I saw a few hundred ordinary citizens collapsed on the road. Driving a truck, the Japanese troops evidently saw them as well, but simply paid no attention and pretended not to see them. They drove directly over the people, transforming the place into a bloodbath.

I will never forget a memory like this:

One day after work, I walked to the entrance of Changshan Park. A man surnamed Tse heard the sound of a Japanese truck, so stuck his head out to take a look. Coincidentally, he caught the eyes of the Japanese troops, who immediately disembarked and tied Old Tse up, forcing him to kneel on the ground. One of them took out a bayonet, and violently hacked at Old Tse's head. Unfortunately, though the back of Old Tse's neck was sliced through, his head hung on by the remaining front part of his neck—he was still breathing and alive, collapsed on the floor. Seeing this, the Japanese soldiers then raised their leather boots, mercilessly kicking him around the Changshan Park's grounds. It was only then, with his head severed and his body trashed, that Old Tse passed away.

I will never forget the violence, the atrocities and the aggression that the Imperial Japanese soldiers enacted during the Nanjing Massacre.[50]

Testimony of Mr. Chen Deshou. Interviewed by Yanming Lu.

Chen: My last name is Chen, spelled with the "ear" and "east", De is the "de" from virtue, and Shou is the "shou" from longevity. My name is Chen De Shou.

Lu: What year were you born?

Chen: 1932

Lu: You were born here in Nanjing?

Chen: Yes, in Nanjing.

Lu: What type of work did your parents do?

Chen: My mother was a housewife, my father was in clothing, he owned a clothing store.

Lu: What did your grandparents do?

Chen: My grandfather was a tailor, he also made clothes.

Chen: My grandmother too.

Lu: So your family ran a tailoring shop?

Chen: No, a clothing shop, a clothing store.

Lu: Do you remember what it was like in your family store at the time?

Chen: Yes.

Lu: Can you talk a little about it?

Chen: Life in our household was a full one. There was my paternal grandfather, my paternal grandmother, my parents and a younger brother. My mother was pregnant. My father's sister also lived with us, and she had two kids who came to live with us. Life was very hard. In 1937, at that time, Japan, the Japanese troops . . . they were setting off bombs, throwing bombs, see at that time, they wanted to . . . to . . . hiding from the planes. Around December of 1937, there were so many people, they fled to escape the troubles. Why didn't our family go? Because our family was in the clothing ordering business, and my father got a contract to make uniforms for the soldiers, uniforms that were for the local army. This money though, was stuck, so there was no cash, and without the money, you couldn't escape, right? So we didn't leave, we lived in this house. Where was our house? It was near Nanjing's Sanshan Rd, in what is now the street just behind the Gan Family Courtyard. My house was #4. . . .

Life was pretty happy and full. Now on December 13, there came change that turned our world upside down. At that time, at the end of the alley, at the end of the alley we lived in, it was called TianQing St. The Japs started a fire, they started a fire at the end of the alley, and the blaze was fierce. My father, being a warm hearted man, he went out to put out the fire. And he never came back. From the moment he left that day, he never came back, he was gone. So only my grandparents, my mother, my aunt, the young and the old, were left at home. On the morning of that day, a *Japanese devil*[51] took a bayonet, a rifle, and with the bayonet he came in. When he came in, we thought everything was as usual, my grandfather even brought out candies for him, telling him to eat, and treating him as a guest. He said he didn't want that, he said one sentence: "I want a woman." My mother was pregnant, with a big belly, so he didn't want her. He dragged my aunt, and at the time she was nursing my little girl cousin. The house we lived in had 3 rooms, each behind the other, we were in the third, in the third room. He took my aunt, and dragged her from the third room to the second room, he was going to humiliate her, he was about to rape her.

My aunt was an educated woman, she would rather die than submit, so she struggled, she struggled with that Japanese devil. Then the devil picked up a knife, and stabbed my aunt, piercing her 6 times, in her thigh as well, she was bleeding there as well as from her chest. At the time when he dragged her to the front, my grandmother, and I was an obedient little boy, she brought me forward, so I witnessed my aunt's death with my own eyes. I was 6 at the time, only 6, but I was old enough to remember things. My aunt handed my little cousin over to my grandmother, and said, "Mother, my heart aches, please give me some sweetened water."

So my aunt, my grandmother, my grandmother carried my little cousin to the back, and poured a bowl of sweetened water, from the third room to the second and back to the front. When she got there, my aunt had already stopped breathing, she didn't get to taste the bowl of sweetened water her mother brought. So, just like that, my aunt died. And then that very night, my mother, she gave birth to her child, at that time she gave birth. Giving birth at that time, when there was no one there to help, was extremely difficult. So we stayed at home.[52]

At this time, we kept my aunt's body in the second room, within that room's entry we put down a door, and her on it, she lay there close to 3 days, we had no other choice, grandfather was old, around 70, he was an old man. We had no one in the house who could work, we couldn't get a coffin, right. The child my mother bore didn't have anything to eat, in a few days our household food ran out. The Japanese devils, were really hateful to the extreme, see, he could kill without batting an eyelid. He could rape and kill without batting an eyelid. And then, on the third day, a Japanese soldier arrived—this was a soldier, not a *Japanese devil*. He had a short gun on him, a short gun. And then he also spoke Chinese, he could understand my grandfather, and he could talk so my grandfather understood. He said that back in Japan he was a shop keeper, not a soldier, he was conscripted, he didn't have a choice, he was conscripted here, and from the looks of him he wasn't a soldier, he was a petty official. He took my grandfather out to the streets, found a couple of youths, and then found a few able bodies and went with them to a coffin shop and brought back a coffin to our second room, that is the room before ours, and put my aunt in the coffin. We couldn't bury her, so we had to put her on the ground open to the sky, like that. And then he took my grandfather, and went out, to a rice shop and a soy sauce shop and found some food, then put it in a bag and carried it back to us, and so we survived this hardest of hard times, see.

Now the Japanese devils, they wouldn't let a single woman off the hook, right. After my mother gave birth, she put the bloodied paper on the floor. When they came they'd want to see it, and after they saw it, they knew she'd had a baby, they didn't want her and they'd leave. This harassment went on everyday, there was nothing we could do.[53]

---

47 The first two are published in a collected volume distributed at the Nanjing Massacre Memorial Hall in China, and the third is transcribed from the USC Shoah Visual History Archive of oral testimonies. Throughout the testimonies some survivors refer to the events from December 13, 1937, through the end of March 1938 as the "massacre."

48 Hutchinson International was a major British company with significant industries and investments in China, and is part of today's Hutchinson Wampoa Limited.

49 Zhu Chengshan, ed., *Japanese Invaders in Nanjing Massacre Survivor Testimony* (Beijing: Social Sciences Academic Press, 2005), 469.

50 Ibid., 9.

51 This term is a pejorative term used for a Japanese Imperial soldier.

52 Here the transcription reads 家中没得人, which sounds like it means they couldn't find someone to help with the birth. The next line, 所以留在家里面, does not provide a subject, so it is assumed Chen refers to the entire family staying at home, rather than just his mother.

53 Chen Deshou, interview by Yanming Lu, December 15, 2012, interview 52120, trans. USC Shoah Foundation, Visual History Archive, USC Shoah Foundation, Los Angeles, CA.

READING 8

HELL ON EARTH: GEORGE FITCH

In many places in China foreigners were bystanders to the conflict, but in Nanjing something very different occurred. In China's capital city a small group of Westerners chose to remain while others stood by or fled the city. This small group formed the Nanjing Safety Zone Committee and provided immediate refuge for those Chinese remaining in the city. While these foreigners were not trained diplomats but missionaries and businessmen, their voices, abundant letters, and diaries documented the atrocities and served as firsthand accounts to the violence engulfing the city. They regularly appealed to the Japanese embassy, wrote to friends, family, and international organizations all in a desperate effort to spread awareness in order to stop the horror raging through Nanjing.

One member of the Nanjing Safety Zone Committee, George Ashmore Fitch (1883–1979), was born in Soochow (Suzhou), China, and was the son of Presbyterian missionaries. He graduated from the College of Wooster in Ohio and obtained a bachelor of divinity at Union Theological Seminary in New York. In 1909 he was ordained by the Presbyterian Church and returned to China to work with the Young Men's Christian Organization (YMCA) in Shanghai.[54]

By 1937 Fitch was head of the YMCA in Nanjing when the city was invaded. He promptly joined efforts to form and maintain the Safety Zone Committee, soon serving as its director. When the Chinese government fled the city, Fitch also served as acting mayor of the city until the Japanese occupational forces installed their administration.

During the first several months after Nanjing was occupied, Fitch took and collected still and moving pictures depicting the Japanese atrocities. In February 1938 Fitch smuggled these images back to the United States in the lining of his overcoat and traveled throughout the country giving lectures and showing his collection of films and other evidence of the Japanese atrocities. *(See Source 4: Eye-Witness Tells of Horror Seen in the Fall of Nanjing.)*

In the following letter home, Fitch describes what struck him as a "hell on earth" with "no parallel in modern history," urgently depicting conditions that he knew few people could testify to and he feared few would even hear of. His account was not written retrospectively but as the events unfolded in front of his eyes. Fitch also sent the letter to Wellington Koo (Koo Wei -jun), the Chinese representative to the League of Nations, and to Australian reporter Harold J. Timperly of the Manchester Guardian. Portions of Fitch's letter were later published in anonymity in Timperly's book *What War Means.*[55] An excerpt from George Fitch's letter:

Nanking, X'mas Eve, 1937.

What I am about to relate is anything but a pleasant story; in fact, it is so very unpleasant that I cannot recommend anyone without a strong stomach to read it. For it is a story of such crime and horror as to be almost unbelievable, the story of the depredations of a horde of degraded criminals of incredible bestiality, who have been and now are, working their will, unrestrained, on a peaceful, kindly, law-abiding people. Yet it is a story which I feel must

be told, even if it is seen by only a few; I cannot rest until I have
told it, and perhaps fortunately I am one of a very few who are
in a position to tell it. It is not complete—only a small part of the
whole; and God alone knows when it will be finished. I pray it may
be soon—but I am afraid it is going to go on for many months to
come, not just here but in other parts of China. I believe it has no
parallel in modern history.

It is now X'mas eve. I shall start with say December 10th. In these
two short weeks we here in Nanking have been through a siege;
the Chinese army has left, defeated, and the Japanese have come
in. On that day Nanking was still the beautiful city we were so
proud of, with law and order still prevailing; today it is a city laid
waste, ravage, completely looted, much of it burned. Complete
anarchy has reigned for ten days—it has been a hell on earth.
Not that my life has been in serious danger at any time; though
turning lust-mad, sometimes drunken soldiers out of houses
where they were raping the women is not, perhaps, altogether a
safe occupation; nor does one feel too sure of himself when he
finds a bayonet at his chest or a revolver at his head and knows
the Japanese Army is anything but pleased at our being here after
having advised all foreigners to get out. They wanted no observ-
ers. But to have to stand by while even the very poor are having
their last possession taken from them—their last coin, their last
bit of bedding (and it is freezing weather), the poor rickshaw man
his rickshaw; while thousands of disarmed soldiers who had
sought sanctuary with you together with many hundreds of innocent civilians are taken out before your eyes to be shot or used
for bayonet practice and you have to listen to the sound of the
guns that are killing them; while a thousand women kneel before
you crying hysterically begging you to save them from the beasts
who are preying on them; to stand by and do nothing while your
flag is taken down and insulted, not once but a dozen times, and
your own home is being looted; and then to watch the city you
have come to love and the institution to which you had planned to
devote your best years deliberately and systematically burned by
fire—this is a hell I had never before envisaged.

We keep asking ourselves "How long can this last?" Day by day we are assured by the officials that things will be better soon, that "we will do our best"—but each day has been worse than the day before. And now we are told that a new division of 20,000 is arriving. Will they have to have their toll of flesh and loot, of murder and rape? There will be little left to rob, for the city has well nigh been stripped clean. For the past week the soldiers have been busy loading their trucks with what they wanted from the stores and then setting fire to the buildings. And then there is the harrowing realization that we have only enough rice and flour for the 200,000 refugees for another three weeks and coal for ten days. Do you wonder that one awakes in the night in a cold sweat of fear, and sleep for the rest of the night is gone? Even if we had food enough for three months, how are they going to be fed after that? And with their homes long ago burned, where are they going to live? They cannot much longer continue in their present terribly crowded conditions; disease and pestilence must soon follow if they do.

Every day we call at the Japanese Embassy and present our protests, our appeals, our lists of authenticated reports of violence and crime. We are met with suave Japanese courtesy, but actually the officials there are powerless. The victorious army must have its rewards—and those rewards are to plunder, murder, rape, at will, to commit acts of unbelievable brutality and savagery on the very people whom they have come to protect and befriend, as they so loudly proclaimed to the world. In all modern history surely there is no page that will stand so black as that of the rape of Nanking. [56]

George Fitch continued to advocate on behalf of aid to China throughout the span of World War II. His images, diaries, and letters later proved instrumental in an affidavit he filed during the Nanjing portion of the International Military Tribunal for the Far East where he also personally testified. Fluent in Chinese, Fitch did not leave China after the war but remained in the country working for relief organizations until the Communists took over in 1949. He then lived in Taiwan for many years and returned to live in the United States in the early 1960s. He died at the age of 95 in Pomona, California.

54 The YMCA was founded in 1844 in London, England, by 22-year-old George Williams. The original organization was established as a refuge for Bible study and prayer for young men seeking to escape the hazards of life on the streets of London. The YMCA in China was established in Shanghai in 1900 and in Beijing in 1909. See http://www.ymca.int/where-we-work/ymca-country-profiles/asia-and-pacific/china/.
55 In the United States this same book was published under the title *The Japanese Terror in China*.
56 George Fitch letter home, January 6, 1938, Yale Divinity School Library, http://divdl.library.yale .edu/ydlchina/images/NMP0335.pdf.

READING 9

POLITICS AND THE ATROCITIES

Western, Chinese, and Japanese diplomats and leaders were also aware of the Nanjing Atrocities. They wrote in private correspondence and issued public statements about the events as they unfolded on the world stage.

On February 2, 1938, the first representative of the Chinese republic to the League of Nations, Koo Wei-jun (Wellington Koo), denounced Japan's military actions, calling for the delegates to condemn the actions of the Imperial Army. Regrettably the council only adopted a resolution expressing their moral support to China and recommending that no actions be taken by the member states to strengthen the current Chinese resistance. Several months later on May 10, 1938, Koo again requested that the league take effective measures to deter Japanese aggression. In stressing the barbarous and cruel acts of the Japanese forces he said:

> The wanton slaughter of noncombatants by the indiscriminate bombing of undefended towns and nonmilitary centers has been continuing unabated. The unprecedented violence to women and ruthlessness to children and the deliberate massacre of hundreds of adult males amongst the civilian population, including those removed from refugee camps under false pretenses, form the subject of many reports by impartial foreign eyewitnesses. The cruel and barbarous conduct of Japanese troops towards the Chinese people in the occupied areas not only shows the want of regard on the part of the Japanese army for the accepted rules of warfare, but also betrays a disgraceful lack of discipline in rank and file.[57]

Koo appealed several more times to the league for assistance to the Chinese and for an international public stand against Japanese aggression. Unfortunately his plea largely fell on deaf ears.

Roger George Howe, the top British diplomat in Nanjing from September 1937 to March 1938, reflected on questions of responsibility. In a letter dated January 10, 1938, Howe wrote:

> I should have said from the start that the Chinese armies in an ill-conceived military program burned down many villages and blocks of houses outside of the wall, and did some casual looting of shops and houses for food. Otherwise they caused little trouble, though there was great anxiety over their obvious collapse, their preparations for street fighting that never occurred, and their possible injuring of the civilian population. The Chinese failure was disgraceful in the flight of high offices, and in its lack of military coordination and determination. But comparatively considered, the ordinary soldiers were very decent.[58]

In Japan, the occupation of Nanjing was largely couched within the larger war on the Asian mainland. Japanese politicians provided rationalizations for the brutality of Japanese troops in China as early as September 1937. Prince Konoe, prime minister of Japan, addressed the Diet explaining that the army's military actions were not directed against the Chinese people but against the Chinese government and its armies. Konoe said, "The only measure Japan can adopt is to administer a crushing blow to the Chinese army and make it completely lose its will to fight. If China fails to realize her mistakes and persists in her resistance, Japan is prepared for protracted hostilities."[59]

Several months later, Japanese ambassador to the United States Saito Horoshi elaborated on Konoe's position in a speech printed in the journal World Affairs at the same time the events were occurring in Nanjing (December 1937):

> The conflict in the Far East is by no means as simple in origin as some Europeans and Americans seem to think. The trouble did not begin last July. It is a result of the conditions of China, which has caused the invasion of foreign armies for more than a century and is the reason for the presence there today of British, French, Italian, Dutch and American troops. If China's house were in order, there would be no need for the presence of these foreign

~~forces of of Japan's present actions. In fact, if law and order were~~
maintained in China, if China were a unified and stabilized nation,
it would be able to "drive all foreigners into the sea"—which has
been the objective of many of its anti-foreign movements.

Who is to blame for the condition of China? Is it Great Britain,
which sought for decades to help successive Chinese governments to organize their two principal sources of revenue? Is it
France, which has sent more missionaries and teachers to them
than to all other backward nations combined? Is it Japan, which
almost staked her existence in a war with Russia to prevent "the
break-up of China"? . . . It is difficult for many Japanese to understand how so many people of the West can fail to see that the
trouble is not of foreign but of Chinese making.

The present conflict has been forced upon Japan, and Japan wants
it to end as quickly as possible. But she is determined to end it in
a way so decisive that a situation like the present can never recur.
Our objective, therefore, is a genuine change of heart on the part
of those in power at Nanjing. We insist that the organized campaign to stir up hate against Japan be discontinued and that the
Central Government renounce the union with Communism which
was solidified at Xi'an [i.e., the "Second United Front"]. . . .[60]

---

57 League of Nations, *Official Journal* 19, 5–6 (May–June 1938): 307, quoted in Takashi Yoshida, "Wartime Accounts of the Nanking Atrocity," in *The Nanjing Atrocity 1937–1938: Complicating the Picture*, ed. Bob Tadashi Wakabayashi (New York: Berghahn Books, 2007), 251–52.

58 Suping Lu, ed., *A Dark Page in History: The Nanjing Massacre and Post-Massacre Social Conditions Recorded in British Diplomatic Dispatches, Admiralty Documents, and U.S. Naval Reports* (Lantham, Maryland: University Press of America, 2012), 40–41.

59 "Threat of 'CRUSHING BLOW,'" *The Sydney Morning Herald*, September 6, 1937, 9, accessed September 2, 2013, http://trove.nla.gov.au/ndp/del/article/17400315.

60 Pei-kai Cheng, Michael Lestz, and Jonathan D. Spence, eds., *The Search for Modern China: A Documentary Collection* (New York: W. W. Norton & Company, 1999), 316–19.

WOMEN IN WAR

Violence against women during war is now an international war crime. At the time of the Japanese occupation of China, it was not. As in many wars, women were raped as a form of power and dehumanization. In an interview conducted with scholars Carol Rittner and John Roth, they explain that sexual violence and rape during war and mass atrocities are a "weapon of war and destroys as much as a bullet."[62] They state that sexual violence particularly, but not exclusively, against women is used to humiliate, dominate, destroy, and maim individuals. It is also deliberately used as a strategy to destroy entire communities.

The dehumanization of women (and in some cases men) during war is a recurring element consistent in cases of foreign occupation and civil war.[63] The large-scale raping of women in Nanjing during the Japanese assault of the city is one reason the crimes in Nanjing have been called the "Rape of Nanking." However, preceding the rapes that occurred during the occupation of the city, the Japanese military had established institutions where women were forcibly held as military sexual slaves. These institutions became euphemistically known as "comfort stations." Korean, Filipina, Taiwanese, and other Asian women were systematically rounded up, imprisoned, and repeatedly raped and abused. They were called comfort women, but a more accurate reference is military sexual slaves. According to Japanese military documents the comfort station system was regarded by the military elite as necessary for the war effort. Their belief was that the spread of sexually transmitted diseases among troops could be "controlled" or "curbed" by establishing these locales and thus reign in uncontrolled sexual activity.

The first known documentation of military sexual slavery during Japanese occupation in China dates back to March 1933. Associated with the Fourteenth Brigade stationed in northeastern China, this facility was titled the "Disease Prevention and Hygiene Facility" and had 35 Korean women and three Japanese women. One General Staff member of the Japanese army made the following observation in 1932:

> The Chinese value honor very highly, and for appearances' sake
> treat their wives with respect. Among all immoral and violent acts,

the Chinese regard rape to be the worst and consider it an
extremely serious social problem. [Bandits and thieves] lie,
deceive, loot, and steal with no compunctions; but they rarely
commit rape.[64]

As this staff member reports, it was clearly understood that rape would be
an assault on China on many different levels and rapes would be considered
an obstacle to maintaining order in the occupied regions. Comfort stations
existed in China and elsewhere for years prior to the occupation of Nanjing.
But by July 1937 Japan began its full-scale aggressive war in China and the
policy of establishing such institutions shifted. This was the first time that
the Japanese army had such a large number of military men on active duty
on the Asian mainland. By the end of 1937 the Japanese army began to
increase the building of their military comfort stations. On December 11,
merely six days before Japanese troops entered the city wall of Nanjing, the
Central China Area Army ordered the establishment of military comfort
stations. Iinuma Mamoru, the chief of the Shanghai Expeditionary Force,
wrote in his diary on this day, "On the matter of the establishment of
military comfort stations, documents from the [Central China] Area Army
arrived, and [I will] oversee the execution of these orders."[65]

Ample documentation from Japanese soldiers' diaries and from the Japanese
Ministry of War only confirms the wide-scale construction of such stations
throughout occupied China, as do the following excerpts from two documents. The first is a summary report sent out by the Ministry of War in
1938 and the second in September 1940.

"Matters Concerning the Recruitment of Women to Work in Military Comfort Stations." March 8, 1938

Notice from the Adjutant to the Chiefs of Staff of the North China
Area Army and Central China Expeditionary Force. . . .

There are many things [about the rounding up of comfort women]
that require careful attention. In the future, armies in the field will
control the recruiting of women and will use scrupulous care in
selecting people to carry out this task. This task will be performed
in close cooperation with the military police or local police force of
the area. You are hereby notified of the order [of the Minister of
War] to carry out this task with the utmost regard for preserving
the honor of the army and for avoiding social problems.[66]

"Measures to Enhance Military Discipline in Light of the Experiences of the China Incident" September 19, 1940.[67]

Judging from reports since the sudden outbreak of the China Incident, behind the undeniably brilliant military exploits, many criminal acts contrary to the true nature of the Imperial Army such as looting, rape, arson, and massacres of prisoners of war have occurred. [Such acts] incur animosity toward the sacred war at home and abroad and regrettably impede the achievement of its goals. An investigation into the conditions that gave rise to these criminal acts confirms that they frequently occurred immediately after combat. . . . It is necessary to restore order in the areas affected by the China Incident, give careful consideration to the setting up of comfort facilities, and attend to restraining and pacifying savage feels and lust. . . . The emotional effects of sexual comfort stations on soldiers should be considered the most critical. It must be understood that the competence or lack thereof in overseeing [the operation of comfort stations] has the greatest influence on the promotion of morale, the maintenance of military discipline, and prevention of crimes and sexually transmitted diseases.[68]

---

61 Facing History and Ourselves, Carol Rittner and Joth Roth film, untitled. Still in production at time of publication, August 2014.

62 See Jeffrey Burds, "Sexual Violence in Europe in World War II, 1939-1945," *Politics & Society* 37 (2009): 35, accessed January 1, 2014, doi: 10.1177/1059601108329751, http://www.sovhistory.neu.edu /Burds-Sexual-Violence-COURSE.pdf.

63 Yoshimi Yoshiaki, *Jugun ianfu* [Comfort Women], trans. Suzanne O'Brien (New York: Columbia University Press, 2000), 49.

64 Ibid., 50.

65 Ibid., 59, 105–06.

66 *China Incident* was a term used during the war by some Japanese to refer to the Nanjing Atrocities. Decades after the war, Japanese nationalists who attempt to minimize the violence that occurred choose this terminology.

67 Yoshimi Yoshiaki, *Jugun ianfu* [Comfort Women] , 60, 166–67.

THE CONDUCT OF SOLDIERS

There were two particular periods of intense violence by Japanese soldiers in Nanjing. The first occurred with the initial assault of the city from December 15 through December 21, 1937, and the second from January 28 to February 3, 1938. Replace sentence with: While the first weeks of the initial occupation of the city was extremely important, it was six weeks later that mass rape and violence by soldiers in the Imperial army escalated.

When the Imperial Army ordered all Chinese residing in the Nanjing Safety Zone to return to their homes by February 4, 1938, the excuse for an escalation of violence was set in place.[68] Chinese refusal to leave by this date would result in their forcible removal by Japanese soldiers. With this ultimatum in place, Chinese refugees had little alternative. Complicating matters was the fact that by late January almost half of all homes within Nanjing had been destroyed or burned down during the city's occupation. Those that still had a home to return to were lucky; others simply had to rebuild from nothing. With assurances by Westerners administering the Safety Zone that it was necessary to leave, Chinese refugees reluctantly departed. As feared, instead of rebuilding their lives, an outbreak of rape and murder occurred

Ullstein Bild/The Granger Collection

Japanese soldiers shoot at Chinese citizens in December of 1937.

once outside the Safety Zone boundaries. In fact, almost half of all documented acts of rape during the Nanjing Atrocities happened during this one week of time, a time in which the battle for the city was over and the city was already under full occupation.[69]

In one of the final cases documented by a member of the Safety Zone Committee, No. 425, this gratuitous violence is evident. Dated Monday, February 7, 1938, it stands as only one of hundreds of examples:

> Monday morning, February 7, it was reported to us that four people, three men and one woman, had been killed on February 6 about 5 p.m. by Japanese soldiers back of Pei Tze Ting. . . .

> About 4:30 that same day a Chinese girl came to our office for help because she said the woman that had been killed was her own mother. Her mother had gone home a few days before to start their home again and had taken all their money with her. She hoped to find the money on her mother's body.

> Mr. Rabe and Mr. Mills [Westerners active in the Safety Zone] went with her to the scene and immediately found the four bodies located thus with fresh pools of blood: Number one is the old man who was shot first; number two is the woman who brought aid; numbers 3 and 4 are the men who came to get the wounded men; the oblong object is the door.

> The story was that the old man was carrying two chairs along the path by the wire fence and a Japanese soldier stopped him and shot him on the spot. The woman, who was walking with him, noticed that he was only wounded and not dead, so she went and got two men to come with a door to take the wounded man away. When the three of them arrived at the spot, the soldier shot all three of them.[70]

How do we explain why soldiers would engage in the horrific violence documented in Nanjing? Author Ian Buruma offers some compelling questions to begin probing this question:

> The numbers [killed] don't convey the savagery of what happened in Nanking, and in many other Chinese villages, towns and cities as well. Nor do they explain why it was allowed to happen. Was it a deliberate policy to terrorize the Chinese into submission? The

complicity of the officers suggests there was something to this. But it might have been a kind of payoff to the Japanese troops for slogging through China in the freezing winter without decent pay or rations. Or was it largely a matter of a peasant army running out of control? Or just the inevitable consequence of war, as many Japanese maintain?[71]

---

68 The Nanjing Safety Zone was a neutral zone within the city of Nanjing in which Chinese civilian refugees were protected from the Japanese occupational forces from mid-December 1937 to February 1938. See Chapter Five in this resource; "FOREIGNERS' ROLE IN NANKING PRAISED; Group Stayed Throughout the Siege, Caring for Wounded and Scores of Refugees," *New York Times*, December 19, 1937, 1, accessed January, 1, 2014, http://query.nytimes.com/mem/archive/pdf?res =F30D15FB3A59177A93CBA81789D95F438385F9; and Brook, *Rape of Nanking,* 114.
69 Brook, *Rape of Nanking,* 8.
70 Ibid., 161.
71 Ian Buruma, *Wages of Guilt* (New York: Farrar, Straus and Giroux, 1994), 112.

READING 12

PRISONERS OF WAR IN NANJING

During the occupation of Nanjing, massacres of Chinese prisoners of war (POWs) by the Imperial Japanese Army occurred. What is clear from the historical record is that when the Imperial Army entered Nanjing, Japanese soldiers specifically targeted and captured Chinese men, some of whom were soldiers and some of whom were not. Because they were Chinese men, many were assumed to be soldiers and were captured and indiscriminately treated as POWs—as enemy combatants.

Since 1929 when the Geneva Convention on the Treatment of Prisoners of War was codified, signatory nations to the convention agreed to uphold the 97 articles outlined. These include the conditions in which prisoners should be evacuated, organization of POW camps, food and clothing for prisoners, hygiene, religious practice, mental and physical recreation, and prison labor, to name a few.[72] Article 2 specifically states, "Prisoners of War in the power of the hostile Government . . . shall at all times be humanely treated and protected, particularly against acts of violence."[73]

In 1937 Japan had not formally ratified the 1929 Geneva Convention. But, on the brink of war with China the Japanese Ministry of Affairs agreed to apply the convention even without formal ratification. As an occupational force it was legal to fire upon soldiers believed to be enemy combatants but illegal under the Geneva Convention to kill POWs once captured. According to the laws of the time, it was also legal to capture men as enemy combatants even if they were fleeing an advancing army and uniforms had been shed and weapons discarded. The fear remained that weapons could still be concealed.[74] What remains uncertain, however, is the chain of communication that subsequently occurred between the Japanese ministry and the leadership within the Japanese Imperial Army regarding compliance with certain articles within the Geneva Convention.

Complicating this reality are the memoirs, field reports, diaries, and official records of Japanese military operations documenting the large-scale roundup and massacre of Chinese men, all under the guise of eliminating enemy combatants. Lieutenant General Nakajima Kesago, commander of Japan's Sixteenth Division, wrote in his diary on December 13, 1938:

> To begin with, it is our policy not to take prisoners, so we decided to get them out of the way. But when it became a group of one thousand, five thousand, and finally ten thousand, we couldn't even disarm them all. We were safe simply because they had absolutely no will to fight back and followed us slovenly. . . . I have never imagined that we would have to deal with this large-scale disposition. The staff officers were extremely busy.[75]

Westerners administering the Nanjing Safety Zone also witnessed the roundup and massacre of Chinese men and confronted what became a moral and legal quandary. One of the most important provisions Westerners had made to the Japanese High Command in order for the Safety Zone to be established was to maintain the parameters as a demilitarized zone. John Rabe, chairman of the Safety Zone Committee, wrote of the pangs of guilt he felt for being unable to keep Japanese troops entirely out of the zone's boundaries. Once Chinese troops had been discovered within the Safety Zone, it was increasingly difficult to keep Japanese troops from entering at will and rounding up suspected soldiers. Rabe knew of the laws of war at the time. He feared that troops who did not surrender but fled an advancing army would be treated as hostile enemy combatants because of the possibility of their concealing weapons. At one point in the early weeks of the war, and at the height of the violence and chaos, a large cache of weapons had presumably been discovered within the zone's parameters, giving the Imperial Army the pretext to re-enter and search throughout the zone again and again and again.[76]

In one postwar testimony submitted at the International Military Tribunal for the Far East, witnesses recount searches of plain-clothed soldiers. One witness, Professor Miner Searle Bates of Nanking University, and a member of the Nanjing Safety Zone Committee, appeared on behalf of the prosecution:

> **Q [IMTFE]:** What was the conduct of the Japanese soldiers toward the civilians after the Japanese were in control of the city of Nanking?
>
> **A [Searle]:** I, myself, observed a whole series of shootings of individual civilians without any provocation or apparent reason whatsoever.
>
> **Q:** What were the circumstances under which the former soldiers or alleged soldiers were killed?
>
> **A:** Large parties of Chinese soldiers laid down their arms, surrendered immediately outside the walls of the city and there, within the first seventy two hours, were cut down by machine gun fire, mostly upon the bank of the Yangtze River.
>
> We, of the International Committee, hired laborers to carry out the burials of more than thirty thousand of these soldiers. That was done as a work relief project inspected and directed by us. The number of bodies carried away in the river, and the number of the bodies buried in other ways, we cannot count.
>
> Within the safety zone a very serious problem was caused by the fact that the Japanese officers expected to find within the city a very large number of Chinese soldiers. When they did not discover the soldiers, they insisted that they were in hiding within the zone and that we were responsible for concealing them. On that theory, Japanese military officers and non-commissioned officers were sent among the refugees in the safety zone day after day for about three weeks attempting to discover and seize former

soldiers. It was their common practice to require all able-bodied men in a certain section of the zone, or in a certain refugee camp, to line up for inspection and then to be seized if they had calluses upon their hands or the marks of wearing a hat showing on the skin of the forehead.

I was present throughout several of these inspections and watched the whole process. It was undoubtedly true that there were some soldiers—former soldiers among the refugees, men who had thrown away their arms and uniforms and secured civilian clothes. It was also clearly true that the majority of the men so accused or seized—were ordinary carriers and laborers who had plenty of good reasons for calluses on their hands. The men so accused of having been soldiers were seized, taken away, and in most cases, shot immediately in large groups at the edges of the city.

In some cases a peculiar form of treachery was practiced to persuade men to admit that they had been soldiers. Using the proclamation issued by General Matsui before the Japanese army took Nanking, and distributed widely by airplane, the proclamation which declared that the Japanese Army had only good will for peaceful citizens of China and would do no harm to those who did not resist the Imperial Army, Japanese officers tried to persuade many Chinese to come forward as voluntary workers for military labor corps. In some cases these Japanese soldiers urged Chinese men to come forward, saying, "If you have previously been a Chinese soldier, or if you have ever worked as a carrier or laborer in the Chinese Army that will all now be forgotten and forgiven if you will join this labor corps." In that way, in one afternoon, two hundred men were secured from the premises of the University of Nanking and were promptly marched away and executed that evening along with other bodies of men secured from other parts of the safety zone.[77]

Historian Bob Tadashi Wakabayashi offers further insights to consider in understanding the treatment of POWs during the occupation of Nanjing:

[I]t was illegal at the time to execute POWs until military tribunals judged that they were spies or guerillas. But deniers [of the Nanjing Atrocities] justify summary executions on the grounds that Chinese captives had already violated the laws of war by not surrendering under a responsible commanding officer, by changing into plainclothes, and by fleeing into the NSZ [Nanjing Safety Zone] where they [believed they] had access to hidden arms caches that included tanks, howitzers, machine guns, revolvers, rifles and hand grenades. As this logic goes, Chinese soldiers chose to be unlawful combatants within reach of weapons, so the Japanese could dispense with the due process and humanitarian treatment reserved for bona fide POWs. . . .[78]

Wakabayashi also notes that in Japanese private diaries and records there are accounts of Chinese troops who ambushed Imperial troops by pretending to surrender and then uncovering their concealed guns and attacking. He says that it is difficult to know how frequent these acts of deception were, but he is not suggesting these occurrences explain or exonerate the mistreatment of Chinese POWs. Simply, such acts are one more piece of information to consider in evaluating the very extreme circumstances within which Japanese soldiers were operating.[79]

---

72 Geneva Convention (III) Relative to the Treatment of Prisoners of War, July 27, 1929, 75 U.N.T.S. 135, accessed January 1, 2014, http://www.icrc.org/ihl/INTRO/305?OpenDocument.

73 Ibid., Part I: General provisions, Art. 2.

74 The International Red Cross of the 1920s took steps toward laying down supplemental rules for the protection of civilians in time of war. A draft convention was approved by 1934 in Tokyo and is referred to as the Tokyo draft. The plan was to submit this to a diplomatic conference to be held in 1940. Because of the outbreak of war, the draft was never approved and the absence of a convention for the protection of civilians in wartime remained until the approval of the Fourth Geneva Convention in 1949. See International Committee of the Red Cross website, accessed June 2, 2014, http://www.icrc.org/ihl/INTRO/380. See also Source 6 of Chapter 6 in this resource, "Report of the United Nations' Secretary General on the Protection of Civilians in Armed Conflict (United Nations S/2007/643)."

75 *Nanking Senshi Shiryoshu I* [Historical Records of the Battle of Nanjing I] (Tokyo: Kaiko, 1989), 220, quoted in Masato Kajimoto, "Confessions of Former Soldiers: I. Killing prisoners of War," in "Online Documentary: The Nanking Atrocities" (University of Missouri-Columbia, 2000), accessed January 1, 2014, http://www.nankingatrocities.net/Confession/confession_01.htm.

76 Bob Tadashi Wakabayashi (professor, York University), personal communication with the author, January 1, 2014. It is also important to note that it remains unverifiable when the cache of arms may have entered the Safety Zone and if, in fact, they were stored prior to the zone's establishment.

77 Suping Lu, *They were in Nanjing: The Nanjing Massacre Witnessed by American and British Nationals* (Hong Kong: Hong Kong University Press, 2004), 308.

78 Wakabayashi, *Nanking Atrocity*, 372.

79 Ibid.

LIVING UNDER THE OCCUPATION

After Nanjing was occupied, the Chinese remaining in the city confronted living under the Japanese authority. What choices did Chinese have under Japanese occupation? How did the Japanese occupation affect the way Chinese lived their everyday lives?

Historian Timothy Brook explains, "[S]ome Japanese and some Chinese negotiated a working relationship under a new structure of authority. . . . cooperation with the Japanese or with the Chinese proxy administration was the modus vivendi [way of living] for those who stayed behind in occupied China."[80] Indeed, the Chinese in Nanjing had no choice but to exist under this new power structure. They were the vanquished who negotiated new decisions in order to survive. Some may call this collaboration; some may call it accommodation. By the end of February 1938 the new political structures imposed by the Japanese required people to accommodate a new reality that the occupying forces controlled.

For some Chinese this entailed helping Japanese officers identify defeated combatants who tried to hide among crowds of refugees in order to limit further slaughter of civilians. For others like Jimmy Wang, Nanjing's notorious smuggler of food to refugees within and outside the Safety Zone and smuggler of prostitutes to the Japanese, living under occupation, extreme duress, and violence required constant negotiations in order to survive. While Jimmy Wang may have reaped some financial benefit to his exploits, he also risked his life and provided food and milk to many hungry refugees.[81]

These few examples illustrate the extreme and extraordinary situations individuals were forced to confront in order to simply survive. Celebrated Chinese writer Lao She wrote many short stories during the Japanese occupation. One story, "The Traitor," was written in 1938 and describes one character's life under occupation:

> Everything that a twentieth century Chinese can possibly enjoy and possess, Pao Shan-chin [Bao Shanqin] has been enjoying and possessing. He has money, a western-style house, an American motor car, children, concubines, curios, and books which serve as decoration; he also has reputation, position, and an impressive chain of official titles which can be printed on his visiting card and

ale Divinity School Library

War damage in the southern section of Nanjing in March, 1938.

eventually included in his obituary; he has friends, all kinds of friends, and he has already enjoyed a fair share of longevity and health in a body fortified by varieties of tonics and stimulants.

If only he would allow himself to take things a little easier, to be a bit retiring-minded, he could rest wrapped in comforts. With his children and concubines to attend to his wants, life would be one effortless existence. Should he die at this moment, his wealth would more than provide for the comforts and pleasures of one of two generations of his children, and in the customary biographical sketch written for distribution after his death there would be enough poetic eulogies and lamentations to glorify his name. His coffin would be made of such expensive wood as to stand against erosion for scores of years. And he would, of course, have sixty-four coffin-bearers and be properly paraded through the main thoroughfares.

But Pao Shan-chin could not think of giving up what he and most people in China call "a political career". His political career does not involve any policy, or political ideal. He has only one determination, that is, not to be idle. He could not stand seeing other people in power and in the swim of things. He somehow feels that whatever he has no part in will eventually work against him; he must do all he can to frustrate it or crush it altogether. On the contrary, he misses no chance of getting into something. Like a fisherman, he always makes full use of the wind with his sail in order to reach the exact spot where he is sure to make the biggest catch. It matters little whether the direction of the wind would work havoc to others; so long as it sets his own sail flying he likes it.

That he has been able to sense which way the wind is blowing and to set his own sail to it accounts for the success of his political career. Once the sail is set right and has the full support of the wind, he will reap with the least effort what a politician in China rightfully expects.

Pao Shan-chin has no wish to retire. It would be doing himself injustice, to say the least, to let such foresights and genius as his go to waste. As he grows older, he becomes all the more conscious of the accuracy of his political foresight and the immaturity of others; to deny such gifts of expression would be absurd. He is only just past sixty and is confident that as long as he lives and his facilities remain what they are, there will be political activity wherever he breathes.

He hates those who have newly sprung into political prominence; even recent events seem distasteful to him. The older he grows, the more he feels that his older familiar friends are the best. For the good of his old friends, he would seize every opportunity that comes his way. He seems to have a natural aversion to things new: new terms, new systems, new theories; and that makes him cling to his old ways all the more tenaciously. He is ready to cooperate with anyone, foreign or Chinese, so long as his "abilities" are recognized; for the same reason those who deny him power at once become his enemies. He admits that his "political views" are extraordinarily tolerant; and that in dealing with people he is at times unscrupulous, and not entirely unoccupied from jealousy and prejudice. By why shouldn't he be so? All statesmen, he thinks, have been more or less like him. He is proud of the fact that he understands himself so thoroughly and that he is no hypocrite. Before those he can afford to challenge, he is capable of a kind of defiant showdown, expressed in a smile on his plum face which seems to say: "Be my friend, or be my enemy; take your choice now!"

He has just celebrated his sixtieth birthday, and his photograph appears again in all the newspapers in the occupied territories. This time it bears the caption: Mr. Pao Shan-chin, newly appointed head of the Commission on National Reconstruction. Glancing a few times at his photograph in the paper, he nods to himself complacently as if to say: "The old guard, they can't do without me?" He thinks of his past political career and the experiences he has gone through, all of which seem to lend weight and prestige to his present new title, which in turn will give him still more experience, more prestige, paving the way for even higher titles to come. For what the future may yet hold in store for him, he can't help feeling expansively ambitious. For over two years, his picture has not appeared widely in the papers. To him, it is evidence enough that he is still going strong. New men may crop up from time to time, but he, old Pao Shan-chin, is like the firs and cypresses, which grow greener, firmer, and more luxuriant with age. For him, the consistent formula has always been to have and to hold. There is no other way to get along in this world, and for the *kuanliao* [officials] in China, this has always been and still is the golden rule to success.[82]

---

80 Timothy Brook, *Collaboration: Japanese Agents and Local Elites in Wartime China* (Cambridge: Harvard University Press, 2005), 9.
81 The examples are redrafted from Brook, *Japanese Agents and Local Elites*, 240–48.
82 Lao She, "The Traitor," in *The Chinese People at War: Human Suffering and Social Transformation, 1937-1945*, ed. Diana Lary (Cambridge: Cambridge University Press, 2010), 72.

READING 14

CHINESE RESISTANCE

Many individual Chinese resisted the Japanese occupation from the very early years of the war and communicated their sentiments in different forms of popular culture and literature. Upon leaving Nanjing on December 7, 1937, Nationalist leader Chiang Kai-shek wrote in his wartime diary of the necessity to keep the "revolutionary spirit" alive. This included education programs fostering the belief that a War of Resistance was essential for the lifeblood of China during occupation as well as in the reconstruction of the nation in the future. Chiang's justifiable fear was that the Chinese would be seen by the Japanese, and the international community, as cowering before an all-conquering Imperial army.

Passionate discussions arose in these organizations as to how best to spread and keep the revolutionary spirit and words alive and reach the largest number of people. With so many Chinese writers working in this effort, the challenge of communicating their messages across the many ethnic dialects and range of literacy throughout China was an important decision and ongoing challenge. What language should they use in these forms of popular literature? What kinds of books should be written? What sources should these writings be based upon? Should we create new forms of art or should old cultural forms be used? In a sense this discussion was rooted in an old Chinese dictum of "new wine in new bottles" (which has the disadvantage of being unfamiliar or even unrecognizable to the masses) or "new wine in old bottles" (which has the disadvantage of being heavily contaminated with old Chinese feudal ideas).[83]

Such discussion resulted in the establishment of the All China Resistance Association of Writers and Artists (ACRAWA), founded directly after the occupation of Nanjing in January 1938. Under the leadership of its first president, writer Lao She, ACRAWA gained a large following and spread the slogan "Literature must go to the countryside! Literature must join the army!"[83] The belief of the organizers was that literary activities could play a vital role in resistance efforts against Japan and if organized and disseminated effectively, literary expression could actually become a decisive factor in the outcome of the war. Literature, in these Chinese organizers' minds, was more than a weapon. They believed it could have the potential of unifying the minds of all Chinese against the occupation forces. Traveling drama troupes were dispatched into the interior of China to reach the masses,

~~spreading messages of resistance against Japanese occupation through~~ informal theater, while cartoons, poems, and other print materials were published in journals throughout the country. Small organizations sprung up throughout China to coordinate and consolidate these efforts given the vast geographic area necessary to cover.

The number of literary figures who participated in the organization ranged from 100 to as many as 400 writers. By spring 1938 ACRAWA published its first magazine, Resistance Literature, and continued to publish up through May 1946. According to their mission, writing was only one avenue of spreading their resistance message. Another was to engage with popular "entertainment" or popular education. This took shape in the creation of over 100 different kinds of popular literary works such as plays, street theater, drum songs, games, and stories.

International Institute of Social History

The caption of this Anti-Japanese propaganda poster reads "Defeat Japanese Imperialism."

Directly after the occupation of Nanjing, Lao She wrote the following two pieces as an expression of ACRAWA's efforts and purpose for wartime literature:

"Wang Xiao gan lü," 1938 [Wang Xiao drives a donkey]— a drum song

I shall go enlist in the army,
I am a man of indomitable spirit,
To die for my country I feel no regret,
It is better than living as a slave under the bayonets of the enemy.[85]

Another piece, a rhythmic talk with accompanying bamboo clappers, is titled Nü'er jing [Classic for Women], 1938:

They are women, but as courageous as men.
Patriots who won't live with a false peace.
Hardworking, they never dress up,
They donate their savings to the nation
And deliver winter clothing to the barracks . . . ,
Full of courage, they take up their guns.
They are heroines like Hua Mulan . . .
Women of a new era, their arms hold up the sky,
And the names of the heroines spread far and wide.[86]

While the official headquarters of ACRAWA moved to Chongqing with the Nationalists, the backbone of the organization remained in the network of writers and artists located throughout China. The literary figures involved subscribed to a wide and varied political spectrum but inclusion of all perspectives was accepted. What was shared by all was the idea that cultural interventions were essential in nurturing and maintaining a patriotic spirit so critical in times of war and conflict.[87] If some believed that the Chinese government was not doing enough to resist, others believed the government had its eyes fully open and understood the role of popular culture in disseminating resistance literature.

One such organization was the Disabled Soldiers Vocational Training Center. They published a series of patriotic songbooks in support of the government's efforts of resistance. One of the songs follows:

Smashing Little Japan

This is a little songbook
Despite its plain language and colloquial expressions,
Every word in it is true and sincere.
I hope you fellow readers will read it with great care,
So that the exact nature of the Sino-Japanese War becomes
    crystal clear.
With evil intention, the Japanese want to conquer China.
We no longer endure any more provocation;
We will become a subjugated people unless we stand up and
    fight.
It is easy to sing using a songbook,
But to save a nation is far more difficult.
Unless we Chinese join hands together
Our nation will never be strong.
If you can gather all your neighbors together,
Be they young or old.
Sing this song to them
And follow with explanation.
This will be a great contribution [to your nation.][88]

---

83 Chi-chen Wang, *Stories of China at War* (New York: Columbia University Press, 1947), v–vi.
84 Chang-tai Hung, *War and Popular Culture: Resistance in Modern China, 1937–1945* (Berkeley: University of California Press, 1994), 6, 188.
85 Lao She, "Wang Xiao gan lü," *Wenyi zhendi* 1, no. 3 (May 16,1938): 77, quoted in Chang-tai Hung, *War and Popular Culture*, 200.
86 Lao She, "Nü'er jing,"quoted in Chang-tai Hung, *War and Popular Culture*, 200.
87 Charles Laughlin, "The All China Resistance Association of Writers and Artists," in "Essay Descriptions," Literary Societies in Republican China Project website.
88 *Da xiao Riben* (N.P.: Ronguy junren shiye xunliansuo, n.d.), 1–2 (abridged), quoted in Chang-tai Hung, *War and Popular Culture*, 214.

PRIMARY SOURCES

SOURCE 1

SONG, "EIGHT HUNDRED HEROES"

The song "Eight Hundred Heroes," also known as "China Will Not Perish," was written in 1939 to commemorate the three month–long battle of Shanghai in the fall of 1937. From October 26 through November 1, 1937, there was a pivotal battle that took place, known today as "The Defense of the Sihang Warehouse," that signals the beginning of the end of the first phase of Chinese resistance to the Japanese occupation of Shanghai. The defenders of this warehouse were referred to as the Eight Hundred Heroes for their perseverance and success at defending against a series of Japanese assaults.

中国不会亡, 中国不会亡,

你看民族英雄谢团长。

中国不会亡, 中国不会亡,

你看那八百壮士孤军奋斗守战场,

四方都是炮火, 四方都是豺狼,

宁愿死不退让, 宁愿死不投降。

我们的国旗在重围中飘荡飘荡, 飘荡飘荡, 飘荡。

八百壮士一条心, 十万强敌不能挡,

我们的行动伟烈, 我们的气节豪壮,

同胞们起来! 同胞们起来!

快快赶上战场, 拿八百壮士做榜样。

中国不会亡, 中国不会亡,

中国不会亡, 中国不会亡!

不会亡! 不会亡! 不会亡!

China will not die. China will not die.

Look at our national hero Colonel Xie.

China will not die. China will not die.

Watch the eight hundred heroes of the lone battalion fight for every inch of land,

From four sides come the gunfire, from the four sides come the wolves,

With shell fire all around, with savage beast all around

They would rather die than retreat, they would rather die than surrender

Amidst the sea of chaos our nations's flag flies proudly, flies proudly, flies proudly, flies proudly.

Eight hundred heroic hearts all beat as one, unstoppable to the thousands of enemies,

Our actions are mighty, our integrity heroic

Comrades, arise! Comrades, arise!

Let's answer the call to arms, and follow the example of the eight hundred heroes

China will not die, China will not die!

Will not die! Will not die! Will not die![89]

---

89 "800 Heroes Song," Wikipedia, accessed May 28, 2104, http://en.wikipedia.org/wiki /800_Heroes_Song.

SOURCE 2

SECONDARY SOURCE FROM SCHOLAR— DISSENTING OPINION OF RADHABINOD PAL (CLOSE READING)

In *Documents on the Rape of Nanking* historian Timothy Brook includes the dissenting opinion of Radhabinod Pal, one of the judges appointed to the International Military Tribunal for the Far East, also referred to as the Tokyo War Crimes Trials. In his written dissent, Justice Pal references the following order issued from the Supreme Headquarters in Tokyo to attack Nanking.

The Chief of Staff of [the] Central China Area Army to [General] Tsukada, and six staff officers under him, prepared an order to the following effect:

1. The Central China Area Army intends to capture Nanking Castle ["Castle" is a Japanese mistranslation of *ch'eng,* walled city].

2. The Shanghai Expeditionary Forces and the Tenth Army shall capture Nanking in accordance with the main points as to the capture of Nanking.

The main points, in the order as to the capture of Nanking, referred to above, were set out as follows:

1. Both armies (Shanghai Expeditionary Forces and Tenth Army) shall stop and prepare for capture of Nanking 3 to 4 kilometers away from Nanking Castle when they so far advance.

2. On December 9th, scatter from airplanes, the bills advising surrender of the Chinese Army, stationed within the Castle of Nanking.

3. The case of the surrender of the Chinese Army, only two or three battalions, chosen from among the various divisions and military police, shall enter the castle and guard the assigned area with[in] the castle as indicated on the map. Especially, perfectly carry out the protection of foreign interests and cultural facilities, as indicated on the map.

4. In cases of the Chinese Army refusing to surrender, begin attack against Nanking Castle on the afternoon of December 10. Even in this case, the movements of troops that enter the castle shall be the same as described above, *especially making military discipline and morality very strict* and restoring peace within the castle.[90]

---

90 Timothy Brook, *Documents on the Rape of Nanking* (Ann Arbor: University of Michigan, 1999), 289–90.

SOURCE 3

PHOTOGRAPH: 100-MAN KILLING CONTEST

⁹¹

91 Shinju Sato, photog., "百人斬の' 超記録'" [100-Man-Beaheading's "Super-Record"],
Tokyo Nichi Nichi Shimbun, December 13, 1937, in Wikipedia, accessed January 1, 2014,
http://en.wikipedia.org/wiki/File:Contest_To_Cut_Down_100_People.jpg.

SOURCE 4

EYE-WITNESS TELLS OF HORROR
SEEN IN THE FALL OF NANKING

The destruction of Nanking was the blackest page in modern history, according to George Fitch, who was director of the safety zone in Nanking from Dec. 13 to Feb. 20 and an eye-witness of the destruction of the city by the Japanese.

Fitch spoke yesterday at Cleveland Heights Presbyterian Church. During the reign of terror which followed the Japanese entry into the city, Fitch was in charge of the food administration and protection of 250,000 Chinese and others crowded into the safety zone.

The Japanese for two months kept up continuous looting, burning, robbing, and murdering, Fitch said.

"Chinese men by the thousands were taken out to be killed by machine guns or slaughtered for hand grenade practice," he asserted. "The poorest of the poor were robbed of their last coins, deprived of their bedding and all that they could gather out of a city systematically destroyed by fire. There were hundreds of cases of bestiality inflicted upon Chinese women.

"But in spite of the dark horizon there is a new hopefulness among the Chinese. China is going to win this war, I'm confident. The whole business would be brought to a quick close if the United States would stop helping Japan by selling her gasoline, scrap iron, and nitrates.

"The challenge to the Christian church in America is to help put a stop to this damnable traffic in munitions and to give until it hurts for China."[92]

---

92 Eye-Witness Tells of Horror Seen in Fall of Nanking," *The Cleveland Plain Dealer,* May 23, 1938.

CHAPTER 5

RESCUE AND RESISTANCE IN NANJING

The readings in Chapter Five draw from diaries, letters, and documents recorded by a range of individuals who chose to resist imperial Japan's occupation in Nanjing and elsewhere. Chinese nationals resisted the Japanese occupation from the beginning of the war in 1937 until its conclusion in 1945. But the largest body of materials specifically documenting the Nanjing Atrocities comes from the handful of foreign missionaries and businessmen who remained in the besieged capital city. After the Battle of Shanghai and the escalation of violence continued, a small community of Westerners chose to remain and establish what became the Nanjing Safety Zone. Sociologist Helen Fein writes that nations express what she calls a "universe of obligation." She defines that universe as "the circle of individuals and groups toward whom obligations are owed, to whom rules apply, and whose injuries call for amends." While originally Fein's concept referred to the way nations perceive their responsibilities to their citizens, the choices made by members of the Nanjing Safety Zone Committee stand as powerful examples of a community of people exercising and expanding their universe of obligation. As one member of the Safety Zone committee wrote explaining the the zone's establishment, "In case the situation becomes anti-foreign and our staying endangers our church co-workers, certainly we would leave, but if we can be of service to our particular groups we desire to remain with them."[1]

The readings chosen for this chapter are arranged to follow a chronological sequence of what occurred during the months directly preceding Nanjing's occupation to the fall of the city. They are firsthand accounts from witnesses who chose to do everything they could to resist and rescue as many people as possible. The following questions may be helpful to consider as you deepen your study of these topics:

- In times of mass violence, why do some individuals help while others stand by?

- What dilemmas were faced by those who tried to save lives in Nanjing?

- Is it possible to truly create a "safe zone" in a city besieged by war?

For media and classroom materials such as discussion questions and additional primary sources, visit www.facinghistory.org/nanjing-atrocities.

INTRODUCTION

Beginning in August 1937 the Japanese Imperial Army initiated an aerial assault of the Chinese capital city of Nanjing (Nanking). In response to this assault, thousands of Chinese able to flee left the city while the elderly, sick, and poor remained behind. Many that left continued to actively fight the Japanese. Others actively resisted. In Nanjing, like in other cities throughout China in the late nineteenth and early twentieth century, Western merchants, missionaries, physicians, and educators had settled seeking economic opportunities or fulfilling religious or professional aspirations. Hundreds of these Westerners considered Nanjing initially their home.

Despite calls from their respective governments and organizations to leave China as the full force of the aerial invasion continued, a small group of individuals elected to remain to do what they could and provide aid to the remaining Chinese refugees. Their motives varied with their situations. Some businessmen had their company's financial interests in mind while others, including missionaries, doctors, and teachers, felt intimately connected and held a sense of duty to the people of Nanjing who remained. In response to the onslaught of refugees to the city and the poor left to fend for themselves, the International Committee for the Nanking Safety Zone was officially formed on November 22, 1937. Inspired by the efforts of Jesuit Father Robert Jacquinot de Besange in Shanghai, who successfully established a similar zone in Shanghai in the summer of 1937, Westerners in Nanjing began to negotiate the details with city officials. Two days later the Chinese newspaper *Hankow Ta-kung-pao* reported on the formation of the Safety Zone in which a neutral zone would exist in Nanjing to protect civilian refugees from the Japanese occupational forces.[2] The Westerners hoped to use their privileged status as foreigners to coordinate relief and provide noncombatants with refuge as the Japanese moved closer.

Hang Liwu, chairman of the board of trustees of the University of Nanking, presided over the first meeting on November 22 to discuss the establishment and provisions of the neutral zone. One of the first orders of business was to compose a telegram to be sent to the Japanese ambassador in China by way of the American consulate detailing the Safety Zone's purpose. A portion of the telegram reads as follows:

> An international committee composed of nationals of Denmark, Germany, Great Britain, and the United States, desires to suggest to the Chinese and Japanese authorities the establishment

of a Safety Zone for Civilian Refugees in the unfortunate event of hostilities at or near Nanking. The International Committee will undertake to secure from the Chinese authorities specific guarantees that the proposed "Safety Zone" will be made free and kept free from military establishments and offices, including those of communications; from the presence of armed men other than civilian police with pistols; and from the passage of soldiers or military officers in any capacity. The International Committee would inspect and observe the Safety Zone to see that these undertakings are satisfactorily carried out. . . .

The International Committee earnestly hopes that the Japanese authorities may find it possible for humanitarian reasons to respect the civilian character of this Safety Zone. The Committee believes that the merciful foresight on behalf of civilians will bring honor to the responsible authorities on both sides. In order that the necessary negotiations with the Chinese authorities may be completed in the shortest possible time, and also in order that adequate preparations may be made for the care of refugees, the Committee would respectfully request a prompt reply from the Japanese authorities to this proposal.[3]

While the Japanese embassy never publically supported the Safety Zone, they tacitly gave their consent as long as the zone remained solely for Chinese noncombatants and free of any weapons and Chinese soldiers— former or current. Chiang Kai-shek supported the idea as well, offering $100,000 to support their efforts (although only $40,000 of his pledge was paid out).[4] Once this agreement was made, several groups were initially formed and tasked with different responsibilities such as medical care, food distribution, and housing. As the city came under assault, the International Red Cross Committee agreed to care for the wounded soldiers and the International Committee for the Nanking Safety Zone agreed to administer the distribution of food and overall organization of shelter. Twenty-seven foreigners were reported to be in the city when it fell, eventually working together by coordinating efforts and creating what we now refer to as the Nanjing Safety Zone, or the Safety Zone.[5] John Rabe, a German businessman and engineer working for the Siemens Company who was also a member of the Nazi Party, was elected the Safety Zone's first chairman. Spanning approximately 3.4 square miles, the Safety Zone included the western district of the city from Nanking University to the northern gates of the city.

ale Divinity School Library

Members of the Nanjing Safety Zone Committee pose for a photograph at the Safety Zone headquarters in December 1937. Left to right: Mr. Zial, Mr. Hatz, Mr. Rabe, Rev. John Magee, Mr. Cola Podshivaloff.

This included Ginling Women's Arts and Science College, the American embassy, and various Chinese buildings. This small contingency of individuals working within a very small amount of physical space eventually became the caretakers of tens of thousands of Chinese during one of the most violent episodes in the opening phase of World War II in China.

Alongside offering safe refuge to upward of 200,000 Chinese during the occupation of the city from mid-December through its eventual dissolution at the end of February, the Safety Zone Committee served several other critical functions. After committee members met with the civic leaders of the city at the end of November, it quickly became apparent to the Safety Zone Committee's leadership that they would be shouldering many more civic responsibilities than originally imagined.[6] A week after this initial meeting, the entire city leadership and staff of the Nanjing government left the capital city, leaving behind both a large civilian population and a large number of Chinese soldiers to fend for themselves. With the absence of any civic leadership, Safety Zone Committee leaders stepped in and served as the city's temporary government, organizing vital services of police, utilities, fire department, food supply, and sanitation. It also allowed for critical institutions to remain open, such as the three remaining hospitals led by the International Committee for the Red Cross.

Finally, the Safety Zone Committee fastidiously documented the events and misconduct of soldiers through detailed documentation and letters.

The first letter, sent by John Rabe to the Japanese commander in Nanking on December 14, begins this invaluable documentary record. As the Japanese soldiers' conduct quickly turned unlawful and violent, Safety Zone Committee members sent daily letters of protest directly to the Japanese embassy in Nanjing and to international organizations detailing numerous incidences of mass violence and rape. They also recorded every incident of Japanese misconduct as they heard it or witnessed it firsthand and delivered them regularly to the Japanese consulate. Records of food supply and security matters were also kept alongside compiling a chronological listing of atrocities committed. This extraordinary effort created a body of firsthand accounts published in newspapers and journals in the United States and Europe. In July 1938 the American publication *Reader's Digest* published two stories detailing what was occurring in Nanjing and by 1939 three bodies of materials and evidence were assembled and published by Chinese political scientist Hsu Shuhsi.[7]

One of the most difficult issues that quickly arose within the Safety Zone, and the one that led to very dire choices, was the state of noncombatants and combatants within the boundaries of the Safety Zone. Of primary concern for the Japanese forces was the harboring of Chinese soldiers (combatants) within the boundaries of the zone. With thousands of refugees fleeing into the Safety Zone as the city came under siege and only a handful of foreigners administering the day-to-day tasks, it was difficult to ensure a foolproof filter. But John Rabe's agreement with the Japanese commanding officers was based upon the understanding that Imperial forces would leave the Safety Zone alone so long as the committee would not knowingly harbor Chinese soldiers. Once the city came under occupation some Chinese soldiers discarded their uniforms and arms and appealed to the committee to enter the zone, many pleading for their lives. When told by Safety Zone Committee members that they could not be protected, and in fact if identified they would be lawful POWs, the soldiers understood their circumstances. At the same time the committee members explained that if arms were surrendered, the Japanese would hopefully treat them mercifully by upholding the 1929 Geneva Convention on the Treatment of POWs and the soldiers would be given shelter and treated humanely.

Upon suspicion that some Chinese soldiers were, in fact, living within the Safety Zone boundaries, Japanese forces entered the zone and frequently rounded up old and young men indiscriminately, including some soldiers but many civilians as well. Often the suspicion alone of soldiers within the Safety Zone was used as an excuse for Japanese forces to enter the zone's boundaries and commit rape or kidnap women and commit rape outside the zone's perimeter. Despite these acts, and what some consider the porous nature of the refugee zone, the Nanjing Safety Zone sheltered thousands who would have otherwise been left vulnerable and without any assistance whatsoever.

In the end, the International Committee for the Nanking Safety Zone achieved two great feats—preserving the dignity and life of thousands of Chinese refugees during the height of violence in Nanjing and leaving an authoritative body of material behind to be used as evidence and as a first-hand historical record. The varied documentation was used as vital evidence during the International Military Tribunal for the Far East, and several com-mittee members testified as key witnesses in the prosecution and indictment of Japanese leaders for the atrocities committed in Nanjing. *(See Source 1: Brief Time Line, Nanjing Safety Zone, August 1937–February 1938.)*

---

1   Minnie Vautrin, Entry in Diary, (November 17, 1937), from manuscript at "The Nanking Massacre Project" website, Yale University Divinity School Library, accessed February 11, 2013, http://web.library.yale.edu/.

2   Takashi Yoshida, "Wartime Accounts of the Nanking Atrocity," in *The Nanjing Atrocity 1937–1938: Complicating the Picture,* ed. Bob Tadashi Wakabayashi (New York: Berghahn Books, 2007), 249–50.

3   John Rabe, *The Good Man of Nanking: The Diaries of John Rabe,* trans. John E. Woods (New York: Vintage Books, 1998), 28.

4   Mitter, *Forgotten Ally,* 128.

5   Timothy Brook, *Documents on the Rape of Nanking* (Ann Arbor: University of Michigan Press, 1999), 3. The recorded members were 17 Americans, 6 Germans, 2 Russians, 1 Austrian, and 1 British. This number is incomplete but is the one stated by John Rabe, quoted in Brook.

6   On November 27 the committee met with Chiang Kai-shek and General Tang Shengzhi, the general in charge of defending Nanjing. Several days later on December 1 the committee met with the mayor of Nanjing, Ma Cha'o-chun.

7   "The Sack of Nanking," *Reader's Digest* (July 1938): 28–31; "We Were in Nanking," *Reader's Digest* (October 1938): 41–44; and Brook, *Documents on the Rape of Nanking,* 4. According to historian Timothy Brook, Hsu Shuhsi's slim volume of documents "is still the best source of what happened to the people of Nanking between December 1937 and February 1938."

NANJING AND ITS SAFETY ZONE (1937–1939)

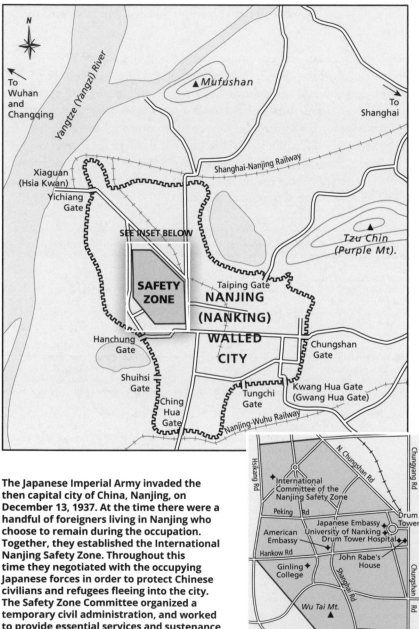

The Japanese Imperial Army invaded the then capital city of China, Nanjing, on December 13, 1937. At the time there were a handful of foreigners living in Nanjing who choose to remain during the occupation. Together, they established the International Nanjing Safety Zone. Throughout this time they negotiated with the occupying Japanese forces in order to protect Chinese civilians and refugees fleeing into the city. The Safety Zone Committee organized a temporary civil administration, and worked to provide essential services and sustenance to civilians during the height of violence in the city.

CONVICTION AND COURAGE: MINNIE VAUTRIN

In the days and months leading up to the occupation of Nanjing, foreign nationals living in the capital city played a key role in resisting the Japanese assault. Those who chose to remain served both as witnesses to history and as emblems of courage.

Minnie Vautrin, one of only two foreign women who remained in Nanjing, was one such individual. She was a woman of courage and conviction. As a key member of the International Committee for the Red Cross, Vautrin directed the efforts to specifically protect women and girls from the Japanese soldiers. Born in Secor, Illinois, on September 27, 1886, Vautrin graduated from the University of Illinois with a major in education in 1912. She was commissioned by the United Christian Missionary Society to serve as high school principal in Luchowfu, then promoted to become the first chairman of the education department of Ginling College in Nanking in 1916.[8]

The selections chosen from Vautrin's diary chronicle her days and weeks preceding the siege of Nanjing on December 13, 1937. They illuminate her internal struggles during these extreme circumstances and the many dilemmas she faced to survive while upholding her commitment to the work of the Nanjing Safety Zone Committee:

July 2–18, 1937

> For these sixteen days I have been having a holiday with friends in the seaside summer resort of Tsingtao—the city which belonged to the Germans before the Great War, then was given to Japan, and finally because of the Washington Agreement was returned to China. . . .

> Word came through to us in Tsingtao that on July 7th trouble started a few miles south of Peiping [Beijing] when a Japanese soldier disappeared—how? Nobody really knows, and why? Again nobody really knows. Since then fighting has increased and what the end of it will be we dare not say. Of the Great War, Milne said "Two people were killed in Sarajevo in 1914 and the best Europe could do about it was to kill eleven million more." And Milne did

not include in this summary all the personal loss and anguish, the deaths from disease, the economic dislocation and the increased and deepened hatreds. China does not want war and knows that she is not prepared for it. I believe that the Japanese people do not want war but Japan cannot control her military machine.

July 19–20, 1937

Yesterday morning I left Tsingtao and this afternoon arrived in Nanking coming through by train. During that journey I passed five troop trains—just open cars they were, filled with soldiers and horses and equipment of war. The soldiers looked so miserable in the terrific heat and some of them were mere lads.

Today's English paper has in it the speech of Generalissimo Chiang Kai-shek which he delivered to leaders at a conference in Kuling on July 9th. I hope that it appeared in American papers as that you were able to read it for it seemed to me to be sane and reasonable. He had a minimum of four points which China cannot yield and retain her national integrity. He seemed to be giving a reply to the unreasonable demands and at the same time he was explaining to his own people what the final sacrifice for them might be. He said, "Weak nation as we are we cannot neglect to uphold the integrity of our nation. It is impossible for us not to safeguard to our utmost the heritage of our forefathers, a duty which we must fulfill to the utmost. Let us realize, however, that once war has begun there is no looking backward, we must fight to the bitter end."

July 22, 1937

Tonight after the lights went out on our campus, for more than two hours I listened to the tramp, tramp, tramp of soldiers and horses and the clanking of guns on the road outside. By day all is calm, but at night war preparations are moving forward. Can nothing stop these two nations? Truly we seem like sheep without a shepherd when the passion for war is let loose, and yet we know that in every country there are enough people opposed to war to really put a stop to it. I cannot forget the tramping of those men!

July 29–31, 1937

Japan's reaction has come more quickly than I imagined. Word is coming through that not only has she taken the cities momentarily lost but she is driving all Chinese troops past Tientsin and Peiping. It seems that nothing has been destroyed in Peiping, but Tientsin has been bombarded by an air force, and much destruction has taken place. Nankai University [in Tientsin] has been totally destroyed we are told, because Japanese felt that it was a center of propaganda. Naturally the Chinese are furious and even the calmest say that China must fight even though she may be defeated. Some even say that China must herself destroy her great coastal cities and retreat to the mountain regions and from there carry on guerilla warfare until Japan is exhausted economically.

August 2, 1937

. . . Yesterday it was said that an announcement was made to officials to get their families out of the city [Nanking]. The reason was to lessen the number in Nanking and to free officials of family responsibility—but the result has been to frighten the people terribly. Trains and boats are packed and tickets have been sold for days in advance. Thousands are leaving.

August 14, 1937

11 a.m. Anna Moffet, Ronald Rees, John Magee and I spent about an hour and a half over in Anna's office trying to see what Christians can do in a situation like the present one. Are we to stand by hopelessly and see if war comes upon the Orient or is there something that we can do—and if so, what? This morning at 5 o'clock I got up and drafted a plan for International Moral Mobilization which I believe we could at least start and no one can say how far it would go. . . . 1 p.m. Over the radio at Anna's we learned that air raids and fighting are now going on in Shanghai.

November 17, 1937

Last night 50,000 Chinese soldiers came into the city and unfortunately they were not assigned places so they occupied empty buildings of their own choosing. . . . Searle Bates came over this afternoon to ask me two questions that the American Embassy is asking each citizen. 1. Can we leave now or do we feel needed? 2. If the city is in great danger would we be willing to go to [the] Embassy bomb-proof dugout? We agree in our answers to these. In case the situation becomes anti-foreign and our staying endangers our church co-workers, certainly we would leave, but if we can be of service to our particular groups we desire to remain with them. You cannot imagine the number of people who have come in today to ask what I am planning to do. . . .

November 18, 1937

Conditions seem slightly improved today although the trek out of the city continues. Almost all who can go are going. . . . At our informal publicity meeting today we heard reports on the plan for a "Zone of Safety." It is remarkable how much has been accomplished. The idea was only mentioned two days ago. An influential committee was formed yesterday and tomorrow morning will interview the Mayor of Nanking. The American Embassy is willing to help them get through to the Japanese authorities later. A vast amount of organization must be done if it goes through. . . .

November 21, 1937

Last night Mrs. Twinem brought us back home about midnight. Never in all my life will I forget that experience. We found the wounded soldiers scattered rather thickly at the railway station. Perhaps there were 200 there, I do not know. There were no doctors or nurses present and some of the men were in great agony. . . . I wish that all who last July and August felt war a necessity could first have seen that mass of suffering mutilated men of last night. I feel sure they would admit with me that war is a crime when it produces such results. The soldiers were just ordinary looking men and boys such as we see in our neighborhood. They looked untrained and unequipped for modern warfare. . . .

December 1, 1937[5]

At 10 a.m. was called to Embassy for a conference with leaders of other mission institutions. Mr. Paxton, Secretary in U.S. Embassy, divided us into three groups—those who can and should get away today on a commercial boat; those who must stay on for time being and will out at the last minute on the U.S.S. Panay—going down over city wall by rope if necessary; and those who expect to stay through. . . . At 11:50 the Emergency Committee met and appointed Mr. Li to organize six men servants into a police squad, to drill them and prepare arm bands for them; also asked Miss Hsueh, Neighborhood School teacher, to organize her pupils and older children on the campus into a Service Group for refugees to train them and prepare badges for them. . . . Took about $2000, Mrs. Thurston's wedding silver and receipts of college deeds to American Embassy for safe keeping. We had decided to leave vault open. As for me and mine, I think I shall not pack a thing. At Press Conference tonight, the Safety Zone was definitely announced and four Commissions named to look after Food, Housing, Finance and Sanitation. City has given rice and $20,000.

Hulton-Deutsch Collections/Corbis

Chinese citizens, and American and British visitors, evacuate Nanjing in preparation for an attack by the Japanese.

December 3, 1937

. . . Last call from Embassy today. We had to choose one of the three alternatives and sign our names. (1) Go now, (2) Expect to go later (3) Under no conditions leaving. I signed under 3, although if my Chinese colleagues felt I was endangering them, surely I would go. . . .

December 10, 1937

Refugees continue to come in this morning. . . . This afternoon F. Chen and I went to our west boundary to help put up Safety Zone flags. . . . While we were out, there were severe air raid and several bombs were dropped west of the Seminary. For the first time I heard the whirr of a dropping bomb, and saw the flash from the anti-aircraft guns. . . . The Japanese are said to be very near Gwang Hwa Gate. Fires have been seen around the city a good part of the day, and tonight the sky to the west is aflame—the destruction of the houses of the poor just outside the city wall. . . . At the Press Conference tonight the question was raised of the poor when the city is turned over. Who will take care of them during coming months?

December 13, 1937

(Have heard that Japanese entered Gwang "[Hwa]" Gate at 4 a.m.). . . . 4 p.m. The report came to me that there were Japanese soldiers on the hill west of us. I went up to South Hill Residence, and sure enough our West Hill had a number on it. . . . 7:30 p.m. The men managing the rice kitchen report that Japanese soldiers are occupying the house opposite our gate in which the rice is stored. . . . Tonight Nanking has no lights, no water, no telephone, no city paper, no radio. We are indeed separated from all of you by an impenetrable zone. So far Ginling, people and buildings, has come through safely—but we are not sure of the coming days. We are all fearfully tired.[10]

8   "The Nanking Massacre Project," Yale University Divinity School Library, accessed February 11, 2013, http://web.library.yale.edu/. Note: Luchowfu is near Hefei, roughly 180 km (112 miles) from Nanjing.
9   On this day Mayor Ma Chao-chun ordered all Chinese citizens remaining in Nanjing to move into the Safety Zone. Many, including the mayor, fled the city by December 7, leaving the international committee to take over as the de facto government in Nanjing.
10 Yale University Divinity School Library, Ibid.

READING 2

WRESTLING WITH THE REALITY OF WAR: TSEN SHUI-FANG

While most Chinese with a higher social standing chose to leave Nanjing, there were a handful of Chinese nationals who chose to remain and help. Some were well educated and helped manage and serve as translators while others helped prepare and distribute food, helped with sanitation, or served as police. Professor Zhang Lianhong said of these Chinese:

> Chinese rescue workers in the Safety Zone labored frequently under tremendous difficulty and stress. For unlike Westerners, if they did not handle matters with extreme discretion, they would easily be singled out by Japanese soldiers and killed. Therefore, not only did they have to work very hard, they had to be on constant alert for possible Japanese cruelties. After witnessing the Japanese atrocities, seeing how fellow Chinese were brutalized and slaughtered, the only thing the Zone workers could do was to hide the hatred in their hearts and endure the disgrace as well as the insults in order to complete the tasks at hand. In short, the Chinese workers were important components of the rescue undertakings; nothing could have been accomplished in the Safety Zone without their strenuous efforts.[11]

Yale Divinity School Library

Minnie Vautrin (front, third from left), Tsen Shui-fang (front, fourth from left), and others from the Committee that organized religious work for refugee women and girls stand in front of Ginling College.

Tsen Shui-fang was one such Chinese national working within the Safety Zone. The tremendous amount of coordination and details to administer often fell in her hands as she remained Minnie Vautrin's most trusted assistant. Because Tsen was a Chinese national and a woman, she was particularly vulnerable to the wrath of the Japanese soldiers. For many years she served as the guardian for the dormitories at Ginling College in Nanjing. Along with several other Chinese men and women, Tsen chose to remain in Nanjing throughout the occupation and served many essential roles, including protecting the very vulnerable and providing information and supplies for the thousands living within the zone's borders.

Tsen Shui-fang kept a daily diary documenting her experiences during the occupation of her homeland. As her written words convey strength and courage, she also shares the shame and humiliation she feels living under occupation. As we read her entries, how does she share insights about her nationality? What particular challenges does she write about and face as a Chinese woman surviving under occupation?

Wednesday, December 8th

The Safety Zone was established two months ago. Because Japan denied the need for establishing a safety zone [in Nanjing], it delayed its response. . . . Later, Japan replied that it might or might not recognize [the neutrality of] the Safety Zone. Two months ago, the International Committee decided to establish the Safety Zone with or without Japan's recognition but did not raise its flags at the boundaries of the zone until today. . . .

According to the International Committee's regulations, all the private residences [in the zone] should be available for borrowing or renting. The public buildings have yet to be opened [to receive refugees]. The city's south and Hsia Kwan are all on fire. Some fires were set by our army for the sake of strategy; some started by the Japanese troops from outside of the city. . . . We have decided only to receive women and children, but not men. Currently we plan to receive 2,700 people. . . . This is our plan. However, we have no idea how many will eventually come.

Saturday, December 11th

There is no law and order on the streets. Our soldiers are about to flee shortly, nor are there any policeman. Some foot soldiers looted the North Gate Bridge areas and so did the civilians. A few military policemen who maintain order have shot several looters.

Sunday, December 12th

Now, the artilleries are shelling continuously. Our soldiers are probably going to retreat. We heard they say that the Japanese army is approaching Wuhu and will probably surround the army. No one is on the street, nor are any goods for sale. Only refugees fleeing for their lives.

Monday, December 13th

Last night, our troops retreated, and no artillery sound could be heard this morning. This afternoon at 2:00 p.m., the Japanese soldiers entered the city from Shuihsi Gate. When our [campus] policeman Huang spotted Japanese soldiers on Canon Road from the South Hill, he ran, taking off his police uniform. After he reached #400 Building, he was so scared that he fell down, his face becoming pale. He was really a coward. We, at once, went to the South Hill to observe and saw more than ten soldiers standing behind Old Shao's house. All the workers were frightened. . . .

I feel so sad. Nanking has not had peace since four months ago and fell only after three days' fighting. It is really pathetic. I have no idea what's going to happen tomorrow. Today, two more poor babies were born.

Tuesday, December 14th

Many more refugees came [to the college] today. All fled to here from the Safety Zone because the Japanese soldiers came to their homes to demand money and to rape. Quite a few people were bayoneted to death on the streets. The situation in the Safety Zone is [terrible] like this and it is even worse outside the Zone. Nobody dares to go out of the Safety Zone. Most of the dead were young men.

Yale Divinity School Library

Refugee children at Ginling College during the war in Nanjing.

Friday, December 17th

Now it is midnight. I am sitting here to write this diary and cannot go to sleep because tonight I have experienced the taste of being a slave of a toppled country. . . . This kind of slavery life is very difficult to endure. If I were not struggling for the survival of our Chinese race, I would commit suicide. . . .

~~These several days, I have been frustrated to death, having no~~ idea what's going on with the war, no communication with the outside world. Embassies have no Westerners left. Not many Americans are here, and they are helpless. The refugees come here to seek shelter and insist on coming in. It really made me angry to death. It's better not to let them in than see them being dragged from here; it is better not to see what happens to them outside. Each night, outside, every place is burning. . . . Why must Chinese people suffer like this? Today, several times soldiers went to the South Hill. I do not want to write any more. When thinking about the Chinese people, I cannot help but feel heartbroken. Another boy was born today.

Sunday, December 19th

Today at noon, Riggs came. He intended to ask married women with husbands to go home so the Japanese soldiers would not come [to Ginling] to find [women] so often. Because they have all run into refugees camps, no women are left outside. What [Riggs] meant was that it is okay for women with husbands to return home, but not for maidens. If a husband stays home alone, Japanese soldiers would accuse him of being a [Chinese] soldier because he has no family. Although there is nothing wrong with this reasoning, yet, as soon as I heard it, I cried. I thought that my own country is not strong, so it suffers this kind of humiliation. When can we shed the shame?

Tuesday, December 21st

The [Japanese] soldiers dispatched here last night were for pro-tection in name only. They came to change shift. Vautrin thought that the officer was so nice to send people to protect [us]. In fact, he is resentful of losing face because no matter how [we] receive girls from [the] outside, the soldiers still come to take them away, day and night. I told Vautrin, "You should not forget that we are their enemies. You should not believe their sweet words." What they say is not what they believe in their hearts. Now, they [the Westerners] all see every inhuman deed and empty words sweet words which the Japanese engaged in. Sometimes, when Vautrin went to the Japanese consulate to report their troops' bad deeds, I said to her that the more you report, the more harm they would do. Fortunately, there are still two Germans here. Not adequate to have only Americans. Now, the several Americans are also helpless, deadly tired too. But, on the other hand, if there were not several Americans here, the Chinese would only face a death road. . . . [Vautrin's] days are simply unbearable; sometimes at mealtime, the Japanese soldiers came and everybody left, but Vautrin had to face them. They come several times a day. And we have no idea what they will do. It really makes people tremble. Last night again, two soldiers came and took [raped] two girls on the ground. It's really heart-rending. In the past, I heard people say that they [the Japanese soldiers] were inhuman. Now, it has indeed become a reality.[12]

---

11 Zhang Lianhong, "Chinese Rescue Workers in the Nanking Safety Zone," trans. Monica Brick, in *The Nanking Massacre and Other Japanese Military Atrocities, The Asia-Pacific War 1931–1945: A Curriculum Guide for Secondary Educators,* 2nd edition, vol. 1, New Jersey Commission on Holocaust Education, NJ-ALPHA, and Global Alliance, (2010), 131, accessed January 1, 2014, http://www.state.nj.us/education/holocaust/curriculum/NankingCurriculum2010.pdf.
12 Hu Hualing and Zhang Lianhong, *The Undaunted Women of Nanking: The Wartime Diaries of Minnie Vautrin and Tsen Shu-fang* (Carbondale, IL: Southern Illinois University Press, 2010), 35-79.

A SIMPLE SENSE OF OUTRAGE: DR. ROBERT O. WILSON

Dr. Robert O. Wilson (1906–1967) was one of the few surgeons remaining in Nanjing and one of the few skilled to treat the severity of the wounded soldiers. Like Fitch, Wilson was the child of missionaries who knew China intimately. He was born in Nanjing and in 1936, after medical school, he began work at the University of Nanjing Hospital. As the Imperial troops

~~approached Nanjing, Wilson was among the first Westerner to assist in es~~ tablishing the Safety Zone. He worked in the hospital until June 1938 when he left to live in Shanghai. After World War II, he was among the members of the Safety Zone Committee to testify at the International Military Tribunal for the Far East.

Fitch's testimony carries the added weight of reporting on an unceasing stream of medical cases—the stark, constant, immediate effects of Nanjing's events that he shouldered with the meager aid of his colleague, Dr. C. S. Trimmer, and a few nurses. One of the particular challenges he encountered within the hospital was when Chinese soldiers living within the Safety Zone arrived wounded and in need of care.

What follows are two letters that he wrote to his family directly while in Nanjing. The second letter alludes to a complex relationship with the Germans working within the Nanjing Safety Zone. While Americans and Germans worked together in the Safety Zone, Wilson and other Americans struggled to reconcile the admirable deeds of John Rabe with his allegiance to the Nazi Party.

December 15, 1937

. . . The hospital gets busier every day. We are about up to our normal capacity as far as patients go. There were about thirty admissions today and no discharges. We can't discharge any patients because they have no place to go. About ten of the hundred and fifty cases are medical and obstetrical and the rest are surgical. Neither of our Chinese doctors have the ability to care for them except under careful supervision so that keeps me humping. Yesterday I wrote that I had eleven operations. Today I had ten operations in addition to seeing the patients on the ward. I got up early and made ward rounds on one ward before coming home to breakfast. After breakfast I spent the morning seeing the other wards and then started operating after lunch.

The first case was a policeman who had had a bomb injury to his forearm shattering the radius and severing about three-fourths of the muscles. He had had a tourniquet on for about seven hours and any attempt to stop the hemorrhage would have completely shut off the remainder of the circulation to the hand. There was nothing to do but amputation. The next case was a poor fellow who had had a large piece of metal enter his cheek and break off a portion of the lower jaw. The metal was extracted as well as several teeth imbedded in the broken off portion of the jaw. Then came a series of cases under the fluoroscope with Trim's assistance. One fellow had a piece of shrapnel in his parotid gland, it having severed his facial nerve. Another had a bullet in his side. It had entered his epigastrium and gone straight through his stomach. He vomited a large quantity of blood and then felt better. His condition is excellent and I don't believe I will have to do a laparotomy on him at all. I got the bullet out of the side without difficulty. Another case had his foot blown off four days ago. He was very toxic and I did an open flap amputation of his lower leg. Another case was that of a barber bayonetted by Japanese soldiers. . . . He was in shock and will probably die. He is the only survivor of the eight in the shop, the rest having all been killed.

The slaughter of civilians is appalling. I could go on for pages telling of cases of rape and brutality beyond belief. Two bayonetted cases are the only survivors of seven street cleaners who were sitting in their headquarters when Japanese soldiers came in and without warning or reason killed the five or six of their number and wounded the two that found their way to the hospital. I wonder when it will stop and we will be able to catch up with ourselves again.

Christmas Eve

This seems like anything but Christmas Eve. It is sort of tough to sit in a small X-ray room to keep Japanese soldiers from looting a hospital in the center of what was a few weeks ago a great city while the rest of the family is scattered all over the globe. My baby will be six months old in four days and I have only seen her for seven weeks of that time.

The burning seems almost over. Only a half a dozen fires were started today to finish up the job of wiping out the shops on both sides of all the main streets. The looting continues. They carried off the Daniels' rugs today, one of them requiring four men to take. The poor people who stay in the house can of course do nothing about it and can only tell about it later. J. Lossing Buck has no idea now extremely lucky he is to date. His house, by virtue of the fact that there are eight Americans in it, has so far been spared the ravages of looters. Thompson's house next door has also been left untouched. The remaining houses are mere shells. . . .

Tonight we invited Trim and three of the five Germans in town to Christmas Eve dinner. Mr. Rabe, head of the International Committee, didn't feel he could come and leave the 600 refugees that are crowding every corner of his house and yard. Every time he leaves them they are looted. He is well up in Nazi circles and after coming into such close contact with him as we have for the past few weeks and discovered what a splendid man he is and what a tremendous heart he has it is hard to reconcile his person-ality with his adulation of Der Fuhrer [Adolf Hitler]. He has labored incessantly for the thousands of poor people that have crowded into the Zone. The other two Germans, Kruger and Sperling, have given themselves wholeheartedly to the work of the committee and its attempt to save some of these poor people. No one will ever know how many have been ruthlessly slaughtered.

One man who just got in today says he was a stretcher bear-er and was one of four thousand marched to the banks of the Yangtze and machine-gunned. He has a bullet wound through his shoulder and dares not talk above a whisper and then only after carefully peering about to see if he is going to be overheard. One of the two burned wretches died this morning but the other is still hanging on for a while. Searle Bates went over this afternoon to the place described as the scene of the burning and found the charred bodies of the poor devils. And now they tell us that there are twenty thousand soldiers still in the Zone, (where they got their figures no one knows), and that they are going to hunt them out and shoot them all. That will mean every able-bodied male be-tween the ages of 18 and 50 that is now in the city. How can they ever look anybody in the face again?

Simburg was back in the city today with some more horror tales. He says that the big trenches that the Chinese built for tank traps along the way were filled with the bodies of dead and wounded soldiers and when there weren't enough bodies to fill the trench so that the tanks could pass they shot people living around there indiscriminately to fill up the trenches. He borrowed a camera to go back and take some pictures to bear out his statement.

Good night and Merry Christmas![13]

---

13 "The Nanking Massacre Project," Yale University Divinity School Library, accessed February 11, 2013, http://divdl.library.yale.edu/ydlchina/images /NMP0016.pdf.

READING 4

A PLEA FOR HUMANITY: MINER SEARLE BATES

Much of the international committee's efforts were spent writing almost daily letters of protest to the Japanese embassy as well as publishing pamphlets for disseminating the information abroad. These appeals often included records of the Japanese troops' atrocities. They had little immediate effect on the authorities or in stopping the carnage, but they do provide excellent documentation of the events that occurred in occupied Nanjing.

Miner Searle Bates, an American professor of history, became one of the committee's leaders. He published several pamphlets that were intended to be circulated abroad and wrote a significant body of its letters to the embassy including the letter listed below:[14]

> University of Nanking,
> Nanking, 27 December, 1937.
> Officers of the Japanese Embassy,
> Nanking.
>
> Gentlemen: -
>
> Beginning more than a week ago, we were promised by you that within a few days order would be restored by replacement

of troops, resumption of regular discipline, increase of military police, and so forth. Yet shameful disorder continues, and we see no serious effort to stop it. Let me give you a few examples from University property close to you, without covering all portions of the University.

(1) Yesterday afternoon a soldier [threw] out the rope and took away the American flag from our Rural Leaders' Training School at Yin Yang Ying and Shanghai Roads.

(2) Last night between eleven and twelve o'clock, a motor car with three Japanese military men came to the main University gate, claiming that they were sent by headquarters to inspect. They forcibly prevented our watchman from giving an alarm, and kept him with them while they found and raped three girls, one of whom is only eleven years old. One of the girls they took away with them.

(3) Stray soldiers continue to seize men to work for them, causing much fear and unnecessary inconvenience. For example, a soldier insisted on taking a worker from the Hospital yesterday; and several of our own servants and watchman have been taken.

(4) Several of our residences are entered daily by soldiers looking for women, food, and other articles. Two houses within one hour this morning.

Example (5) is from the Bible Teachers' Training School for Women, Chien Ying Hsiang, a place which has suffered terribly from your soldiers for a long time, and which I believe you once promised to protect especially—but where no military policeman has appeared. Yesterday seven different times there came groups of three or four soldiers, taking clothes, food, and money from those who have some left after previous lootings of the same type. They raped seven women, including a girl of twelve. In the night larger groups of twelve or fourteen soldiers came four times, and raped twenty women.

The life of the whole people is filled with suffering and fear, all caused by soldiers. Your officers have promised them protection but the soldiers every day injure hundreds of persons most seriously. A few policemen help certain places, and we are grateful for them. But that does not bring peace and order. Often it merely shifts the bad acts of the soldiers to nearby buildings where there are no policemen.

Does not the Japanese Army care for its reputation? Do not Japanese officers wish to keep their public promises that they do not injure the common people?

Yale Divinity School Library

A Chinese woman is carried into the hospital for gunshot wounds inflicted by a Japanese soldier who threatened to rape her.

While I have been writing this letter, a soldier has forcibly taken a woman from one of our teachers' houses, and with his revolver refused to let an American enter. Is this order?

Many people now want to return to their homes, but they dare not because of rape, robbery, and seizure of men continuing every day and night. Only serious efforts to enforce orders, using many police and real punishments, will be of any use. In several places the situation is a little better, but it is still disgraceful after two weeks of army terrorism. More than promises is now needed.[15]

14 Bates published the pamphlets *Crop Investigation in the Nanking Area December 1937 through March 1938 and Sundry Economic Activity* and *The Nanking Population: Employment, Earnings and Expenditures*. Both were published in 1938.
15 "The Nanking Massacre Project," Yale University Divinity School Library, accessed February 11, 2013, http://divdl.library.yale.edu/ydlchina/images/NMP0162.pdf.

READING 5

A QUESTION OF MORALITY: JOHN RABE

If you can do some good, why hesitate.

—JOHN RABE, DECEMBER 10, 1937[16]

John H. D. Rabe's story presents a paradox. He is remembered as a great humanitarian despite remaining a loyal member of the Nazi Party. Born in 1882 in Hamburg, Germany, Rabe first came to Shanghai in 1908. He began working for the Chinese branch of the Siemens Company in 1911 and 20 years later in 1931 transferred to Nanjing and served as director of the Siemens branch office with his wife and two children. Siemens was largely responsible for building the Nanjing telephone lines and supplying turbines for the electrical plant and equipment for the city's hospitals.

In 1934 Rabe founded a German school in Nanjing and decided to locate the building on his property. While both of his children were past elementary school age, Rabe served as chairman of the school board and it was in this capacity that he first came in formal contact with the Nazi leadership of Germany and joined the NSDAP (the Nazi Party). Throughout World War II Rabe remained a loyal member of the Nazi Party.

Like several of the other foreigners who chose to remain in Nanjing and help, Rabe kept almost a daily journal of the events leading up to the Japanese occupation as well as the occupation itself. Like all the foreigners in Nanjing, Rabe faced many dilemmas: should he stay in the face of the eminent assault by the Japanese army or should he return to Germany?

What policy should the Safety Zone Committee uphold in regard to Chinese soldiers that had deserted? How could such a small number of foreigners administer to the many needs of Chinese refugees simply trying to survive? The detailed account of his daily life in Nanjing provides an invaluable window into the days leading up to the occupation of the city:

21 September 1937

All the rich or better-off Chinese began some time ago to flee up the Yangtze to Hankow. . . . Many Americans and Germans have departed as well. I've been seriously considering the matter from all sides these last few nights. It wasn't because I love adventure that I returned here from the safety of Peitaiho [vacation destination for many foreigners in China], but primarily to protect my property and to represent Siemens interests. Of course the company can't—nor does it—expect me to get myself killed here on its behalf. Besides, I haven't the least desire to put my life at risk for the sake of either the company's or my own property; but there is a question of morality here, and as a reputable Hamburg businessman, so far I haven't been able to side-step it.

Our Chinese servants and employees, about 30 people in all including immediate families, have eyes only for their "master." . . . I cannot bring myself for now to betray the trust these people have put in me. And it is touching to see how they believe in me. . . .

Under such circumstances, can I, may I, cut and run? I don't think so. Anyone who has ever sat in a dugout and held a trembling Chinese child in each hand through the long hours of an air raid can understand what I feel.

Finally—subconsciously—there's a last, and the not least important, reason that makes my sticking it out here seem simply a matter of course. I am a member of the NSDAP, and temporarily held the office of local deputy leader. When I pay business calls on the Chinese agencies and ministries who are our customers, I am constantly asked questions about Germany, about our party and government, and my answer always is:

~~Yes indeed—~~
We are soldiers of labor;
We are a government of workers,
We are friends of the working man,
We do not leave workers-—the poor-—
in the lurch when times are hard!

To be sure, as a National Socialist I was speaking only of German workers, not about the Chinese; but what would the Chinese think? Times are bitterly hard here in the country of my hosts, who have treated me well for three decades now. The rich are fleeing, the poor must stay behind. They don't know where to go. They don't have the means to flee. Aren't they in danger of being slaughtered in great numbers? Shouldn't one make an attempt to help them? Save a few at least? And even if it's only our own people, our employees?[17]

As air raids increased over Nanjing and more and more Chinese fled the city, the efforts to organize the Nanjing Safety Zone were solidified. In October 1937 Rabe was unanimously elected as the first chairman of the Nanjing Safety Zone (NSZ) Committee. On November 25, 1937, approximately three weeks before the Imperial Army laid siege to the city, Rabe sent the following telegram to Adolf Hitler:

Undersigned Deputy Group Leader Nanking, chairman of local International Committee, asks his Führer kindly to intercede with the Japanese government to grant permission for creation of a neutral zone for noncombatants, since imminent battle for Nanking otherwise endangers the lives of over two thousand people stop

With German greetings from Rabe Siemens agent in Nanking stop[18]

It is uncertain if Hitler ever received the telegram, but Rabe never received a reply. Nonetheless, Rabe hung the Nazi flag at his home, draped the Nazi flag on the hood of his car, and wore a swastika armband to confront Japanese soldiers at even the hint of misconduct. Rabe's home was within the parameters of the NSZ so he was able to shelter hundreds of refugees inside and around the grounds of his residence during the siege of the city.

Many entries in John Rabe's diary also record the tremendous amount of time he spent negotiating with the Japanese military leadership to keep the NSZ safe from marauding Japanese soldiers. They consistently accused the Safety Zone Committee of sheltering Chinese soldiers who had deserted the army. Even though all Chinese refugees were notified that only Chinese civilians were permitted within the borders of the Safety Zone, and in fact the committee was unable to protect soldiers if they were discovered, it was almost impossible to ensure a foolproof method to bar their entrance. Rabe struggled with this dilemma a great deal, knowing that Chinese soldiers would still be treated as enemy combatants in Japanese eyes even if they gave up their weapons. *(See Source 2: Notice for Chinese Refugees Issued by the Nanjing Safety Zone Committee.)* Prior to the Japanese occupation, Rabe wrote:

> *9 December 1937*
>
> . . . The streets of the Safety Zone are flooded with refugees loaded down with bundles. The old Communication Ministry (arsenal) is opened to refugees and in no time fills to the rafters. We cordon off two rooms because our weapons and ammunition are in them. Among the refugees are deserters, who hand over their uniforms and weapons.[19]

> *11 December*
>
> The streets of our Zone are packed with people who aren't even bothered by the din of the shelling. These people have more faith in our "Safety Zone" than I do. The Zone is a long way from being safe; there are still armed soldiers inside, and all our efforts to get them out have thus far been to no avail. We cannot tell the Japanese, as was our intention, that the Zone is now free of all military.[20]

The day before the city was occupied Rabe wrote:

> *12 December*
> 8 p.m.
>
> The sky to the south is all in flames. The two dugouts in the garden are now filled to the brim with refugees. There are knocks at both gates to the property. Women and children plead to be

let in. Several plucky fellows seeking shelter on my grounds climb
over the garden wall behind the German School.

And I can't listen to their wailing any longer, so I open both gates
and let everyone in who wants in. Since there's no more room
in the dugouts, I allocate people to various sheds and to corners
of the house. Most have brought their bedding and lie down in
the open. A few very clever sorts spread their beds out under the
large German flag we had stretched out in case of air raids. This
location is considered especially "bombproof."[21]

Once the Imperial Army arrived and unleashed the full force of their occupation, Chinese soldiers were shown no mercy. The Japanese military used the possibility of Chinese soldiers hiding in the NSZ as an excuse to enter the premises again and again and search for supposed combatants. Rabe wrote:

16 December

Almost all the houses of the German military advisors have been
looted by Japanese soldiers. No Chinese even dares set foot
outside his house! When the gates to my garden are opened to
let my car leave the grounds—where I have already taken in over
a hundred of the poorest refugees—women and children on the
street outside kneel and bang their heads against the ground,
pleading to be allowed to camp on my garden grounds. You simply cannot conceive of the misery. . . .

I've just heard that hundreds more disarmed Chinese soldiers
have been led out of our Zone to be shot, including 50 of our
police who are to be executed for letting soldiers in. . . . We
Europeans are all paralyzed with horror. There are executions everywhere, some are being carried out with machine guns outside
the barracks of the War Ministry.

Katsuo Okazaki, the consul general, who visited us this evening,
explained that while it was true that a few soldiers were being
shot, the rest were to be interned in a concentration camp on an
island on the Yangtze.

As I write this, the fists of Japanese soldiers are hammering at the
back gate to the garden. Since my boys don't open up, heads ap-

pear along the top of the wall. When I suddenly show up with my flashlight, they beat a hasty retreat. We open the main gate and walk after them a little distance until they vanish in dark narrow streets, where assorted bodies have been lying in the gutter for three days now. Makes you shutter in revulsion.

All the women and children, their eyes big with terror, are sitting on the grass in the garden, pressed closely together, in part to keep warm, in part to give each other courage. Their one hope is that I, the "foreign devil," will drive these evil spirits away.[22]

By late February 1938 his leadership role in Nanjing precipitated the home office of Siemens to recall Rabe back to Berlin, Germany. Never again to resume a large leadership role in the company, Rabe gave lectures that included films and photographs of the atrocities he had witnessed. When Rabe returned to Germany he was also detained and interrogated by the Gestapo. Only through the intervention of Siemens was he released and allowed to keep some evidence (excluding footage) of his time in Nanjing.

In the aftermath of World War II, John Rabe was denounced for his Nazi Party membership and arrested first by the Soviet NKVD (the primary enforcement agency of the Soviet Union and predecessor of the KGB) and then by the British army. Both discharged him after their investigations. He was declared "de-Nazified" by the Allies in June 1946. Denied his full pension, Rabe's final years were lived largely in poverty supplemented by monthly food and money parcels provided by the Chinese government and sent to him as recompense. In 1947 John Rabe retired at the age of 65 and died two years later on January 5, 1949.

---

16 John Rabe, *The Good Man of Nanking: The Diaries of John Rabe,* trans. John E. Woods (New York: Vintage Books, 1998), 58.
17 Ibid., 5-6.
18 Ibid., 33.
19 Ibid., 57.
20 Ibid., 60.
21 Ibid., 64.
22 Ibid., 76–77.

RESCUE OUTSIDE THE SAFETY ZONE

While rescue efforts within the agreed-upon Safety Zone were perilous at best, there were other individuals, often working alone, who saved lives as well. One such man was a Danish man by the name of Bernhard Arp Sindberg, or Mr. Xin.

Sindberg was born in February 1911 in Aarhus, Denmark, into a wealthy and politically active family. At the age of 17 he left home first to California to visit an uncle and eventually joined the Foreign Legion to travel the world. After only 10 months, he left this effort, escaped into the mountains of Morocco where he was stationed, and eventually found passage to China in 1934. At the time the Danish government was supplying weapons to the Chinese in the fight against the Japanese, so his arrival into Shanghai garnered little suspicion.

Sindberg was quite lucky from the beginning of his stay in Shanghai, for he was offered a position with the Danish company Nielsen & Winther to demonstrate the efficiency of Danish manufactured weapons to the government in Nanjing. By 1937 this position had ended and Sindberg was then hired as a driver for the British war correspondent Pembroke Stephens, who was covering the Japanese Imperial Army's assault on Shanghai for the London Daily Telegraph. Stephens had been expelled from Germany in June 1934 for his openly critical reporting of Nazism and for campaigning on behalf of German Jews. As a driver for a war correspondent, Sindberg found himself touring the war zone. On what was to become the last day of the siege of Shanghai, November 11, 1937, Sindberg found himself on top of a water tower in the French concession overlooking Shanghai with Stephens and another journalist, Mental Berg. A Japanese airman attacked them from above and fatally wounded Pembroke Stephens.

The day after this aerial attack, Sindberg was hired as a guardsman to protect an unfinished cement factory owned by F. L. Smith and Company and operated by the Shanghai Portland Cement Works in Nanjing. Known as the Kiangnan Cement Works in Hsi Sha Shan, it was located some 1½ hours outside the city center of Nanjing. According to Sindberg, the unfinished building had over two million Chinese dollars' worth of machinery inside as the Japanese army's assault turned toward Nanjing. He signed a contract on December 1, 1937, and a week later he arrived with funds in hand that had been wired from Denmark. The factory itself had been built by Danes but the machinery was manufactured in Germany, and the company had close ties with Germany as well.

From the day he arrived at the abandoned cement factory, Sindberg met flee-ing Chinese refugees seeking shelter in the skeleton of the factory, hoping his foreign presence would provide some protection. Sindberg, who had arrived with German engineer Karl Günther, found themselves sheltering thou-sands of refugees. Painting a Danish and German swastika flag above the factory, they were able to avoid aerial bombings. To the best of his ability and by flying both flags he was largely able to ward off marauding soldiers. While there was no large-scale murder on the grounds of the cement fac-tory, Sindberg could not fully protect the women refugees from rape. He recorded these assaults and other crimes he witnessed outside the city walls of Nanjing and delivered the reports to the International Committee for the Nanking Safety Zone in Nanjing.

On December 20, 1937, Sindberg delivered a petition from the refugees he was harboring requesting help from the Safety Zone or from any foreign government who would listen. No help came. He was able to provide some meager supplies of food, but the cold and hunger that ensued over the next few months were extremely difficult. John Rabe described meeting Sindberg from a diary entry dated January 28, 1938:

> Memorandum of Chancellor R. Scharffenberg to the German Embassy in Hankow
>
> The situation in Nanking as of 28 January 1938
>
> The food supply provided by the Japanese is completely inade-quate. If we were to rely on them, we would starve. Yesterday Sindberg, the Dane from the cement factory, brought us another little pig, eggs, two ducks. Granted, he was arrested on the way here, but by subsidizing the sentries with a crate of beer he got through under the guard of three men and an officer.

And on February 3, 1938, Rabe documented:

> Report from the China Press in Shanghai, 25 January (Excerpt)
>
> Dr. Günther's report, passed on to us by Herr Sindberg of the Kiangnan Cement Factory, proves that it is not just Nanking that is suffering at the hands of the Japanese soldiery. The same reports

are coming in from all sides about rapes, murder and mayhem.
One might be led to think that the entire criminal population of
Japan is in uniform here.[23]

By February 1938, the consulate general sent some supplies to Sindberg, but the Japanese assaults in the area began to increase again and soon he became a liability to the Danish firm. In the end the Japanese pressured the F. L. Smith Company to recall Sindberg. Before his departure, the Danish newspaper Aarhus Stiffstidende published letters Sindberg had sent dated March 6, 1938. He wrote:

On a trip like this [to Nanjing] you see destruction all around. All villages are torched. All cattle and poultry is taken. Wherever you look, lie the corpses of killed peasants and Chinese soldiers, serving as food for stray dogs and animals.[24]

Almost immediately after returning to Europe, Sindberg emigrated to the United States, where he lived the rest of his life. He died in 1983. On the 70th anniversary of the Nanjing Atrocities, Bitten and Mariann Stenvig Andersen, Sindberg's sister and niece, traveled to Nanjing to receive a special accommodation from the Chinese government on behalf of Bernhard. They have also met Nanjing survivors over the years who have recounted stories of how Bernhard Arp Sindberg saved their lives. One survivor, Wang Yongli, stayed 100 days in the cement factory as a teenager and said, "Without his help we would not have had any chance of survival. We hope that the goodness in people like Sindberg will live on."[25]

---

23 Rabe, *Good Man of Nanking*, 161, 173.
24 Sindberg, "The Good Dane in Nanjing 1937," NACS 8th Biennial Conference in Stockholm, June 11-13, 2007, accessed January 1, 2014, http://www.nacsorg.com/stockholmconf/NACSindbergHinrup.htm.
25 Ibid., accessed January 2, 2014, http://www.nacsorg.com/stockholmconf/NACSindbergHinrup.htm.

PRIMARY SOURCES

SOURCE 1

TIME LINE, NANJING SAFETY ZONE, AUGUST 1937–FEBRUARY 1938

1937

- August 13—Japanese attack Shanghai.

- August 15—First air raid occurs over Nanjing.

- November 12—Shanghai falls.

- November 15—International Committee for the Nanking Safety Zone is conceived.

- November 22—Safety Zone proposal is sent to the Japanese authorities and rejected weeks later.

- November 25—John Rabe wires Hitler for help establishing the Safety Zone.

- December 1—The mayor of Nanjing, Ma Chao-chun, orders all Chinese citizens remaining in the city to go to the Safety Zone.

- December 8—Chiang Kai-shek and advisers flee the city.

- December 9—Japanese Imperial Army begin to surround the capital city. Assault on city begins.

- December 12—Chinese soldiers are ordered to withdraw from Nanjing.

- December 13—Soldiers of the Japanese Imperial Army capture Nanjing. General Matsui Iwane, commander of the expeditionary forces sent to China during this period, does not arrive in Nanjing until December 17.

- December 14—The International Committee for the Nanking Safety Zone lodges the first protest letter against Japanese atrocities with the Japanese embassy.

- December 14–21—First major wave of rape, pillage, and murder occurs.

- December 21—Japanese military is reorganized to complete "mop-up"; second major wave of violence begins.

1938

- January 28–February 3—Second wave of violence occurs.

- February 19—The last of the 69 protest letters against Japanese atrocities is sent by the Safety Zone Committee to the Japanese embassy and announces the renaming of the committee as the Nanking International Relief Committee.

- May—Safety Zone is dissolved; relief efforts continue.

SOURCE 2

NOTICE FOR CHINESE REFUGEES ISSUED BY THE NANJING SAFETY ZONE COMMITTEE

14 December 1937: Important Notice to the Refugees in the Safety Zone

1. From now on people should stay off the streets as much as possible.

2. At the most dangerous moment, everyone should get in houses or out of sight.

3. The Safety Zone is for Refugees. Sorry, the Safety Zone has no power to give protection to soldiers.

4. If there is any searching or inspection, give full freedom for such search. No opposition at all.[26]

---

26 John Rabe, *The Good Man of Nanking: The Diaries of John Rabe,* trans. John E. Woods (New York: Vintage Books, 1998), 267–68.

CHAPTER 6

AFTERMATH
AND JUDGMENT

The readings in Chapter Six explore the aftermath of World War II in China and Japan and the challenges of rebuilding a nation after the devastation of war. The chapter explores ways of seeking justice by using the rule of law and holding leaders accountable for their acts of aggressive war and atrocities.

The following questions may be helpful as you explore the range of topics examined in this chapter:

- What needs to happen for there to be justice after mass violence or atrocities?

- To what extent should efforts to rebuild Japan be connected to making amends for the crimes of war?

- What role should the law play in the pursuit of justice? What nonlegal efforts can help bring comfort to victims and help prevent future violence?

- How should individuals, groups, institutions, and nations be held accountable for war crimes and mass atrocities?

- How do you decide who is most responsible? The leaders or soldiers?

- What significance is there to the term "aggressive war"?

For media and classroom materials such as discussion questions and additional primary sources, visit www.facinghistory.org/nanjing-atrocities.

INTRODUCTION

Efforts to seek accountability for the atrocities in Nanjing (Nanking) continue to be deeply tied to the larger legacy of World War II in East Asia. In mainland China, World War II continued for nearly seven more years after the occupation of Nanjing. As a nation Japan knew as early as November 1943 that unconditional surrender and defeat were a possibility, yet their aggressive war efforts continued in mainland China and in the Pacific. Meeting in Cairo, Egypt, President Chiang Kai-shek of the Republic of China, Prime Minister Winston Churchill of the United Kingdom, and President Franklin Roosevelt of the United States issued the Cairo Communiqué in November 27, 1943, which declared:

> The several military missions have agreed upon future military operations against Japan. The three Great Allies are fighting this war to restrain and punish the aggression of Japan. They covet no gain for themselves and have not thought of territorial expansion. It is their purpose that Japan shall be stripped of all the islands in the Pacific which she has seized or occupied since the beginning of the First World War in 1914, and that all the territories Japan has stolen from the Chinese, such as Manchuria, Formosa, and the Pescadores, shall be restored to the Republic of China. Japan will also be expelled from all other territories which she has taken by violence and greed. The aforesaid Three Great Powers, mindful of the enslavement of the people of Korea, are determined that in due course Korea shall become free and independent.

> With these objects in view the Three Allies, in harmony with those of the United Nations at war with Japan, will continue to persevere in the serious and prolonged operations necessary to procure the unconditional surrender of Japan.[1]

When Nazi Germany surrendered on May 8, 1945 (V-E Day), World War II in Europe was over.[2] By late July 1945 the Allied powers convened for the Potsdam Conference to negotiate the military occupation and reconstruction of postwar Germany. Also at Potsdam US president Harry Truman publically revealed to Secretary-General Josef Stalin of the Soviet Union a critical factor that would ultimately lead to Japan's surrender—the first successful detonation of an atomic bomb by the United States at Alamogordo, New Mexico, one month prior. Out of this meeting came the

Potsdam Declaration issued by Truman, Churchill, and Chiang demanding the "unconditional surrender" of Japan. If anything other than unconditional surrender was given, the Allied forces clearly warned Tokyo that such actions would invite "prompt and utter destruction." As John Dower notes, "The Potsdam [Declaration] was by no means a tame document. It assured the Japanese that they would not be enslaved or destroyed as a nation, although they would lose their empire."[3] *(See Source 1: Potsdam Declaration [excerpt].)*

But the war in East Asia and the Pacific continued on months after V-E Day even as intensive aerial bombardment by Allied forces persisted against Japan. After the largest amphibious assault of the Pacific War, the Battle of Okinawa (April–June 1945), was over, diplomatic negotiations and peace terms between Japan and the Allied nations began to materialize.[4] The Japanese Imperial General Staff drew up a final operational blueprint for Japan's strategy to end the war. It aimed to inflict heavy losses to the Allies so American and British leaders would be forced to accept a negotiated peace. In case of failure, it would at least buy time for the Imperial forces to regroup their homeland defenses. Even if Japan did agree to the Allied forces' demands, there was no guarantee that Japan's overseas armies would capitulate to the Chinese.

When pressed by journalists to respond to the demands of the Potsdam Declaration, Prime Minister Suzuki of Japan stated, "The Potsdam [Declaration], in my opinion, is just a rehash of the Cairo Declaration, and the government therefore does not consider it of great importance. We must *mokusatsu* it." The Japanese term *mokusatsu* is defined as: (v.) take no notice of; treat (anything) with silent contempt; ignore [by keeping silence]; remain in a wise and masterly inactivity.[5] After the English-speaking press interpreted the term to mean "ignore" or "treat with silent contempt" and the *New York Times* headline of July 30, 1945, read "Japan Officially Turns Down Allied Surrender Ultimatum," a rapid succession of events unfolded, forever altering modern warfare.[6]

On August 6, 1945, the first atomic bomb was dropped on Hiroshima, Japan, by the United States military; on August 8 the Soviet Union entered the war in East Asia; on August 9 the second atomic bomb was dropped on Nagasaki, Japan; and on August 10 the Japanese government opened communication with the Allied forces to negotiate their surrender. Japan's formal surrender to the Allied powers occurred on August 13, 1945 and on August 14 after the Japanese Supreme War Council had convened, Japan communicated with the Allied powers its decision to surrender and end the war and accept the Potsdam Declaration. On August 15 Emperor Hirohito broadcast his unprecedented radio address of surrender to the nation and an end to the war.

By the end of August 1945 American troops began their formal postwar occupation of Japan under the leadership of General Douglas MacArthur's "SCAP" bureaucracy (SCAP, an acronym for Supreme Command[er] for the Allied Powers, was used to refer to MacArthur's command in Japan.) The Americans set out to do what no other occupation force had ever done before: remake the political, social, cultural, and economic fabric of a defeated nation, and in the process attempt to change the very way of thinking.[7]

However many survivors of the Nanjing Atrocities, in particular, do not feel the crimes they endured have been properly acknowledged. One way to consider questions of justice after the atrocities in Nanjing is to examine them through the contemporary lens of transitional justice. The International Center for Transitional Justice defines this process as:

> A range of approaches that societies undertake to reckon with legacies of widespread or systematic human rights abuse as they move from a period of violent conflict or oppression towards peace, democracy, the rule of law, and respect for individual and collective rights.

> In making such a transition, societies must confront the painful legacy, or burden, of the past in order to achieve a holistic sense of justice for all citizens. . . . A variety of approaches to transitional justice are available that can help wounded societies start anew. These approaches are both judicial and nonjudicial.[8]

While international conversations around transitional justice did not exist in 1945[9], in the immediate aftermath of the war, Japan undertook several of these steps. They included rewriting civil laws, rebuilding civil institutions, and participating international trials for some Japanese leaders held accountable for atrocities committed under their command. But decades after the war's conclusion, there are still open questions about what else can and should be done to acknowledge the grievances of victims, their descendants and what would constitute a full accounting by the Japanese government for war crimes committed in Nanjing and elsewhere during World War II. These old memories remain open wounds and can be passed down for generations, igniting new hatreds and grievances.

By January 1946 the charter for the International Military Tribunal for the Far East, also known as the Tokyo Trials, was announced with the aim of holding the High Command of Japanese leadership accountable for the crimes committed during World War II. Now Japan, after less than a century of modernization efforts, lay in ruins, a nation defeated.

---

1 "The Cairo Communiqué," December 1, 1943, The National Diet Library, accessed on January 1, 2014, http://www.ndl.go.jp/constitution/e/shiryo/01/002_46/002_46_001l.html.

2 V-E Day, May 8, 1945, is commonly used as a reference to mean "Victory over Europe."

3 Dower, *Embracing Defeat: Japan in the Wake of World War II,* Kindle edition.

4 An amphibious assault uses naval ships to carry ground and air military power onto shore. The 82-day long Battle of Okinawa is infamous for the ferocity of fighting that took place. The losses incurred by both the Allied and Japanese forces are believed to be the highest of any battle fought during the Pacific War.

5 *Kenkyusha's New Japanese-English Dictionary,* 4th edition, (French and European Publishing House, 2003), 1129.

6 John Toland, *The Rising Sun: The Decline and Fall of the Japanese Empire, 1936-1945* (New York: Modern Library, 1970), 774.

7 Dower, *Embracing Defeat,* Kindle edition.

8 "What is Transitional Justice?" International Center for Transitional Justice website, accessed January 1, 2014, http://ictj.org/about/transitional-justice.

9 It is important to keep in mind that the United Nations, the Universal Declaration of Human Rights and the Convention for the Prevention and Punishment of the Crime of Genocide were codified and institutionalized by December 1948. For further investigation see Facing History and Ourselves' resource, *Fundamental Freedoms: Eleanor Roosevelt and the Universal Declaration of Human Rights.*

READING 1

ACCEPTING DEFEAT

In the spring of 1945 Emperor Hirohito reportedly said, "If we hold out long enough in this war, we may be able to win, but what worries me is whether the nation will be able to endure it until then."[10] The emperor issued an imperial rescript ordering the nation to "smash the inordinate ambitions of the enemy nations and achieve the goals of war."[11] At this point he refused to surrender out of fear for the destruction of the emperor system and imperial, as opposed to popular, sovereignty.

Operation Ketsugo, a policy of defending the Japanese homeland by relying heavily on suicide missions, was Japan's military strategy. This included manufacturing weapons, or special attack planes, solely for the purpose of kamikaze missions, human torpedoes shot from submarines and dynamite-filled crash boats. By early June 1945 the Imperial Diet took one further step and passed a Wartime Emergency Measures Law, designed to mobilize the entire nation for one last battle.

By mid-June 1945 Hirohito's stance began to shift as his empire was collapsing. Japan's oil supply had been completely cut off for months and huge sections of more than 60 Japanese cities were in ruins. Once the first atomic weapons were dropped on Hiroshima and Nagasaki by the United States, and Soviet forces further encroached into regions of China held by Japan, Emperor Hirohito finally agreed to surrender. On August 15, 1945, he read *Gyokuon-hoso,* or "Jewel Voice Broadcast," a four-minute radio address surrendering to the United States and its Allied forces.

The speech was a watershed moment in modern Japanese history. It was the first time the emperor had spoken to the "common people" of Japan and the first time they had ever heard the sound of his voice. His announcement ended the war, set the nation on another course of transformation some 87 years after the beginning of the Meiji era, and sealed the end of imperial Japan. Portions of the speech are included below:

> To Our Good and Loyal Subjects:
>
> After pondering deeply the general trends of the world and the actual conditions obtaining in Our Empire today, We have decided to effect a settlement of the present situation by resorting to an extraordinary measure.
>
> We have ordered Our Government to communicate to the Governments of the United States, Great Britain, China and the Soviet Union that Our Empire accepts the provisions of their Joint Declaration [Potsdam Declaration].
>
> To strive for the common prosperity and happiness of all nations as well as the security and well-being of Our subjects is the solemn obligation which has been handed down by Our Imperial Ancestors and which lies close to Our heart.
>
> Indeed, We declared war on America and Britain out of Our sincere desire to ensure Japan's self-preservation and the stabilization of East Asia, it being far from Our thought either to infringe upon the sovereignty of other nations or to embark upon territorial aggrandizement.

But now the war has lasted for nearly four years. Despite the best that has been done by everyone—the gallant fighting of the military and naval forces, the diligence and assiduity of Our servants of the State, and the devoted service of Our one hundred million people—the war situation has developed not necessarily to Japan's advantage, while the general trends of the world have all turned against her interest. . . .

Moreover, the enemy has begun to employ a new and most cruel bomb, the power of which to do damage is, indeed, incalculable, taking the toll of many innocent lives. Should We continue to fight, not only would it result in an ultimate collapse and obliteration of the Japanese nation, but also it would lead to the total extinction of human civilization.

Such being the case, how are We to save the millions of Our subjects, or to atone Ourselves before the hallowed spirits of Our Imperial Ancestors? This is the reason why We have ordered the acceptance of the provisions of the Joint Declaration of the Powers.

We cannot but express the deepest sense of regret to Our Allied nations of East Asia, who have consistently cooperated with the Empire towards the emancipation of East Asia.

The thought of those officers and men as well as others who have fallen in the fields of battle, those who died at their posts of duty, or those who met with untimely death and all their bereaved families, pains Our heart night and day.

The welfare of the wounded and the war-sufferers, and of those who have lost their homes and livelihood, are the objects of Our profound solicitude.

The hardships and sufferings to which Our nation is to be subjected hereafter will be certainly great. We are keenly aware of the inmost feelings of all of you, Our subjects. However, it is according to the dictates of time and fate that We have resolved to pave the way for a grand peace for all the generations to come by enduring the unendurable and suffering what is unsufferable.

United States National Archives

General Douglas MacArthur observes as Japanese Foreign Minister Shigemitsu Mamoru signs the Instrument of Surrender.

Having been able to safeguard and maintain the structure of the Imperial State, or *kokutai,* We are always with you, Our good and loyal subjects, relying upon your sincerity and integrity.

Beware most strictly of any outbursts of emotion which may engender needless complications, or any fraternal contention and strike which may create confusion, lead you astray and cause you to lose the confidence of the world.

Let the entire nation continue as one family from generation to generation, ever firm in its faith in the imperishability of its sacred land, and mindful of its heavy burden of responsibility, and of the long road before it. Unite your total strength, to be devoted to construction for the future. Cultivate the ways of rectitude, foster nobility of spirit, and work with resolution—so that you may enhance the innate glory of the Imperial State and keep pace with the progress of the world.

All you, our subjects, we command you to act in accordance with
our wishes.

Hirohito
(The Seal of the Emperor)
The fourteenth day of the eighth month of the twentieth year
of Showa
Countersignatures of the Ministers of the State)[12]

Less than a month after the broadcast, the formal surrender of Japan was
convened with the signing of the Instruments of Surrender documents
aboard the battleship USS *Missouri* in Tokyo Bay. Representatives of the
Allied and Axis powers met to "conclude an agreement by which peace can
be restored." After General Douglas MacArthur read his opening remarks,
the Japanese representatives of the Empire of Japan stepped forward to sign
the two copies of the Instruments of Surrender. (*See Source 2: Text of the
Instruments of Surrender of Japan [close reading].*)

In China the formal surrender of Japanese forces occurred several weeks
later on September 9, 1945, in Nanjing. The former capital city, which endured rape, murder, and destruction of property of unimaginable scale in the
early months of World War II, now accepted the surrender of the Japanese
Imperial forces.

---

10 Herbert Bix, *Hirohito and the Making of Modern Japan* (New York: Harper Perennial, 2001),
     489.
11 Ibid., 494.
12 Wm. Theodore de Bary, Carol Gluck, and Arthur L. Tiedemann, eds., *Sources of Japanese
     Tradition*, 2nd edition, vol. 2 (New York: Columbia University Press, 2005), 1016–17.

WAR CRIMINALS AND AGGRESSIVE WAR

A very few throughout the world, including these accused, decided to take the law into their own hands and to force their individual will upon mankind. They declared war upon civilization. . . .

—US ASSISTANT ATTORNEY GENERAL JOSEPH B. KEENAN'S OPENING AT THE INTERNATIONAL MILITARY TRIBUNAL FOR THE FAR EAST (JUNE 4, 1946)

Associated Press

This is a general view of the International Military Tribunal for the Far East meeting in Tokyo in April, 1947.

As Emperor Hirohito prepared for surrender in the summer of 1945, Japanese military leaders also saw that capitulation was imminent. Unlike other times in history when war was concluded, surrender to Allied forces this time included their arrest and prosecution for war crimes. The 1943 Moscow Declaration confirmed that the Allied forces sought to conduct trials against major war criminals, and Article 10 of the Potsdam Declaration stated that "stern justice shall be meted out to all war criminals, including those who have visited cruelties upon our prisoners."[13] Alongside these provisions, Japanese military leaders could not ignore the fate of leading Nazi officials awaiting trial at the International Military Tribunal (IMT) at Nuremberg.

Because of the efforts of the foreigners involved in the Nanjing Safety Zone to collect evidence, photograph, film, and send letters and other documentation to family and colleagues living outside China at the time, there was evidence of the atrocities committed in and around Nanjing. There were also women and men from Nanjing who survived the violence who were willing to step forward and tell their stories publically.

Other cities and locations where war crimes and atrocities occurred did not have the same body of evidence. In a frantic attempt to avoid prosecution, Japanese military leaders took full advantage of the lag of time between their surrender (August 15, 1945) and Allied occupation (August 30, 1945.)[14] A policy of systematically destroying and burning vast amounts of incriminating evidence, including transcripts of imperial conferences, records of the Supreme Council for the Direction of the War, all files on prisoners of war, orders and plans relating to the attack on the Philippines and Southeast Asia, and documents relating to the Manchurian and Chinese campaigns, were put in force.[15] Many high- and low-ranking Japanese leaders also chose to end their lives and practice what Prime Minister Tojo termed as the "frontline code of honor" rather than be "judged before a conqueror's court."[16]

Despite the tremendous loss of evidence and desperate acts by Japanese leaders, on January 19, 1946 General Douglas MacArthur, Supreme Commander of Allied Powers, established by Special Proclamation the International Military Tribunal for the Far East (IMTFE) and approved its Charter. MacArthur appointed a panel of 11 judges, 9 of whom were from nations who signed the terms of surrender.[17] The IMFTE used crimes against peace, war crimes, and conspiracy to commit these crimes in their indictments of Japanese war criminals and relegated them into a total of 55 separate counts to prosecute leading Japanese officials.

The counts were further divided into three levels, Class A, B, and C. Those most deemed responsible for aggressive war or crimes against peace were Class A war criminals. These counts included the following:

Count

1: As leaders, organizers, instigators, or accomplices in the formulation or execution of a common plan or conspiracy to wage wars of aggression, and war or wars in violation of international law.

27: Waging unprovoked war against China.

29: Waging aggressive war against the United States.

31: Waging aggressive war against the British Commonwealth.

32: Waging aggressive war against the Netherlands.

33: Waging aggressive war against France (Indochina).

35, 36: Waging aggressive war against the USSR.

54: Ordered, authorized, and permitted inhumane treatment of Prisoners of War (POWs) and others.

55: Deliberately and recklessly disregarded their duty to take adequate steps to prevent atrocities.[18]

Two of the Class A defendants, Prince Asaka Yasuhiko and General Matsui Iwane, were key military officers involved in the Nanjing Atrocities. Prince Asaka had spent his career in the Imperial Army, was the son-in-law of Emperor Meiji and uncle to Hirohito. He was never indicted, questioned as a witness, or brought to testify at the IMTFE because of his imperial affiliations. General Matsui was commander of both the Shanghai Expeditionary Forces beginning in August 1937 and the Central China Area Army (CCAA) by December 1937. Matsui directed the campaign to capture Nanjing and was deactivated from this position in March 1938. A third Class A defendant, Hirota Koki, was the foreign minister of the CCAA at the time of the occupation of Nanjing. Evidence was also gathered against Class B acts, war crimes, and Class C, crimes against humanity. These accused individuals would only be tried at the IMTFE if they were already being prosecuted for Class A acts.

Finally, the prosecutors at Tokyo faced the decision whether to prosecute Japan's leader (Emperor Hirohito), who remained alive at the conclusion of the war. MacArthur was instructed by Washington and a Joint Chiefs order on September 12 to "take no action against the Emperor as a war criminal."[19] This order was in direct conflict with Article 6 of the Nuremberg Charter, which the IMTFE Charter was loosely based upon. This article held heads of state responsible for committing acts of aggressive war, stating, "Leaders, organizers, instigators and accomplices participating in the formulation or execution of a common plan or conspiracy to commit any of the foregoing crimes are responsible for all acts performed by any persons in execution of such plan."[20] But General MacArthur and the personnel working for SCAP reasoned that the success of their occupation depended upon the stability of Japan. The prosecution and possible removal of the emperor could undermine this effort and jeopardize the American interests in the region.[21] MacArthur even received direct instruction from Washington to "take no action against the Emperor as a war criminal."[22]

This rationale was not shared by all of the Allied forces with interests in Japan. For example, the Australians furnished a detailed memorandum advocating for the prosecution of the emperor. It stressed never "at any time was Hirohito forced by duress to give his written approval to any aggressive military action."[23] In the end, the American forces' dominant role politically and militarily in the region won out and the emperor was not indicted. This decision was supported by the Soviet delegation, on instruction from Stalin, calling for Hirohito's indictment only if the Americans agreed to it. Similarly the three Asian countries participating in the tribunal, China, the Philippines, and India, would only pursue prosecuting the emperor if the Americans agreed to. Ultimately, 28 Japanese defendants were indicted but Emperor Hirohito was not included. *(See Source 3: International Military Tribunal for the Far East Fact Sheet.)*

Less than one year after Japan's surrender, former US assistant attorney general Joseph B. Keenan opened the IMTFE on June 4, 1946. The statement was given at Ichigaya Court in Tokyo, the former headquarters of the Imperial Army in Tokyo during the war:

> Mr. President and members of the International Military Tribunal for the Far East: . . .
>
> This may be one of the most important trials of history. It is important to the eleven nations here represented, constituting orderly governments of countries containing much more than

one-half of the inhabitants of this earth. It is important to all other nations and to the unborn generations, because these proceedings could have a far reaching effect on the peace and security of the world. . . .

Our broad aim is the orderly administration of justice; our specific purpose is to contribute all we soundly can towards the end—the prevention of the scourge of aggressive war. . . .

Mr. President, this is no ordinary trial, for here we are waging a part of the determined battle of civilization to preserve the entire world from destruction. This threat comes not from the forces of nature, but from the deliberate planned efforts of individuals, as such and as members of groups. . . . A very few throughout the world, including these accused, decided to take the law into their own hands and to force their individual will upon mankind. They declared war upon civilization. They made the rules and defined the issues. They were determined to destroy democracy and its essential basis—freedom and respect of [sic] human personality; they were determined that the system of government of and by and for the people should be eradicated and what they called a "New Order" established instead. And to this end they joined hands with the Hitlerite group. . . . Together they planned, prepared, and initiated aggressive wars against the great democracies enumerated in the indictment. . . .

No one needs even the slight reminder to realize that wars in our time are quite different from those of old. Today, and far more important still, tomorrow and forever hereafter wars can be nothing other than total wars.[24]

While some have criticized the Tokyo trials for selective prosecution or as an example of victor's justice, others see the trials as an important legal milestone in the prosecution of crimes against humanity.

---

13 The Moscow Conference, Joint Four-Nation Declaration, USA-UK-USSR-China, October 1943, published in *A Decade of American Foreign Policy: Basic Documents, 1941-49*, prepared at the request of the Senate Committee on Foreign Relations by the Staff of the Committee and the Department of State, (Washington, DC: Government Printing Office, 1950) and online at http://avalon.law.yale.edu/wwii/moscow.asp; and Harry S. Truman, Winston Churchill, and Chiang Kai-shek, The Potsdam Declaration, US-UK-China, July 26, 1945, accessed May 28, 2014, http://afe.easia.columbia.edu/ps/japan/potsdam.pdf.

14 This is the date General Douglas MacArthur arrived in Tokyo but Allied personnel had officially arrived on August 28, 1945.

15 Arnold C. Brackman, *The Other Nuremberg: The Untold Story of the Tokyo War Crimes Trial* (New York: William Morrow, 1987), 40.

16 Ibid., 44. By the end of August 1945 roughly 1,000 officers and men of the Imperial forces committed suicide. Tojo himself unsuccessfully attempted to end his life as the US military police moved in to arrest him in on September 8, 1945. He was resuscitated by US Army medics and would later stand trial at the IMTFE.

17 These included Australia, Canada, the Republic of China, France, British India, the Netherlands, New Zealand, the Philippines, the United Kingdom, the United States, and the USSR.

18 "The Tribunal - An Overview", The Tokyo War Crimes Tribunal: A Digital Exhibition website, accessed January 1, 2014, http://lib.law.virginia.edu/imtfe/tribunal.

19 David M. Crowe, *War Crimes, Genocide, and Justice: A Global History* (New York: Palgrave MacMillan, 2013), 198.

20 "Article 6.," in "Nuremberg Trial Proceedings Vol. 1; Charter of the International Military Tribunal," at the Avalon Project website, accessed January 1, 2014, http://avalon.law.yale.edu/imt/imtconst.asp#art6.

21 Herbert Bix, *Hirohito and the Making of Modern Japan* (New York: Harper Perennial, 2001), 587.

22 Dower, *Embracing Defeat*. The international Far Eastern Commission exempted the emperor as a war criminal by April 1946.

23 Ibid., 592.

24 "Item 52 – Opening Statement of the Prosecution," The Tokyo War Crimes Tribunal: A Digital Exhibition website, accessed January 1, 2014, http://lib.law.virginia.edu/imtfe/content/item-52-opening-statement-prosecution.

READING 3

"THE FUTURE EMERGES"

If our people are to occupy a place of honor in the family of nations, we must see to it that our constitution internally establishes the foundation for a democratic government and externally leads the rest of the world for the abolition of war. Namely, we must renounce, for all time, war as a sovereign right of the State and declare to all the world our determination to settle by peaceful means all disputes with other countries.[25]

—JAPANESE PRIME MINISTER SHIDEHARA KIJURO

Postwar Japanese government was organized under the watchful eye of the American occupation. Under Potsdam the traditional social order the Japanese people had lived under for centuries would be changed. General Douglas MacArthur, Supreme Commander for the Allied Powers (SCAP), began to dismantle the institutions of imperial power immediately upon his arrival in Tokyo at the end of August 1945. Stationed throughout the nation to assist, monitor, and largely oversee the actual rebuilding efforts and institutional reforms, the United States determined basic policy and exercised decisive command over all aspects of the occupational governance and remained in Japan from 1945 until 1952, almost twice as long as the war itself.[26] Shortly after the occupation began, Assistant Secretary of State Dean Acheson stated the goal of the occupation was to ensure that "the present economic and social system in Japan which makes for a will to war will be changed so that the will to war will not continue."[27] During this time Japan had no sovereignty and no diplomatic relations. The authority of the emperor and the Japanese government was subject to the authority of General MacArthur and SCAP. Japanese were not allowed to travel abroad until the final months of the occupation, nor were any political, economic, or administrative decisions possible without the approval of the occupational forces.

New laws attend to one necessary aspect of rebuilding a nation after war and ensuring peace.[28] But laws must accompany other changes that need to occur for a nation to begin the reconstruction process. On October 9, 1945, Shidehara Kijuro became the next prime minister of Japan.[29] A leading pacifist during the war, Shidehara faced a state of affairs that required deft leadership in negotiating with the occupational forces. One month after taking office, Shidehara broadcast a historic address to the Diet in which he shared his perspective on the position of his nation at this unprecedented juncture in its history:

> It fills me with trepidation that unworthy as I am, I should have been commanded to head the government at a time when our nation is confronted with a difficult situation unparalleled in history. I only hope to conform to the august will of our Sovereign by doing everything in my power. . . .

> The war has ended between Japan and the Allied Powers. But the way is still long to the final restoration of peace. In our foreign relations, we are incapacitated; we do not possess the power to uphold and carry out our policies, which we ourselves may believe to be just and equitable. Such is the inevitable of a vanquished nation. Of course, there exists in human society a universal sense

self. Only, as you may readily understand, the postwar conditions in all countries of the world are yet too abnormal to permit them to be in full play. Nevertheless, the ultimate power that controls the minds of men and regulates internal and external affairs of all countries must be neither the sword nor the gun but virtue.

There must be a rule of the rational spirit. That this is so will, I think, be admitted readily by world public opinion. What is wanted for our people today is not to be downhearted or bewildered but to march forth bravely toward the construction of a new Japan on the basis of justice and fair play. That is the only way, and there we may find hope for the future. . . .[30]

Six months into the occupation, SCAP took one further step to ensure Japan's future stability by rewriting of the constitution. The new document would replace the Meiji Constitution of 1889 and would be based upon MacArthur's so-called Three Principles, (a) the preservation of the emperor system, (b) the total renunciation of war, and (c) the abolition of the feudal system. Japanese authorities had submitted a draft constitution to the general headquarters (GHQ) at the end of January 1946 only to have most of it rejected by MacArthur because of status quo and lack of adherence to the changes outlined in Potsdam.

Major General Courtney Whitney, senior adviser to MacArthur, spared no time in assembling staff for the drafting of a new constitution. In early February 1946 he called together 24 individuals at the GHQ in Tokyo and announced the following at a top secret meeting: "By order of General MacArthur you are now a constituent assembly. And you will write the new democratic constitution for Japan. And you are to write it in seven days."[31] The new constitution was drafted with the goal of preventing future war in Japan. It retained the imperial system but also established the principle of popular sovereignty and guaranteed a broad range of human rights. It was under this new constitution that Japanese subjects became citizens. Within the week and after being scrutinized by the necessary channels within the Japanese government, the new constitution became effective in May 1947. The beginning of the preamble states:

We, the Japanese People, acting through our duly elected representatives in the National Diet, determined that we shall secure
for ourselves and our posterity the fruits of peaceful cooperation
with all nations and the blessings of liberty throughout the land,

and resolved that never again shall we be visited with the horrors of war through the action of government, do proclaim the
sovereignty of the people's will and do ordain and establish the
Constitution, founded upon the universal principle that government is a sacred trust the authority for which is derived from the
people, the powers of which are exercised by the representatives
of the people, and the benefits of which are enjoyed by the people; and we reject and revoke all constitutions, ordinances, laws
and rescripts in conflict herewith. . . .[32] *(See Source 4: Preamble of
the 1947 Japanese Constitution [close reading].)*

This historic week divided the group into sections, each assigned to draft
the language for particular areas. Among the group, only one was fluent in
Japanese and had any experience in Japanese life and culture: a 22-year-old
Vienna-born Jewish woman named Beate Sirota who had lived in Japan
during her childhood and was the first civilian woman to come to Japan
after the surrender. Assigned with two other staff members to write the
chapter on the rights of the people for the new constitution, they separated
again and Sirota was assigned to write the section on the rights of women.
Keenly aware of the discrimination women faced in Japan from her childhood, Sirota saw the opportunity to contribute to the new constitution as
a way to address gender inequities in Japan. After looking at other nations'
constitutions and after several versions, Sirota's draft language would become Articles 14 and 24, granting legal equality between men and women in
Japan. Sirota later explained:

> Women had no rights at all. The arranged marriages were often
> unhappy. The women sometimes did not even meet their future
> spouses until just before the wedding. Women were not trained
> for careers and thus could not obtain work that interested them.
> Women had no inheritance rights, no rights to choose their own
> domicile.[33]

Aside from the provisions for equal rights, perhaps one of the most dramatic
changes in the constitution was the inclusion of Article 9: Renunciation of
War, sometimes referred to as the "peace clause." Article 9 continues to
remain in place in Japan's constitution and has been reinterpreted by subsequent ruling governments as renouncing the use of force in international
affairs, but not renouncing the right to maintaining a self-defense force. The
article states:

Aspiring sincerely to an international peace based on justice and order, the Japanese people forever renounce war as a sovereign right of the nation and the threat or use of force as means of settling international disputes.

In order to accomplish the aim of the preceding paragraph, land, sea, and air forces, as well as other war potential, will never be maintained. The right of belligerency of the state will not be recognized.[34]

---

25 John W. Dower, *Embracing Defeat: Japan in the Wake of World War II* (New York: W. W. Norton & Company, 1999), Kindle edition.

26 Ibid. The San Francisco Peace Treaty of 1951 was signed by Japan with 48 countries. In exchange for the end of the Allied occupation of Japan, Japan released territorial claims in Taiwan (Formosa), Korea, the Pescadores, Hong Kong, and other islands and accepted the judgments of the Tokyo Trials. See "San Francisco Peace Treaty," Taiwan Documents Project website, accessed January 1, 2104, http://www.taiwandocuments.org/sanfrancisco01.htm.

27 Dean Acheson, *Present at the Creation: My Years in the State Department* (New York: W. W. Norton & Company, 1969), 126, quoted in Dower, Embracing Defeat.

28 Policy makers in Washington drafted three basic documents that established the initial objectives of the occupation: the Potsdam Proclamation which outlined the terms of surrender, the "United States Initial Post-Surrender Policy Relating to Japan" and a comprehensive military directive elaborating postsurrender policy.

29 Shidehara succeeded Prince Higashikuni Naruhiko, who served as prime minister for only 54 days from August 17, 1945, to October 9, 1954.

30 de Bary, Gluck, and Tiedemann, *Sources of Japanese Tradition*, 1026-27.

31 Beate Sirota Gordon, "Mills College Commencement Speech," May 14, 2011, C-SPAN transcript and video, 26:31, http://www.c-spanvideo.org/program/299523-1.

32 "Constitution of Japan (GHQ Draft)," The National Diet Library, accessed on January 1, 2014, http://www.ndl.go.jp/modern/e/img_t/105/105-001tx.html.

33 Gordon, "Mills College Commencement Speech."

34 de Bary, Gluck, and Tiedemann, *Sources of Japanese Tradition*, 1032.

READING 4

REBUILDING

Journalist F. Tillman Durdin returned to Nanjing immediately after the Japanese surrender. In this newspaper account published on September 3, 1945, he reports on what he witnessed in the former Chinese capital city:

Japanese Retain Hold on Nanking. American and Chinese Troops in Midst of 50,000 Japanese, Awaiting Surrender

NANKING, Sept 3

. . . In atmosphere and spirit Nanking is a much different city than the one this writer saw in 1937 when it was the center of Chinese resistance against the Japanese invasion. It still reflects something of the horror, misery, death and violence that followed imme-diately after the Japanese occupation. Physically there has not been much change. No new buildings have been added under the Japanese and, apparently, no civic improvement.

The scars of old bombings by the Japanese in 1937 remain and no visible new ones have been added. An extraordinary number of motor vehicles fill the streets, driven by Japanese or Chinese puppets who now profess loyalty to Chungking. The Metropolitan, in sharp contrast to the primitive accommodations of Chungking remains a well appointed hostelry. It has hot and cold running water and its modern bathrooms are a welcome change from the new China capital. It has been serving as the Japanese officer's residence. . . .

The Americans are being well fed on local supplies. Generally things seem to be going smoother here, if slowly, but uneasiness will remain as long as the well-armed and disciplined former ene-my forces remains a powerful factor.

The Japanese are making most of the interregnum.[35] Their trucks are hauling great amounts of furniture and general commodities somewhere—nobody seems to know where—and railway trains go in and out of Nanking loaded with general effects.

Vast quantities of documents are being burned and properties of all kinds disposed of. Even in a country where almost everything can happen, Nanking today is a strange place.[36]

Outside of Nanjing, China was a nation rebuilding at the end of the war. Historian Rana Mitter describes China at this moment as simultaneously in the strongest global position it had ever occupied and weaker than it had been for over a century:

> When the war began, it [China] had still been subject to extraterritoriality and imperialism. Now, not only had the much-hated system of legal immunity for foreigners ended, but China was about to make its mark on the postwar world. For the first time since 1842, when the Qing empire signed the Treaty of Nanjing, the country was fully sovereign once again. Furthermore, China was now one of the "Big Four," one of the powers that would play a permanent and central role in the formation of the new United Nations Organization, and the only non-European one. In Asia, the decades of power enjoyed by Britain and by Japan were at an end. . . . The war with Japan was fought for Chinese nationhood and sovereignty, the inheritance of the 1911 revolution, and China had achieved that goal.
>
> Yet China had also paid a terrible price. . . . Even now, at the moment of victory, the country was split. It was divided between two parties, Nationalist and Communist, who talked compromise but seemed set for civil war. And it was distorted by an utterly changed geography. . . . So many people had died: bombed, slaughtered in Japanese war crimes, drowned, starved, or killed in combat. Even now, the numbers are not clear, but some 14 million to 20 million Chinese seem to have perished during the eight years of conflict.[37]

The end of the war and its devastation was only one of many challenges the Chinese faced. Mitter goes on to explain:

> [T]he Civil War, once started, went badly for the Nationalists, in large part because of Chiang Kai-shek's judgments. . . . As 1947 ground on, the Communist general Lin Biao's brilliant campaigning in north China drove the Nationalists further and further back. While major cities were still under Nationalist control, along with

the rail lines, the territory was now Communist. . . . In the autumn of 1948 General Wei Lihuang found himself with some 300,000 Nationalist troops facing some 700,000 under Lin Biao. . . . During the first half of 1949 Chiang transferred his naval and air force headquarters to the island of Taiwan; many civilians followed suit. In May Chiang set sail for Taiwan. He would never return to the mainland.

Lt. Gaetano Faillace/Library of Congress

Emperor Hirohito and General MacArthur meet at the US Embassy, Tokyo, September 27, 1945.

The [civil] war continued through the summer, but Chiang knew
that the game was up and all sides expected a Communist victory,
as cities fell one by one—Nanjing, Shanghai, and Chongqing. On
October 1, 1949, the People's Republic of China (PRC) was declared, its capital once more in Beijing.[38]

Japan also faced a long and arduous road of recovery with its military defeated and its cities and countryside in ashes. After the decision to not prosecute Emperor Hirohito was made, the next critical decisions considered was
what to do with his role. Aware of the emperor's tenuous status, General
MacArthur, SCAP, and the emperor himself set about to redefine his image.

These negotiations all resided within the backdrop of the end of World War
II and the beginning years of the Cold War. The need for the United States
to have stability in the region in order to hold off the spread of communism
in the region was of the highest priority. By 1952 Secretary of State John
Foster Dulles issued a peace treaty with Japan that included granting complete amnesty to every Japanese war criminal not currently serving a term of
imprisonment. Unlike Germany, which underwent de-Nazification to prevent former Nazis from entering government posts, Japanese war criminals
did not live under these restrictions.

Another reason Hirohito was not prosecuted is related to the steps he directly took following the surrender. In early January 1946 newspapers in Japan
printed a "Rescript to Promote National Destiny." This was the first formal
address given by Hirohito since Japan's surrender. Commonly known
by foreigners as the "declaration of humanity," the rescript began with a
summary of the Charter Oath issued at the beginning of the Meiji era and
concluded with a new statement, one that the British and American leaders
viewed as the emperor's first attempt to denounce his divinity, the core of
prewar and wartime emperor worship and ultranationalism. His closing
statement read:

> I stand by my people. I am ever ready to share in their joys and
> sorrows. The ties between me and my people have always been
> formed by mutual trust and affection. They do not depend upon
> mere legends or myths. Nor are they predicated on the false
> conception that the Emperor is divine, and that the Japanese are
> superior to other races and destined to rule the world.[39]

MacArthur, who had viewed many versions and contributed edits to the rescript, saw its publication as a positive step in the democratization of Japan.
But the role of religion in state matters did not solely reside in place of the

emperor in postwar Japan. The authority of SCAP had already prohibited Shinto as a state religion. Before the occupation state, Shinto practices perpetuated the belief that the emperor was superior to other heads of state and the Japanese people were superior to the people of other lands.[40] Because of that, historian John Dower notes from the occupying forces' perspective, the perversion of Shinto theory and beliefs into militaristic and ultra-nationalistic propaganda led the Japanese people into wars of aggression."[41] If Japan was to begin on a path toward democracy, such traditions would need to be re-evaluated.

---

35 An interregnum is an interval of time between two successive regimes.
36 Tillman Durdin, "JAPANESE RETAIN HOLD ON NANKING; American and Chinese Troops in Midst of 50,000 Japanese, Awaiting Surrender," *New York Times*, September 5, 1945, accessed January 1, 2014, http://query.nytimes.com/mem/archive/pdf?res=F10B11FB3E5C15738FD-DAC0894D1405B8588F1D3.
37 Rana Mitter (professor, Oxford University), interview with the author, March 11, 2014.
38 Rana Mitter, *Forgotten Ally: China's World War II, 1937-1945* (Boston: Houghton Mifflin Harcourt, 2013), 362-63, 369-70. The People's Republic of China was lead by Mao Zedong.
39 John Dower, *Embracing Defeat: Japan in the Wake of World War II*, (New York: W. W. Norton & Company, 2000), 314, Kindle edition.
40 IIbid. The role of Shinto in postwar Japan is also explored in Helen Hardacre, *Shinto and the State, 1868 -1988* (Princeton, NJ: Princeton University Press, 1991), 167 -70
41 Ibid.

READING 5

THE HISTORY PROBLEM

On August 28, 1945, two days before General MacArthur arrive in Japan as Supreme Commander of the Allied Powers (SCAP), the Ministry of Education sent out this advisement to the prefectual governments and school heads:

> Concerning textbooks and teaching materials, in the light of the objectives of the Imperial Rescript proclaimed on 14 August [Imperial Rescript of the Termination of the War], due care will be exercised in their use and appropriate measures taken to omit parts of the lessons.

One month later, the Ministry of Education further distilled its policy to adapt to the changing climate in postwar Japan by issuing the following:

(1) Although it will be permitted until further notice to continue to use existing textbooks in Middle Schools, Youth Schools and National Schools, it is required that all teaching materials that are inappropriate in the light of the intentions of the Imperial Rescript proclaiming the end of the war be struck out in whole or in part or be handled with the utmost of care. . . .

(2) The following are materials which ought to be used with care, amended or eliminated: (a) Materials that emphasize national defense and armaments; (b) materials fostering the fighting spirit; (c) materials that may be harmful to international goodwill; (d) materials that have become obsolete through being entirely removed from present postwar condition and the everyday life of the students. . . .

(3) In cases where it is necessary to make up for material omitted, select and supplement from the following subjects, keeping in mind place and circumstances: materials concerning the maintenance of the *kokutai* (rule by the emperor and imperial sovereignty) and the establishment of high moral education; materials suitable for the education of the people of a civilized country; materials concerning increased agricultural production; materials fostering the scientific spirit and its practical application; materials on physical education and hygiene; materials on international peace. . . .[42]

Following this order teachers and students all over the country deleted objectionable passages in the wartime textbooks with a "cut first and create later" philosophy followed by a complete ban of texts on morals, Japanese history, and geography.[43] At the core of this process were objections concerning the integration of "State Shinto," which critics regarded as wartime propaganda. All further use of State Shinto tenets in teachers' manuals and textbooks was prohibited.

It was within this climate that four Japanese historians, including Ienaga Saburo, were called to the Ministry of Education on May 17, 1946. At this meeting they received instructions from an American who laid down three conditions in the writing of the first postwar textbook:

1. It will not be propagandistic.

2. It will not advocate militarism, ultranationalism, and Shinto doctrine.

3. It will not be based on the view of history expressed in *Kokutai no Hongi* (Fundamentals of our National Polity).

Their task was also further supported by Article 21 of the 1947 constitution that stated:

> Freedom of assembly and association as well as speech, press and all other forms of expression are guaranteed. No censorship shall be maintained, nor shall the secrecy of any means of communication be violated.[44]

By 1963, less than 20 years after the end of the war, the Japanese government had reversed their stance. New demands declared that sections in Japanese history textbooks delete entire historical episodes and any language describing wartime aggressions, including the Nanjing Atrocities. Two years later Ienaga, with the support of other historians, filed the first of several lawsuits against the Japanese government, charging censorship and initiating what has become known today as Japan's "history problem," the inaccurate accounting of Japan's colonial rule in Korea as well as its involvement in a range of wartime atrocities including what occurred in Nanjing.

Over the years Ienaga gained some successes including the inclusion and historical truth about the crimes of Unit 731, the "military comfort women," and the Japanese Imperial Army's role in the atrocities in Nanjing.[45] But conservative factions denounced these efforts and continued their campaign to reconstruct Japan's national history, particularly around World War II. In 2001 the Japanese Society for History Textbook Reform waged another successful campaign to soften, and at times remove, entire sections of texts related to the new treatment of the Nanjing Atrocities that had previously been changed. Their arguments range from claiming the reports and accounting of the atrocities were simply a consequence of war to claiming the history has been greatly exaggerated to denying the documentary proof of its occurrence altogether.

Professor Bob Tadashi Wakabayashi, a scholar who believes education and an accurate accounting of the Nanjing Atrocities is important, has read several edits of their textbooks and offers the following perspective on their motivations:

> They [Japanese Society for History Textbook Reform] want Japanese youths to feel pride in their nation by learning about positive, not just negative, dimensions in history. They argue that, until recently, a "masochistic" view of Japan's history has . . . pervaded public education and the media.[46]

In reflecting on the lawsuit years later, Ienaga shared his motives a for dedicating the majority of his adult professional life to confronting the system of government-approved textbook circulation:

> I am a member of the prewar generation and because of that
> reckless war, millions of my countrymen suffered wretched
> deaths in the wilds of the continent, the depths of the sea, and
> the recesses of the jungle. And they died miserable deaths in the
> air raids and atomic bombings. Fortunately, I survived. But I was
> unable to make any effort for the sake of my ancestral country
> to stop the reckless war, and I felt heartfelt remorse for the sin
> of having been a futile bystander to the tragedy of my country.
> If I were to die today without opposing educational policies that
> extol war ... on my deathbed I would ask why I had once again
> done nothing to prevent it. I never want to repeat the experience
> of such remorse. Although I am a single citizen with little power, I
> embarked on this lawsuit with the desire to atone for even a tiny
> fraction of the sin of not having resisted the war.[47]

Ienaga Saburo died in 2002. Today, the Japanese government does not designate a singular textbook to be used across the nation. Instead local school boards decide which texts will be used within their specific jurisdiction.

---

42 Kindai Nihon Kyoiku Seido Shiryo Hensan Kai (Editorial Committee for Materials on the Modern Japanese Educational System), *Kindai Nihon Kyoiku Seid Shiryo* [Materials on the Modern Japanese Educational System], (Kodansha, 1957) XVIII, 488, quoted in John Caiger, "Ienaga Saburo and the First Postwar Japanese Textbook Author," *Modern Asian Studies*, 3, no. 1, (1969): 2–3.

43 Herbert John Wunderlich, "The Japanese Textbook Problem and Solution, 1945-1946" (dissertation, Stanford University, 1952), 236, quoted in Caiger, "Ienaga Saburo."

44 de Bary, Gluck, and Tiedemann, *Sources of Japanese Tradition*, 1033.

45 Both Unit 731 and military sexual slavery are important topics for research on their own and will not be covered in depth in this resource. Unit 731 was the biological and chemical warfare research and development program within the Japanese Imperial Army. The unit conducted human experimentation from 1937-1945 in Harbin, China. For further reading about Unit 731, see Sheldon Harris, *Factories of Death: Japanese Biological Warfare 1932-45 and the American Cover-Up* (New York: Routledge, 2002).

46 Bob Tadashi Wakabayashi (professor, York University), email to the author, January 1, 2014.

47 Ienaga Saburo, *Ienaga Saburo kyokasho saiban*, 2–7, quoted in de Bary, Gluck, and Tiedemann, *Sources of Japanese Tradition*, 1285.

RESPONSIBILITY OF COMMAND

The Tokyo trial's contribution to humanitarian jurisprudence was the concept of criminal liability for permitting, *as distinct from intending, atrocities: this was the "command responsibility" theory.*[48]

—BRITISH BARRISTER GEOFFREY ROBERTSON

Holding leaders accountable for atrocities committed under their command was a leading argument used during the prosecution of what occurred in Nanjing. Count 55 of the charges at the IMTE was "deliberately and recklessly disregarded their duty to take adequate steps to prevent atrocities."

Two Class A defendants, Matsui Iwane and Hirota Koki, and their association with the Nanjing Atrocities were both charged with count 55. When Matsui and Hirota were convicted, Justice Radhabinod Pal was the sole dissenting justice. While Pal did not deny that soldiers had perpetrated crimes against civilians and noncombatants in Nanjing, he did argue that those men were not the men being tried in court, instead the defendants were more senior level officers. He believed the Class A defendants being prosecuted could not be held criminally responsible for what the soldiers had done. Pal also took issue with the idea that military leaders must be expected to always exercise effective control over troops in the field.[49]

However, during the trial, Matsui Iwane, the commander of the Imperial forces occupying Nanjing, revealed knowledge about the atrocities as they were being committed and failure to effectively halt their escalation. He admits he was told of some degree of misbehavior of his Army by the Kempeitai[50] and by Consular Officials. In fact, daily reports of the atrocities were made to Japanese diplomatic representatives in Nanjing, who, in turn, reported them to Tokyo.[51] According to his diary entry the day after he entered Nanjing (December 17, 1937), Matsui recalls instructing the chiefs of staff from each division to tighten their military discipline and any soldier's disdain for the Chinese people. During a memorial service for Chinese soldiers killed in February 1938, Matsui, in fact, emphasized the necessity of putting an end to various reports affecting the prestige of the Japanese troops. Some have interpreted his remarks as knowledge of atrocities committed by his troops.

On November 24, 1947, prosecuting attorney Henry Nolan questioned Matsui about the responsibility of command:

> **Matsui:** Ordinarily discipline and morals within an army was the responsibility of the Division Commander. The Commander of the Army around the Division Commanders supervised these Division Commanders and maintained the court martial under his jurisdiction. I was above them. I was the Commander then and my Area Army Headquarters had no legal organ nor any military police or gendarmerie under its direct control, and therefore reports were not made to my headquarters or to me directly. It would be more proper to say that the facts were brought to my attention or communicated to me for reference purposes. . . .
>
> **Nolan:** You said something a moment ago about discipline and morals being the responsibility of a subordinate commander to yourself.
>
> **Matsui:** The responsibility of the division commander.
>
> **Nolan:** You were the Commander-in-Chief of the Central China Area Army, were you not?
>
> **Matsui:** Yes.
>
> **Nolan:** Are you suggesting to this Tribunal that that power of command did not carry with it the power to enforce discipline on the troops under your command?
>
> **Matsui:** As Commander-in-Chief of the Central China Area Army I was given the power to command operations of the two subordinate armies under my command, but I did not have the authority directly to handle the discipline and morals within these respective armies.
>
> **Nolan:** No, but you had the power to see that discipline and morals were maintained in the units under your command?
>
> **Matsui:** It would be better to say, and more correct to say, obligation rather than authority—obligation or duty.

Nolan: Yes. And that is the reason why you summoned your officers in Nanking after your entry and talked to them about disciplinary measures, is it not?

Matsui: Yes.

Nolan: So that you are not attempting to say that the power of discipline was not inherent in your command, are you?

Matsui: I do not—I am not trying, nor do I evade all responsibilities in connection with the capture of Nanking as area commander—area army commander—commanding my subordinates. However, I am only trying to tell you that I am not directly responsible for the discipline and morals of the troops under the respective armies under my command.

Nolan: And that is because there is an army commander in the units under your command, and you carry out disciplinary measures through your army commanders?

Matsui: I, myself, did not have the authority to take disciplinary measures, or to hold court-martial, such authority resided in the commander of the army or the division commander.

Nolan: But you could order a court-martial to be held either in the army or in the division?

Matsui: I had no legal right to issue such an order.

Nolan: Well, then, how do you explain your efforts to show that you ordered severe punishment meted out to the guilty of the outrages in Nanking, and that you did everything in your power as Commander of the Central China Area Army to give severe punishment to the guilty?

Matsui: I had no authority except to express my desires as overall Commander-in-Chief to the commander of the army under my command and the divisional commanders thereunder.

Nolan: And I suppose a general officer commanding expresses his desires to those subordinate to him in the form of orders?

Matsui: No, that would be difficult in the light of law.

The following day Myron Cramer, the sole American judge to preside over the IMTFE, continued the cross-examination:

> **Acting President [Myron Cramer]:** Before you proceed, Brigadier [Matsui], I have a question by a member of the Court. If you had no power to give orders relative to the maintenance of discipline, please explain the last sentence of your affidavit, which I will read to you:
>
>> "After entering Nanking on 17 December, I heard about it for the first time, from the commander of the Kempei unit [the Japanese military police organization], and I, at once, ordered every unit to investigate thoroughly and to punish the guilty men."
>
> How do you explain that statement?
>
> **Matsui:** I gathered—by that passage I meant to say that I gathered—together my subordinate Commanders and commanding officers of the various units and expressed to them my desires in regard to the maintenance of discipline and ordered them to take appropriate measures. . . .
>
> **Acting President:** But, I thought you testified yesterday that you had no power to give orders.
>
> **Matsui:** At the time, being Area Commander, I was given authority and power to unify and control the strategy—the joint strategy of the two Armies. . . . Therefore, I could not say that the maintenance of military discipline had no connection with military strategy, and therefore, in so far as the two were interconnected, I thought that I did have the power to interfere in matters relating to military discipline, but in the strict legal sense I did not conceive myself as having the power to give specific orders—orders in detail with regard to the maintenance of military discipline, and this remains my belief to the present day.[53]

Matsui Iwane denied that he had "ordered, caused, or permitted" his troops to destroy the city or butcher its population. However, for his involvement with and probable knowledge of the atrocities committed in Nanjing, combined with his failure to act to prevent those atrocities, the Tribunal convict-

Carl Mydans/Time Life Pictures/Getty Images

Matsui Iwane stands on trial at the War Crimes court, receiving his death sentence from the court.

ed Matsui of count 55, war crimes, and sentenced him to death by hanging. He was executed on December 23, 1948, at Sugamo Prison in Tokyo at the age of 70. His judgment read:

> [Matsui Iwane] organized the wholesale murder of male civilians [that] was conducted with the apparent sanction of the commanders on the pretext that Chinese soldiers had removed their uniforms and were mingling with the population. Groups of Chinese civilians were formed, bound with their hands behind their backs, and marched outside the walls of the city where they were killed in groups by machine gun fire and with bayonets.[54]

Historian Timothy Brook views the case and judgment of Matsui through the following angle:

> As commanding officer at the time of the Rape of Nanking, Matsui was too closely associated with the incident, especially in Chinese eyes, to be excused for his part in the incident. Whatever the general had or hadn't done, and whatever his counsel did or didn't argue, was unlikely to deflect the IMTFE from holding him responsible for what happened in Nanking. The bench dismissed the first eight of the nine counts against Matsui, holding that he had not conspired to wage crimes against humanity or even to commit atrocities at Nanking (Count 54), but it judged that he was guilty of failing to act in such a way as to prevent their occurrence (Count 55). "The Tribunal is satisfied that Matsui knew what was happening" declared the judgment, showing that the defense of partial knowledge had not worked. But he "did nothing, or nothing effective to abate these horrors. He did issue orders before the capture of the City enjoining propriety of their conduct. . . . These orders were of no effect as is now known, and as he must have known." Matsui's knowledge, combined with his failure to act commensurately with that knowledge, amounted to criminal negligence. On this count alone, Matsui was condemned.[55]

Hirota Koki ultimately shared a similar fate with Matsui. He served as minister of foreign affairs from June 1937 to May 1938 and was the only civilian convicted at the Tokyo Trials. However, he was physically never in Nanjing. It was argued that his ministry received information from the Japanese consulate in Nanjing as the atrocities were unfolding and did not intervene strenuously enough with the Army Ministry to halt their escalation. Failing to get an adequate response from the Army Ministry, Hirota should have brought the matters to the higher authorities in the cabinet. He did not. As the verdict states in the final line, "inaction [that] amounted to criminal negligence" is a crime of omission, not of commission. He was never to have alleged to directly order atrocities are war crimes to be committed. He was convicted under Counts 1, 27, and 55 and executed.[56]

His judgment read:

> The Tribunal is of the opinion that Hirota was derelict in his duty in not insisting before the Cabinet that immediate action be taken to put an end to the atrocities, failing any other action open to

him to bring about the same result. He was content to rely on assurances which he knew were not being implemented while two
hundred thousands of murders, violations of women, and other
atrocities were being committed daily. His inaction amounted to
criminal negligence.[57]

---

48 Geoffrey Robertson, *Crimes Against Humanity: The Struggle for Global Justice* (New York: The New Press, 1999), 239.
49 Timothy Brook, "The Tokyo Judgment and the Rape of Nanking," *The Journal of Asian Studies* 60, no. 3 (August 2001): 688.
50 Kempeitai was the military police arm of the Japanese Imperial Army from 1881-1945.
51 Neil Boister and Robert Cryer, eds., *Documents on the Tokyo International Military Tribunal: Charter, Indictment and Judgments,* (Oxford: Oxford University Press, 2008), 612.
52 "Japanese Army Discipline to Be Tightened," *North China Daily News,* February 8, 1938, quoted in Masato Kajimoto, "The Postwar Judgment: I. International Military Tribunal for the Far East," in "Online Documentary: The Nanking Atrocities" (University of Missouri-Columbia, 2000), accessed March 18, 2013, http://www.nankingatrocities.net/Tribunals/imtfe_01.htm.
53 Ushimura Kei, *Beyond the "Judgment of Civilization": The Intellectual Legacy of the Japanese War Crimes Trials, 1946–1949,* trans. Steven J. Ericson (Tokyo: The International Library Trust/ International House of Japan, 2003), 41–45.
54 Brook, "The Tokyo Judgment and the Rape of Nanking," 682.
55 Ibid.
56 Count 1: As leaders, organizers, instigators, or accomplices in the formulation or execution of a common plan or conspiracy to wage wars of aggression, and war or wars in violation of international law; Count 27: Waging unprovoked war against China; Count 55: Deliberately and recklessly disregarded their duty to take adequate steps to prevent atrocities. See "The Tribunal - An Overview," The Tokyo War Crimes Tribunal: A Digital Exhibition website, accessed January 1, 2014, http://lib.law.virginia.edu/imtfe/tribunal.
57 Timothy Brook, *Documents on the Rape of Nanking,* (Ann Arbor: University of Michigan, 1999,) 264-65.

A WARNING
TO THE REST OF THE WORLD

How were the Tokyo Trials understood and reported within Japan? Under
the Allied occupation, all media was highly controlled. Newspapers, radio,
and journals could publish what they wanted as long as they abided by the
authority of the occupational forces, strict conventions. Some media outlets
were known to say things that they did not really believe in order to gain
favor with the occupation authorities. Moreover, the media at the time could

~~not report rapes, murders, assaults, robberies or other crimes committed by~~ the occupation troops.[58]

Japan's leading newspaper, *Asahi Shimbun*, published an article before the trial's conclusion discussing Chief Justice Joseph B. Keenan's statement for his closing argument. The article provides an interesting insight to the discussion of wartime responsibility and the Japanese nation from a Japanese perspective:

> February 28, 1948
>
> The Tokyo trial entered the phase of final arguments for the prosecution delivered by Chief Prosecutor Joseph B. Keenan yesterday when the 371st session of the International Military Tribunal for the Far East was opened more than 21 months after the trial began.
>
> The trial was opened as part of the terms of the Potsdam Declaration and the Japanese people, having accepted those terms unconditionally, are in no position to make comments on the proceedings but we must not neglect to derive lessons from them, to make positive efforts to avail of the suggestions they offer and to appraise them calmly in our minds. For they point the way to a Japan transformed from a militaristic past into a nation newly reconstructed on the basis of peace.
>
> Mr. Keenan's arguments contain such important points as that the responsibility for the irresponsible militaristic actions of which Japan was guilty since the Manchurian incident of September 18, 1931, lies with their leaders and not the people, that militarism dominated the nation during all those years preceding the Pacific War and that the latter war was one of aggression and not of legitimate self-defense. What we would like to take up here is the first point, that the responsibility for the militaristic actions of Japan lies with their leaders and not the people.
>
> It is now a fact not to be denied that throughout the period since the Manchurian incident through the China war to the Pacific War the military clique, which accused Tojo repudiates, substantially dominated government and dogmatically and exclusively directed the course of national policy. Consequently, the top-ranking leaders who were at work at the pivotal center of the military regime must take direct responsibility for the militaristic actions of Japan,

legally and morally. This is only logic and so far as this is so it is quite clear where responsibility lies. On the other hand, simply because those who are directly responsible are so unmistakable, are the people themselves permitted to look on as if the matter did not concern them in the least? What the Japanese today most lack is reflection regarding the past and present of their own selves.

Accused Tojo's testimonies the other day gave the impression of variety. This variety, however, consisted merely in asserting the "inevitableness" of the Pacific War and recognizing his own responsibility to the Japanese people, while almost all other accused endeavored to prove themselves pacifists and to establish their innocence. What he did was merely to justify the international upheavals that he brought about himself while he showed no reflection on his own actions. If such lack of self-introspection were general among the Japanese people, that would prove a serious stumbling block to a real metamorphosis of the nation. Whatever accused Tojo may do or say, we ourselves must ponder deeply on this question.

To be sure, for about 14 years up to the end of the war the people were subjected to powerful dictatorial government. But dictatorships cannot be established by any one man or a group of dictatorial politicians. A dictatorship depends on objective economic and social as well as political conditions making it possible, but above all it must have the support of the great masses.

The people in those days were silenced and blinded, it is true, but, whether consciously or unconsciously, positively or negatively, at any rate they supported the national policies that the dictatorial leaders enforced. If they did not actually support them, they at least followed them. This was the common error of politicians, businessmen, the press and the people at large. Thus, although the people may not be liable to legal responsibility, it would do well to remember that part of the moral responsibility for making the dictatorship possible and enabling the enforcement of militaristic policies for the 14 years in question.

The way that Japan must go is already determined. It is to pursue the doctrine of peace no matter what circumstances should arise.

enthusiasm. In his speech, Mr. Keenan said: "The Powers of the world did not intend merely to drive out irresponsible militarism from Japan but to drive it out of the whole world. This lengthy trial is intended to be something more than a trial of individuals, a warning to the rest of the world." The purpose of the Tokyo trial is here clearly and directly presented. In order that this purpose may be served fully Japan must exert her utmost and that is the foremost mission of a rejuvenated Japan. We must strongly bear in mind not to repeat the past errors, to reflect on the methods of avoiding them and to pursue a policy of peace in the face of all difficulties. We must realize that this requires a greater courage than the momentary uplifting of the spirit on the battlefield.[59]

---

58 Bob Tadashi Wakabayashi (professor, York University), correspondence with the author, January 1, 2014.
59 "Keenan Opening Statement printed in Tokyo News, Page 1," The Tokyo War Crimes Tribunal: A Digital Exhibition website, accessed January 1, 2014, http://lib.law.virginia.edu/imtfe/content/page-1-1118.

READING 8

RAPE AS A WEAPON OF WAR

Rape has always been a weapon of war. But until recently it was neglected as a crime worthy of prosecution on its own. During the Nanjing Atrocities young and old women were repeatedly violated by Japanese Imperial troops. While definitive numbers are difficult to pin down because of the nature of the crime, tens of thousands of rapes were documented, witnessed, and reported.

While postwar courts such as the International Military Tribunal in Nuremberg heard evidence of rape being committed, the actual crime of rape was missing from the tribunal's charter and not mentioned within the definition of a crime against humanity. At the International Tribunal for the Far East, also known as the Tokyo Trials, the record was slightly different.

While the Tokyo Trials did not prosecute leaders in the Imperial Japanese Army for the institution of military sexual slaves, it did reference the atrocities of sexual nature committed in Nanjing by referring to these crimes as the "Rape of Nanking." Two Japanese officials, Matsui Iwane and Hirota Koki, were convicted of failing to prevent rape and while the crime still remained subsumed under crimes against humanity, rape could no longer be ignored as a crime of war.[60]

However, the official record of recognizing sexual violations committed during war did not begin with postwar trials after World War II. The Lieber Code, written during the Civil War in the United States, contained three articles specifically codifying the protection of women against rape during this conflict.[61] Following World War II, the 1949 Geneva Conventions also stated that "Women shall be especially protected against rape, enforced prostitution, or any form of indecent assault."[62]

Not until the International Criminal Tribunal for the former Yugoslavia (ICTY) in 1996, the first international war crimes trial held since Nuremberg and Tokyo, did the world's attention finally move international political will to prosecute rape and other forms of sexual violence as an international war crime. On June 28, 1996 a headline in the *New York Times* read: "U.N. Court, for First Time, Defines Rape as War Crime."[63] The historic ruling included the indictment of eight Bosnian Serb military and police officers for their connection with the rapes of Muslim women during the war in Bosnia (April 1992 through December 1994.) This historic ruling, heard at the International Criminal Tribunal for the former Yugoslovia (ICTY), was a landmark in the efforts to prevent and prosecute sexual violence during war. It was the first international tribunal to try a case exclusively for charges of sexual violence and was being prosecuted as a crime against humanity. No could leaders and soldiers operate with impunity when crimes of sexual nature are committed almost entirely, but not exclusively on women, during armed conflict.[64]

Philosophy professor Claudia Card expands upon the understanding of rape as a war crime by explaining the role rape holds in the crime of genocide. She explains:

> There is more than one way to commit genocide. One way is mass murder, killing individual members of a national, political, or cultural group. Another is to destroy a group's identity by decimating cultural and social bonds. Martial rape [rape committed during war] does both. . . . If there is one set of fundamental functions of rape, civilian or martial, it is to display, communicate, and produce

es of torture, communicate dominance by removing our control.[65]

She continues by explaining that the violation involved in the crime of rape is intended to terrorize the victim and the nation being occupied, to destroy any community bonds that may exist, and to send a clear message of domination, humiliation, and power to both the victim and family members (particularly husbands, fathers, and sons, who may be unable to "protect" their wives, daughters, or children). Card states that rape can be used as a weapon of revenge and as a form of genetic or biologic imperialism. Professors John Roth and Carol Rittner expand upon this idea by explaining acts of rape resulting in unintentional pregnancy by the perpetrator group also can destroy a family's solidarity by "imposing" themselves into future generations.[66]

Today great strides have been made in educating and prosecuting rape as an international war crime. Following the genocide in Rwanda in 1994, the International Criminal Tribunal for Rwanda (ICTR) was held. In 1998 at the trial of Jean-Paul Akayesu, the first conviction of genocide was handed down that included as a component of genocide.[67] That same year, the Rome Statute was passed, establishing the International Criminal Court (ICC). The ICC Statute explicitly defines rape as an individual crime and defines it as a war crime and crime against humanity.[68] *(See Source 5: Summary of Treatment of Sexual Violence in International Law and Source 6: Report of the United Nations' Secretary General on the Protection of Civilians in Armed Conflict.)*

---

60 Matsui Iwane, Japanese Imperial commander of the Central China Area Army, and Hirota Koki, the foreign minister of the Central China Area Army, were the two Japanese officials prosecuted, convicted, and executed for failing to prevent the crimes that occurred in Nanjing beginning in December 1937. For further reading, please refer to Reading 6.2 in this resource, "War Criminals and Aggressive War."

61 Crystal N. Feimster, "Rape and Justice in the Civil War," *New York Times,* April 2, 2013, accessed November 7, 2013, http://opinionator.blogs.nytimes.com/2013/04/25/rape-and-justice-in-the-civil-war/.

62 The United Nations International Criminal Tribunal for the Former Yugoslavia (UN-ICTY), ICTY -TPIY: Crimes of Sexual Violence website, June 20, 2014, http://www.icty.org/sid/10312, accessed June 20, 2014.

63 Marlise Simons, "U.N. Court, for the First Time, Defines Rape as War Crime," *New York Times,* June 28, 1996, Accessed November 12, 2013. http://www.nytimes.com/1996/06/28/world/un-court-for-first-time-defines-rape-as-war-crime.html. In the trial *Prosecutor v. Tadic,* which began on May 7, 1996, Dusko Tadic was specifically charged with rape and sexual violence as a crime against humanity and war crime. While he was not convicted of rape, he was convicted of aiding and abetting crimes of sexual nature. See http://clg.portalxm.com/library/keytext.cfm?keytext_id=200.

64 UN-ICTY, ICTY-TPIY website, accessed June 20, 2014, http://www.icty.org/sid/10312.

65 Claudia Card, "Rape as a Weapon of War," *Hypatia* 11, no. 4: Women and Violence (Autumn 1996): 7.

66 Ibid., 8 and Facing History and Ourselves video with Profesors John Roth and Carol Rittner.

67 As of 2014 the ICTR has indicted 93 persons who were the most responsible for the 1994 geno-
    cide. More than half of these indictments charged rape and other forms of sexual violence as a
    means of perpetrating genocide and as crimes against humanity or war crimes.

68 "Crimes against Women under International Law," *Berkeley Journal of International Law,* 2003,
    accessed January 1, 2014, http://clg.portalxm.com/library/keytext.cfm?keytext_id=204.

PRIMARY SOURCES

SOURCE 1

POTSDAM DECLARATION (EXCERPT)

Proclamation Defining the Terms for the Japanese Surrender, July 26, 1945

(1) WE - THE PRESIDENT of the United States, the President of the National Government of the Republic of China, and the Prime Minister of Great Britain, representing the hundreds of millions of countrymen, have conferred and agree that Japan shall be given the opportunity to end this war.

(2) The prodigious land, sea and air forces of the United States, the British Empire and of China, many times reinforced by their armies and air fleets from the west, are poised to strike the final blows upon Japan. This military power is unstained and inspired by the determination of all the Allied Nations to prosecute the war against Japan until she ceases to resist.

(3) The result of the futile and senseless German resistance to the might of the aroused free peoples of the world stands forth in awful clarity as an example to the people of Japan. The might that now converges on Japan is immeasurably greater than that which, when applied to the resisting Nazis, necessarily laid waste to the lands, the industry, and the method of life of the whole German people. The full application of our military power backed by our resolve, will mean the inevitable and complete destruction of the Japanese armed forces and just as inevitably the utter devastation of the Japanese homeland.

(5) Following are our terms. We will not deviate from them. There are no alternatives. We shall brook no delay.

(6) There must be eliminated for all time the authority and influence of those who have deceived and misled the people of Japan into embarking on world conquest, for we insist that a new order of peace, security and justice will be impossible until irresponsible militarism is driven from the world.

(7) Until such a new order is established and until there is convincing proof that Japan's war-making power is destroyed, points in Japanese territory to be designated by the Allies shall be occupied to secure the achievement of the basic objectives we are here setting forth.

(10) We do not intend that the Japanese shall be enslaved as a race or destroyed as a nation, but stern justice shall be meted out to all war criminals, including those who have visited cruelties upon our prisoners. The Japanese Government shall remove all obstacles to the revival and strengthening of democratic tendencies among the Japanese people. Freedom of speech, of religion, and of thought, as well as respect for the fundamental human rights shall be established.

(12) The occupying forces of the Allies shall be withdrawn from Japan as soon as these objectives have been accomplished and there has been established in accordance with the freely expressed will of the Japanese people a peacefully inclined and responsible government.

(13) We call upon the government of Japan to proclaim now the unconditional surrender of all Japanese armed forces, and to provide proper and adequate assurances of their good faith in such action. The alternative for Japan is prompt and utter destruction.[69]

---

69 Harry S. Truman, Winston Churchill, and Chiang Kai-shek, The Potsdam Declaration, US-UK-China, July 26, 1945, accessed May 28, 2014, http://afe.easia.columbia.edu/ps/japan/potsdam.pdf.

TEXT OF THE INSTRUMENTS OF SURRENDER OF JAPAN (CLOSE READING)

Signed on September 22, 1945, aboard the USS *Missouri,* anchored in Tokyo Bay, Japan

We, acting by command of and in behalf of the Emperor of Japan, the Japanese Government and the Japanese Imperial General Headquarters, hereby accept the provisions set forth in the declaration issued by the Heads of the Governments of the United States, China, and Great Britain on 26 July 1945 at Potsdam, and subsequently adhered to by the Union of Soviet Socialist Republics, which four powers are hereafter referred to as the Allied Powers.

We hereby proclaim the unconditional surrender to the Allied Powers of the Japanese Imperial General Headquarters and of all Japanese armed forces and all armed forces under the Japanese control wherever situated.

We hereby command all Japanese forces wherever situated and the Japanese people to cease hostilities forthwith, to preserve and save from damage all ships, aircraft, and military and civil property and to comply with all requirements which may be imposed by the Supreme Commander for the Allied Powers or by agencies of the Japanese Government at his direction.

We hereby command the Japanese Imperial Headquarters to issue at once orders to the Commanders of all Japanese forces and all forces under Japanese control wherever situated to surrender unconditionally themselves and all forces under their control.

We hereby command all civil, military and naval officials to obey and enforce all proclamations, and orders and directives deemed by the Supreme Commander for the Allied Powers to be proper to effectuate this surrender and issued by him or under his authority and we direct all such officials to remain at their posts and to continue to perform their non-combatant duties unless specifically relieved by him or under his authority.

We hereby undertake for the Emperor, the Japanese Government and their successors to carry out the provisions of the Potsdam Declaration in good faith, and to issue whatever orders and take whatever actions may be required by the Supreme Commander for the Allied Powers or by any other designated representative of the Allied Powers for the purpose of giving effect to that Declaration.

We hereby command the Japanese Imperial Government and the Japanese Imperial General Headquarters at once to liberate all allied prisoners of war and civilian internees now under Japanese control and to provide for their protection, care, maintenance and immediate transportation to places as directed.

The authority of the Emperor and the Japanese Government to rule the state shall be subject to the Supreme Commander for the Allied Powers who will take such steps as he deems proper to effectuate these terms of surrender.

Signed at TOKYO BAY, JAPAN at 0904 on the SECOND day of SEPTEMBER, 1945

> Mamoru Shigemitsu
> By Command and on Behalf of the Emperor of Japan and the Japanese Government

> Yoshijiro Umezu
> By Command and on Behalf of the Japanese Imperial General Headquarters

> Accepted at Tokyo Bay, Japan at 0908 on the second day of September, 1945, for the United States, Republic of China, United Kingdom and the Union of Soviet Socialist Republics, and in the interests of the other United Nations at war with Japan.

> Douglas MacArthur
> Supreme Commander for the Allied Powers

> C. W. Nimitz
> United States Representative

> Hsu Yung-Ch'ang
> Republic of China Representative

> Bruce Fraser
> United Kingdom Representative

> Kuzma Derevyanko
> Union of Soviet Socialist Republics Representative

> Thomas Blamey
> Commonwealth of Australia Representative

> L. Moore Cosgrave
> Dominion of Canada Representative

Jacques LeClerc
Provisional Government of the French Republic Representative

C. E. L. Helfrich
Kingdom of the Netherlands Representative

Leonard M. Isiti
Dominion of New Zealand Representative[70]

---

70 Japan Surrenders," National Archives and Records Administration website, accessed May 28, 2014, http://www.archives.gov/exhibits/featured_documents/japanese_surrender_document/.

SOURCE 3

FACT SHEET, INTERNATIONAL MILITARY TRIBUNAL FOR THE FAR EAST

Twenty-eight Class A Japanese war criminals were tried during the IMTFE.

DEFENDANTS

Civilian officials

- Kōki Hirota, prime minister (1936–1937), foreign minister (1933–1936, 1937–1938)
- Baron Kiichirō Hiranuma, prime minister (1939), president of the Privy Council
- Naoki Hoshino, chief cabinet secretary
- Marquis Kōichi Kido, Lord Keeper of the Privy Seal
- Toshio Shiratori, ambassador to Italy
- Shigenori Tōgō, foreign minister (1941–1942, 1945)
- Mamoru Shigemitsu, foreign minister (1943–1945)
- Okinori Kaya, finance minister (1941–1944)
- Yōsuke Matsuoka, foreign minister (1940–1941)

Military officers

- General Hideki Tōjō, prime minister (1941–1944), war minister (1940–1944), chief of the Imperial Japanese Army general staff office (1944)
- General Seishirō Itagaki, war minister (1938–1939)
- General Sadao Araki, war minister (1931–1934)
- Field Marshal Shunroku Hata, war minister (1939–1940)
- Admiral Shigetarō Shimada, navy minister (1941–1944), chief of the Imperial Japanese Navy general staff (1944)
- Lieutenant General Kenryō Satō, chief of the military affairs bureau
- General Kuniaki Koiso, prime minister (1944–1945), governor-general of Korea (1942–1944)
- Vice Admiral Takazumi Oka, chief of the bureau of naval affairs
- Lieutenant General Hiroshi Ōshima, ambassador to Germany

Fleet Admiral Nagano Osami, navy minister (1936–1937), chief of
the Imperial Japanese Navy general staff (1941–1944)

- General Jirō Minami, governor-general of Korea (1936–1942)
- General Kenji Doihara, chief of the intelligence service in Manchukuo
- General Heitarō Kimura, commander of the Burma Area Army
- General Iwane Matsui, commander of the Shanghai Expeditionary
  Force and Central China Area Army
- Lieutenant General Akira Mutō, chief of staff of the Fourteenth Area
  Army
- Colonel Kingorō Hashimoto, founder of Sakurakai
- General Yoshijirō Umezu, commander of the Kwantung Army, chief of
  the Imperial Japanese Army general staff office (1944–1945)
- Lieutenant General Teiichi Suzuki, chief of the cabinet planning board

Other

- Shūmei Ōkawa, a political philosopher

VERDICT and SENTENCING

The verdict and sentences of the tribunal were confirmed by MacArthur on
November 24, 1948, two days after a perfunctory meeting with members of
the Allied Control Commission for Japan, who acted as the local representatives of the nations of the Far Eastern Commission. Six of those representatives made no recommendations for clemency. Australia, Canada, India,
and the Netherlands were willing to see the general make some reductions
in sentences. He chose not to do so. The issue of clemency was thereafter to
disturb Japanese relations with the Allied powers until the late 1950s, when
a majority of the Allied powers agreed to release the last of the convicted
major war criminals from captivity.

Death by Hanging

Six defendants were sentenced to death by hanging for war crimes, crimes
against humanity, and crimes against peace (Class A, Class B, and Class C):

- General Kenji Doihara, chief of the intelligence service in Manchukuo,
  later air force commander
- Kōki Hirota, prime minister (later foreign minister)

- General Seishirō Itagaki, war minister
- General Heitarō Kimura, commander, Burma Expeditionary Force
- General Akira Mutō, commander, Philippines Expeditionary Force
- General Hideki Tōjō, commander, Kwantung Army (later prime minister)
- One defendant was sentenced to death by hanging for war crimes and crimes against humanity (Class B and Class C):
- General Iwane Matsui, commander, Shanghai Expeditionary Force and Central China Area Army
- All were executed at Sugamo Prison in Ikebukuro on December 23, 1948. MacArthur, afraid of embarrassing and antagonizing the Japanese people, defied the wishes of President Truman and barred photography of any kind. Four members of the Allied Council were brought in and served as official witnesses.

Imprisonment

Sixteen defendants were sentenced to life imprisonment. Three (Koiso, Shiratori, and Umezu) died in prison, while the other 13 were paroled between 1954 and 1956:

- General Sadao Araki, war minister
- Colonel Kingorō Hashimoto, major instigator of the second Sino-Japanese War
- Field Marshal Shunroku Hata, war minister
- Baron Kiichirō Hiranuma, prime minister
- Naoki Hoshino, chief cabinet secretary
- Okinori Kaya, finance minister
- Marquis Kōichi Kido, Lord Keeper of the Privy Seal
- General Kuniaki Koiso, governor of Korea, later prime minister
- General Jirō Minami, commander, Kwantung Army
- Admiral Takazumi Oka, naval minister
- General Hiroshi Ōshima, ambassador to Germany
- General Kenryō Satō, chief of the military affairs bureau
- Admiral Shigetarō Shimada, naval minister
- Toshio Shiratori, ambassador to Italy

General Teiichi Suzuki, president of the cabinet planning board

- General Yoshijirō Umezu, war minister
- Foreign minister Shigenori Tōgō was sentenced to 20 years imprisonment and died in prison in 1949.
- Foreign minister Mamoru Shigemitsu was sentenced to 7 years.

Other

- One defendant, Shūmei Ōkawa, was found mentally unfit for trial and the charges were dropped.
- Two defendants, Matsuoka Yosuke and Nagano Osami, died of natural causes during the trial.
- Shiro Ishii (Unit 731) was never tried, nor was barely anything about biological warfare brought into the trials.

SOURCE 4

PREAMBLE OF THE 1947 JAPANESE CONSTITUTION (CLOSE READING)

We, the Japanese People, acting through our duly elected representatives in the National Diet, determined that we shall secure for ourselves and our posterity the fruits of peaceful cooperation with all nations and the blessings of liberty throughout the land, and resolved that never again shall we be visited with the horrors of war through the action of government, do proclaim the sovereignty of the people's will and do ordain and establish the Constitution, founded upon the universal principle that government is a sacred trust the authority for which is derived from the people, the powers of which are exercised by the representatives of the people, and the benefits of which are enjoyed by the people; and we reject and revoke all constitutions, ordinances, laws and rescripts in conflict herewith.

Desiring peace for all time and fully conscious of the high ideals controlling human relationships now stirring mankind, we have determined to rely for our security and survival upon the justice and good faith of the peace-loving peoples of the world. We desire to occupy an honored place in an international society designed and dedicated to the preservation of peace, and the banishment of tyranny and slavery, oppression and intolerance, for all time from the earth. We recognize and acknowledge that all peoples have the right to live in peace, free from fear and want.

We hold that no people is responsible to itself alone, but that laws of political morality are universal; and that obedience to such laws is incumbent upon all peoples who would sustain their own sovereignty and justify their sovereign relationship with other peoples.

To these high principles and purposes we, the Japanese People, pledge our national honor, determined will and full resources.[71]

---

71 "Constitution of Japan (GHQ Draft)," Modern Japan in archives website, accessed December 8, 2013, http://www.ndl.go.jp/modern/e/img_t/105/105-001tx.html.

SOURCE 5

SUMMARY OF TREATMENT OF SEXUAL VIOLENCE IN INTERNATIONAL LAW[72]

Leiber Codes (1863)

- General Order 100 signed by President Abraham Lincoln to regulate the conduct of the Union army during the U.S. Civil War specifically included "rape" and made it punishable by the death penalty. (article 44)

- The code was later adopted as international law at the 1907 International Peace Conference in Copenhagen and became the basis for Hague Convention IV respecting the laws and customs of war on land, though the rape provision underwent dramatic changes.

Hague Convention (1907)

- In the regulations attached to the Hague Convention, Article 46 states: "Family honor and rights, the lives of persons, and private property, as well as religious convictions and practice must be respected."

- While there is no specific mention of rape, this provision was long relied on as the prohibition.

Nuremberg & Tokyo Tribunals (1945/6)

- The London Charter creating the International Military Tribunal for Nuremberg made no mention of the offense of rape.

- Control Council Law No. 10, the basis for prosecution of lower-level Nazis listed rape as a crime against humanity.

- The Tokyo War Crimes Tribunal charged rape as an offense and relied on the regulation attached to the Hague Provisions relating to "family honor."

Geneva Conventions (1949) and Additional Protocols (1977)

- Common Article 3: This article, common to all four Geneva Conventions, applies to non-international armed conflicts and prohibited "outrages upon personal dignity, in particular humiliating and degrading treatment" against protected persons (i.e. those not taking active part in the hostilities).

- Article 27 of the Fourth Geneva Convention, relating to the protection of civilian persons in time of war, states: "Women shall be especially protected against any attack on their honour, in particular against rape, enforced prostitution, or any form of indecent assault."

- Article 75 Additional Protocol I, relating to the protection of victims of international armed conflicts, prohibits: "outrages upon personal dignity, in particular humiliating and degrading treatment, enforced prostitution and any form of indecent assault." Art. 76 calls for special protection of women in armed conflict.

- Article 4 of Protocol II, relating to internal armed conflict, prohibits: "outrages upon personal dignity, in particular humiliating and degrading treatment, rape, enforced prostitution and any form of indecent assault."

International Criminal Tribunals for the Former Yugoslavia & Rwanda (1993 & 1995)

- The Statutes of the ICTY and ICTR list rape as among the crimes against humanity within the tribunals' jurisdictions but not specifically among the grave breaches or other serious violations of the laws and customs of war.

- Through the jurisprudence of both of these tribunals, rape and other forms of sexual and gender violence have been recognized as among the most serious of offenses and have been charged and prosecuted as such. The cases have recognized that rape and other sexual violence can constitute genocide, torture and other inhumane acts.

Statue of the International Criminal Court (1998)

- Specifically prohibits "rape, sexual slavery, enforced prostitution, forced pregnancy, enforced sterilization and other forms of sexual violence." Article 7(1)g "crimes against humanity; Article 8(2)(b)(xxii); war crimes in international armed conflict; Article 8(2)(e)(vi); war crimes in non-international armed conflict."

- Article 7(1)(h) prohibits "persecution against identifiable group or collectivity on political, racial, national, ethnic, cultural, religious, gender as defined in paragraph 3, or other grounds that are universally recognized as impermissible under international law, in connection with any act referred to in this paragraph or any crime within the jurisdiction of the Court."

- Article 7(1)(c) "Enslavement, meaning the exercise of any or all powers attaching to the right of ownership over a person, including the exercise of such power in the course of trafficking in persons, in particular women and children."

72 "Treatment of Sexual Violence in International Law," Women's Institute for Gender Justice website, accessed August 9, 2013, http://www.iccwomen.org/resources/crimeschart.htm.

SOURCE 6

REPORT OF THE UNITED NATIONS' SECRETARY GENERAL ON THE PROTECTION OF CIVILIANS IN ARMED CONFLICT

(United Nations S/2007/643)

Selections of key paragraphs:

Sexual violence, including rape, is a war crime and may, in some situations, be of such dimensions as to constitute a crime against humanity. Sexual violence has been used as a calculated method of warfare in places such as Bosnia and Herzegovina, Liberia, Rwanda, Sierra Leone and Somalia, and is currently practiced in the Central African Republic the Democratic Republic of the Congo and the Sudan, where its use by Janjaweed and Government soldiers was described by the International Commission of Inquiry on Darfur as widespread and systematic. As a method of warfare, sexual violence is aimed at brutalizing and instilling fear in the civilian population through acts of deliberate cruelty, weakening their resistance and resilience, through humiliation and shame and destroying the social fabric of entire communities. Victims are often left with horrific physical and psychological scars and, worse may have contracted a sexually transmitted disease, including HIV and AIDS. In some cases, they are shunned and abandoned by their families and communities.

The perpetrators of sexual violence regularly go unpunished. Their crimes may go unreported because of shame or fear on the part of the victims, because of the absence of assistance or mechanisms for reporting such crimes; because of a lack of faith in reporting systems; or because the victims did not survive. It is believed that for every rape that is reported, as many as 10 to 20 may go unreported. In most conflict settings, though, impunity frequently prevails because of the lack of action by those with a duty to respond—a failure that denies justice to those affected and reinforces a climate in which violence of this nature is inexplicably considered normal.[73]

---

73 United Nations Security Council, "Report of the United Nations' Secretary-General on the Protection of Civilians in Armed Conflict," United Nations S/2007/643, October 28, 2007, http://daccess-ods. un.org/TMP/783407.762646675.html.

MEMORY, LEGACY, AND CHOOSING TO PARTICIPATE

Chapter Seven considers the legacy and memory of the Nanjing Atrocities. The readings address the efforts of individuals and communities who work to record and account for this history. Despite the disputes over memory, people have found windows of opportunity to shift and expand perspectives.

The readings in this chapter are by no means comprehensive. They highlight some of the more difficult topics surrounding the legacy of the Nanjing Atrocities, including questions about tradition and ritual, the memory of former Japanese perpetrators, the debates about education in Japan today over the Nanjing Atrocities, as well as the politics of apology and remembrance. We hope students will gain a deeper understanding of what has changed in the 75 years since the atrocities and what challenges remain. The readings ask students to consider the following questions:

- What are the enduring legacies of war and war atrocities in China?

- What has been done to preserve the memory of the Nanjing Atrocities? What challenges do those attempting to face history confront today?

- How does the way we remember the past shape the future?

For media and classroom materials such as discussion questions and additional primary sources, visit www.facinghistory.org/nanjing-atrocities.

INTRODUCTION

December 13, 2012, marked the 75th anniversary of the Nanjing Atrocities. In China, air raid sirens sounded throughout Nanjing and thousands attended commemorative events memorializing the victims of the violence. In Japan little national attention was given to mark this date. Why? With the enormous toll World War II had on both nations, and the international visibility given to the Nanjing Atrocities, how can such an important anniversary be honored so differently? Historian Diana Lary offers one viewpoint as to the origin of such a difference:

> The war divided families and communities. It created splits between people who cooperated more with the Japanese, those who cooperated less, and those who opposed any cooperation. China had been previously overwhelmed by horsemen who attacked the more settled peoples, but these conquerors then became part of the more advanced Chinese civilization. Japanese conquest was more humiliating because the Japanese came with more modern technology and more effective organization. How do the Chinese explain to themselves their weaknesses that allowed their country to be subdued by a small country on their periphery that had been learning civilization from China for more than a millennium? How do they heal the scars of the horrors of war inflicted by the Japanese troops? How do they heal the rifts between those Chinese who collaborated more and those who collaborated less or not at all? . . .

> For the Japanese, the China War was the tragic ending of their dream of gaining Asian cooperation while bringing the benefits of modern civilization to backward countries under Japanese leadership. The dream originated almost a century earlier as Japan, more frightened of Western military power, more unified, and led by more enlightened officials who supported modernization, began to industrialize before China. The Japanese had accurately observed that China was, as Sun Yat-sen said, a "loose sheet of sand," but they vastly underestimated the potential for the Chinese nationalism to grow. By the time they became aware of the power of Chinese nationalism, they had already invested heavily in China and they chose to expand their army, strength-

~~en their weapons production, and then resort to military force.~~ As Maruyama Masao said, the invasion of China resulted from a combination of indecision "cowards" at the top of civilian government and "outlaws" at low levels in the military who acted on their impulse. Though the China War brought more suffering to China than to Japan, more Japanese died in the China War than in any war in history. Japanese were subjected to military discipline, to the loss of young men through the draft, and to shortages of food and supplies as they tightened their belts to support the war effort. With defeat came disillusionment with the military and wounded national pride. How could Japan adjust to their first military defeat in history and to the end of their ambitions? How could the Japanese explain to themselves why they should have embarked on a course that brought so much suffering in China and at home? How could Japanese who were called upon to commit inhuman acts in China explain to their children and grandchildren what they had done? Even today, it is tempting to avoid confronting the horrible deaths of the war and hope that the passage of time will heal the rifts with their neighbors.[1]

To this day, the legacy of this period continues to remain both national and very personal. The international community's response to the war crimes committed during World War II, including those in Nanjing, is reflected in the drafting and creation of institutions aimed to uphold the human dignity of all and to hold nations and their leaders accountable for crimes of war and crimes against humanity. The United Nations Convention on the Prevention and Punishment of Genocide (1948), the Universal Declaration of Human Rights (1948), and the International Criminal Court (2002) are the most visible international efforts in this direction.

Despite these advances, the Nanjing Atrocities of 1937–1938, a seminal event in the history of World War II, remains mired in controversy and dispute. It is irrefutable that Japanese troops illegally and unjustifiably massacred thousands of Chinese during their assault of Nanjing. Yet in Japan and China, as well as in the international community, different versions of the event are disputed. One debate is about the numbers of victims: how many Chinese were "massacred" in Nanjing? Depending upon your political or national affiliations, or how you define the parameters of the event, your answer may vary. People debate whether combatants and POWs who were killed should be included in the total number? Should it remain only civil-

Peter Parks/AFP/Getty Images

On December 13, 2012, the 75th anniversary of the atrocity, members of the Chinese military gathered at the Nanjing Museum to remember victims of the Nanjing Massacre.

ians? Should those individuals killed outside the city walls and in the vicinity of Nanjing be included? Or should only those killed within the city walls be the only ones counted? And, as we have seen, the atrocities in Nanjing were not limited to the massacres, so how do we account for the numbers of women sexually assaulted? Each question is historically important in accurately documenting one of the greatest war crimes of World War II. And each is also ultimately connected to issues of responsibility and opportunities for future efforts towards repairing the wounds of the atrocities.

---

1   Ezra F. Vogel, preface to *China at War: Regions of China, 1937–1945*, ed. Stephen R. MacKinnon, Diana Lary, and Ezra F. Vogel (Stanford: Stanford University Press, 2007), xi–xiii.

READING 1

A NATION'S PAST

Decades after the end of World War II in China, Sino-Japanese relations continue to remain strained. Conflicting memories and accounts of imperial Japan's occupation of China and wartime atrocities remain one element of this discord. One of the most visible expressions of this tension arises regularly at the Yasukuni shrine.

Built near Tokyo in 1869 on orders from the Meiji emperor to console the spirits of those who sacrificed their lives to restore political power from the Tokugawa shoguns to the emperor, this Shinto shrine has become a focal point for national tensions between China and Japan. Hua Chunying, a Chinese foreign ministry spokesperson, describes visiting the shrine as a "blatant attempt to whitewash Japanese militarism's history of aggression and to challenge the outcomes of the Second World War and the post war international order." For Japan, state or individual visits to the shrine are explained as simply paying "homage to those who died in the war."[2]

To appreciate the tensions surrounding Yasukuni, it is important to understand the role Shinto shrines play in Japanese society. Shinto is the indigenous faith of the Japanese people and has existed as a unifying system of beliefs and rituals for centuries. One important element of the Shinto faith is *kami,* sacred spirits embodied in forms important to life such as elements found in nature—wind, air, water, and mountains. Human and human forms can also become kami after death and are revered by family members as ancestral kami. The kami of extraordinary people in Japan are preserved in hundreds of shrines throughout the country including those for the imperial family, those dedicated to powerful clans, those for rice, and those dedicated to who died during war in the service of the nation such as at Yasukuni.

What we know as the Yasukini shrine was completed and named in 1879. The name originates from the classical Chinese text *Zuo Zhuan* and literally means "pacifying the nation." Soon after being built, Yasukuni became one of Japan's and one of Shinto's principal shrines combining the values of the State with Shinto beliefs. From this point forward the Meiji emperor visited the Yasukuni shrine twice a year to honor the spirits enshrined—once in the fall and once in the spring. With this ritual and the relationship of the emperor with the shrine, the sacrifice of dying in battle became associated with the highest of Japanese honors. The spirits of those who died in battle would hereafter be enshrined at Yasukuni and be assured of an emperor's visit.

Over time the shrine included kami not only for soldiers but also for those who sacrificed their lives for the "public duty of protecting their motherland." The shrine's official website reads:

> Currently, more than 2,466,000 divinities are enshrined here at Yasukuni Shrine. These are souls of men who made ultimate sacrifice for the nation since 1853 during national crisis such as the Boshin War, the Seinan War, the Sino-Japanese and Russo-Japanese wars, World War I, the Manchurian Incident, the China Incident, and the Greater East Asian War (World War II). These people, regardless of their rank or social standing, are considered to be completely equal and worshipped as venerable divinities of Yasukuni.
>
> Japanese people believe that their respect to and awe of the deceased is best expressed by treating the dead in the same manner as they were alive. Hence, at Yasukuni Shrine, rituals to offer meals and to dedicate words of appreciation to the dead are repeated every day. And, twice every year—in the spring and autumn—major rituals are conducted, on which occasion offerings from His Majesty the Emperor are dedicated to them, and also attended by members of the imperial family.
>
> Thus, Yasukuni Shrine has deep relationship with the Japanese imperial family. Also, five million people visit the shrine every year since it is known as a central institution for commemorating those who died in wars.[3]

Excluded from the description on the shrine's website are the specific rank and role of some of the fallen soldiers from wars past. After World War II 14 convicted Class A war criminals (including both Matsui and Hirota) and 1,054 Class B and Class C war criminals from the Tokyo Trials were all enshrined.[4] The website also avoids explaining the ongoing controversy that erupts when Japanese political leaders choose to visit the shrine, and particularly when they visit on August 15—the day set aside to commemorate Japan's surrender ending World War II.

In December 2013 Japan's prime minister Shinzo Abe visited the Yasukuni shrine. One month later in January 2014 the *New York Times* reported:

On the surface, the Yasukuni compound offers a typical vignette of Japan, with its meticulously maintained gardens and the graceful movements of its Shinto priests. But just a short stroll from the main shrine, the visitor finds a consecration of lies and half-truths that tarnishes Japan's post-1945 ascendancy: the Yasukuni War Museum.

Here are historical narratives that glorify Japan's brutal colonization of Korea from 1910 to 1945 and the 1937 invasion of China, which involved the massacre of hundreds of thousands of Chinese civilians. The attack on Pearl Harbor is even presented as contributing to "world peace."

The museum also houses a memorial to the Indian jurist Radhabinod Pal, who was the sole judge on the postwar International Military Tribunal for the Far East to argue that all the Japanese defendants were not guilty. The message is clear: Japan fought for peace, fell victim to the more powerful Allies, and was served victor's justice. . . .

Mr. Abe may have intended, as he said, simply to pray for the souls of his nation's war dead. But in the eyes of the world, his pilgrimage to the Yasukuni Shrine appeared a willful evocation of Japan's pre-1945 imperialism and repudiation of its post-1945 legacy of peace."[5]

---

2   Justin McCurry, "China summons Japanese ambassador over war shrine visit," *The Guardian*, October 18, 2013, accessed November 13, 2013, http://www.theguardian.com/world/2013/oct/18/china-japan-yasukuni-war-shrine-visit.

3   "About Yasukuni Shrine," Yasukuni shrine website, accessed May 22, 2014, http://www.yasukuni.or.jp/english/about/index.html.

4   Class A war criminals were, generally speaking, leaders at the national level who conspired or ordered to wage aggressive war crimes against peace. Class B and Class C were those who committed war crimes such as the murder of POWs or crimes of omission. The Class A criminals enshrined at Yasukuni are Tojo Hideki, Hirota Koki, Doihara Kenji, Nagano Osami, Matsui Iwane, Matsuoka Yosuke, Muto Akira, Togo Shigenori, Koiso Kuniaki, Hiranuma Kiichiro, Kimura Heitaro, Itagaki Seishiro, Shiratori Toshio, and Umezu Yoshijiro.

5   Sung-Yoon Lee, "Abe's Profane Pilgrimage," *New York Times*, January 6, 2014.

WHAT HISTORY TEXTBOOKS LEAVE OUT

The teaching of Japan's war history, specifically the story of the Nanjing Atrocities and the institution of military sexual slavery during World War II, continues to be a source of controversy within Japan and between Japan and nations it occupied during the war. In 2013 BBC reporter Oi Mariko reflected upon her own childhood education in Japan in the article "What Japanese History Lessons Leave Out":

> When I returned recently to my old school, Sacred Heart in Tokyo, teachers told me they often have to start hurrying, near the end of the year, to make sure they have time for World War II. "When I joined Sacred Heart as a teacher, I was asked by the principal to make sure that I teach all the way up to modern history," says my history teacher from Year Eight. "We have strong ties with our sister schools in the Asian region so we want our students to understand Japan's historical relationship with our neighboring countries."
>
> I still remember her telling the class, 17 years ago, about the importance of Japan's war history and making the point that many of today's geopolitical tensions stem from what happened then. When we did finally get there, it turned out only 19 of the book's 357 pages dealt with events between 1931 and 1945. There was one page on what is known as the Mukden incident, when Japanese soldiers blew up a railway in Manchuria in China in 1931.
>
> There was one page on other events leading up to the Sino-Japanese war in 1937—including one line, in a footnote, about the massacre that took place when Japanese forces invaded Nanjing—the Nanjing Massacre, or Rape of Nanjing. There was another sentence on the Koreans and the Chinese who were brought to Japan as miners during the war, and one line, again in a footnote, on "comfort women"—a prostitution corps created by the Imperial Army of Japan. There was also just one sentence on the atomic bombings of Hiroshima and Nagasaki. I wanted

subject in my spare time. As a teenager, I was more interested in fashion and boys.

My friends had a chance to choose world history as a subject in Year 11. But by that stage I had left the Japanese schooling system, and was living in Australia. . . . I picked history as one of my subjects for the International baccalaureate. My first ever essay in English was on the Rape of Nanjing.

There is controversy over what happened. The Chinese say 300,000 were killed and many women were gang-raped by the Japanese soldiers, but as I spent six months researching all sides of the argument, I learned that some in Japan deny the incident altogether. Nobukatsu Fujioka is one of them and the author of one of the books that I read as part of my research. "It was a battlefield so people were killed but there was no systematic massacre or rape," he says, when I meet him in Tokyo. "The Chinese government hired actors and actresses, pretending to be the victims when they invited some Japanese journalists to write about them. All of the photographs that China uses as evidence of the massacre are fabricated because the same picture of decapitated heads, for example, has emerged as a photograph from the civil war between Kuomintang [Nationalists] and Communist parties."[6]

As a 17-year-old student, I was not trying to make a definitive judgment on what exactly happened, but reading a dozen books on the incident at least allowed me to understand why many people in China still feel bitter about Japan's military past. While school pupils in Japan may read just one line on the massacre, children in China are taught in detail not just about the Rape of Nanjing but numerous other Japanese war crimes, though these accounts of the war are sometimes criticized for being overly anti-Japanese. The same can be said about South Korea, where the education system places great emphasis on our modern history. This has resulted in very different perceptions of the same events in countries an hour's flying time apart.

One of the most contentious topics there is the comfort women. Fujioka believes they were paid prostitutes. But Japan's neighbors, such as South Korea and Taiwan, say they were forced to work as sex slaves for the Japanese army. Without knowing these debates, it is extremely difficult to grasp why recent territorial disputes with China or South Korea cause such an emotional reaction among our neighbors. The sheer hostility shown towards Japan by ordinary people in street demonstrations seems bewildering and even barbaric to many Japanese television viewers.

Equally, Japanese people often find it hard to grasp why politicians' visits to the controversial Yasukuni Shrine—which honors war criminals among other Japanese soldiers—cause quite so much anger.[7] I asked the children of some friends and colleagues how much history they had picked up during their school years.

Twenty-year-old university student Nami Yoshida and her older sister Mai—both undergraduates studying science—say they haven't heard about comfort women. "I've heard of the Nanjing massacre but I don't know what it's about," they both say. "At school, we learn more about what happened a long time ago, like the samurai era," Nami adds. . . .

Former history teacher and scholar Tamaki Matsuoka holds Japan's education system responsible for a number of the country's foreign relations difficulties. "Our system has been creating young people who get annoyed by all the complaints that China and South Korea make about war atrocities because they are not taught what they are complaining about," she said. "It is very dangerous because some of them may resort to the internet to get more information and then they start believing the nationalists' views that Japan did nothing wrong."

I first saw her work, based on interviews with Japanese soldiers who invaded Nanjing, when I visited the museum in the city a few years ago. "There were many testimonies by the victims but I thought we needed to hear from the soldiers," she says. "It took me many years but I interviewed 250 of them. Many initially refused to talk, but eventually, they admitted to killing, stealing and raping." Matsuoka accuses the government of a deliberate silence about atrocities. When I saw her video interviews of the soldiers, it was not just their admission of war crimes which shocked me, it

~~upon their age. Already elderly by the time she interviewed them,~~
many had been barely 20 at the time, and in a strange way, it
humanized them.

I was choked with an extremely complex emotion. Sad to see
Japan repeatedly described as evil and dubbed "the devil", and
nervous because I wondered how people around me would react
if they knew I was Japanese. But there was also the big question
why—what drove these young soldiers to kill and rape? When
Matsuoka published her book, she received many threats from
nationalist groups. She and Fujioka represent two opposing
camps in a debate about what should be taught in Japanese
schools.

Fujioka and his Japanese Society for History Textbook Reform
say most textbooks are "masochistic" and only teach about Japan
in negative light. "The Japanese textbook authorization system
has the so-called 'neighboring country clause' which means that
textbooks have to show understanding in their treatment of
historical events involving neighboring Asian countries. It is just ri-
diculous," he says. He is widely known for pressuring politicians to
remove the term "comfort women" from all the junior high school
textbooks. His first textbook, which won government approval in
2001, made a brief reference to the death of Chinese soldiers and
civilians in Nanjing, but he plans to tone it down further in his next
book.

But is ignorance the solution? . . .

Matsuoka, however, thinks the government deliberately tries not
to teach young people the details of Japan's atrocities. Having
experienced history education in two countries, the way history is
taught in Japan has at least one advantage—students come away
with a comprehensive understanding of when events happened,
in what order.

In many ways, my school friends and I were lucky. Because junior
high students were all but guaranteed a place in the senior high
school, not many had to go through what's often described as the

"examination war". For students who are competing to get into a good senior high school or university, the race is extremely tough and requires memorization of hundreds of historical dates, on top of all the other subjects that have to be studied. They have no time to dwell on a few pages of war atrocities, even if they read them in their textbooks. All this has resulted in Japan's Asian neighbors—especially China and South Korea—accusing the country of glossing over its war atrocities.[8]

---

6   Bob Tadashi Wakabayashi (professor, York University), interview with the author, January 22, 2014. Wakabayashi noted in his review of this resource that Fujioka and his textbook group have never captured even 1% of the market.

7   The opposite is also true. In 2007 Prime Minister Abe chose *not* to visit Yasakuni shrine with the Chinese government, stating it was a gesture intended to improve relations between the two nations. See Brian Walsh, "Japan's Abe a No-Show at Shrine," *Time*, August 15, 2007, http://www.time.com/time /world/article/0,8599,1653265,00.html. However, note that in 2013, Abe returned to the shrine. See previous reading.

8   Mariko Oi, "What Japanese History Lessons Leave Out," *BBC News Magazine*, March 13, 2013, accessed March 20, 2013, http://www.bbc.co.uk /news/magazine-21226068.

READING 3

REFUTING DENIAL

History education and documentation were the focal points for historian Ienaga Saburo. His successful suit against the Japanese government to change the method by which history textbooks were adopted and how events like the Nanjing Atrocities and the institution of military sexual slaves are included greatly impacted Japanese society.

Despite Ienaga's efforts, since the 1970s ardent Japanese nationalists continued to use history education as a platform to promote their political views. Criticizing what they perceived as a liberal view of history, these Japanese public figures, intellectuals, and politicians critiqued the depiction of wartime atrocities in textbooks and called for yet another revision of texts. Some publically dismissed the extent of Japanese wartime atrocities and called for a revision of history texts once again while at the same time expressing nostalgia about the era of prewar empire in Japan and Japanese power in the region.[9]

In response, Japanese historians such as Fujiwara Akira (1922–2003) and his allies within Japan established the "Nanjing Massacre Research Group" in the 1980s. Their efforts to present and publish research on what occurred between 1937 and 1938 in Nanjing, China, within Japan stands as a direct reaction to the escalation of nationalism directed at erasing the culpability of Japan's wartime actions.

As an effort at countering and challenging historical deniers, Fujiwara published the following essay, "Nankin jiken o do miru ka" (How to see the Nanjing incident), on the 60th anniversary of the occupation of Nanjing in 1997:

> Sixty years have passed since imperialist Japan began its total war of aggression in China in July 1937 and, in November of that year, committed large-scale atrocities during the occupation of Nanjing, the Chinese capital. . . .
>
> In Japan today, some forces still refuse to acknowledge the war of aggression and persist in affirming and glorifying the war. And these war glorifiers focus particularly on denying the facts of the Nanjing massacre. Just as Nazi glorifiers focus particularly on denying the facts of the Holocaust, the symbol of German war crimes, their Japanese counterparts are vehement deniers of the Nanjing massacre, which symbolized the war crimes committed by Japan. Now, sixty years later, researchers must investigate the Nanjing incident in order to stop these denial arguments and demolish the glorification of war. . . .
>
> When Japan accepted the Potsdam Declaration and surrendered in August 1945, the state officially acknowledged the war of aggression and the Nanjing massacre committed by the Japanese army. The Potsdam Declaration denounced Japanese aggression and specified the punishment of war criminals. After the surrender, the International Military Tribunal for the Far East convened in Tokyo. In November 1948 the court handed down its judgment that the war was a war of aggression for which Japan was respon-

sible, and it also acknowledged that 200,000 people had been massacred in Nanjing. Then, in article 11 of the San Francisco Peace Treaty concluded in San Francisco in 1951, Japan signaled its acceptance of the judgments of the war crimes trial about the war of aggression and the Nanjing massacre. And because most Japanese, having experienced the horrors of war welcomed the Peace Constitution and were deeply critical of the war, they, too, accepted the treaty.

But this provision was disregarded almost as soon as the treaty came into effect. Because the postwar purge of public officials was lifted around the same time, right-wing activists returned to politics in force. The affirmation and glorification of the war began with a publishing boom in war books and the assault on history textbooks for being critical of the war. . . .

One focus of the present movement of politically motivated historical revisionism is the denial of the facts of the Nanjing massacre. In order to counter the views of these war glorifiers and "liberalists" who distort history for their own purposes, it is up to us to make the facts clear. However abhorrent these events are to Japanese, that they occurred is a fact, and only confronting these facts can they become "lessons for the future. . . ."

Recently the denials of the Nanjing massacre have centered on the question of numbers. At the beginning, the war glorifiers had labeled the massacre as an "illusion" or a fiction, but this view was completely bankrupted by advances in scholarly research. So now they are reduced to arguing about the number of victims, to the effect that because the numbers are small, it was not a massacre. This debate limits the time frame and geographic extent of the events in order to calculate as small a number of victims as possible [calculations refuted by recent scholarly works in both China and Japan]. . . .

. . . Yet another question that must be addressed is why Japanese became the perpetrators. Believing in emperor-system militarism, poisoned by sexism and ethnocentrism, without offering any resistance whatsoever, they became the perpetrators of a massacre. Understanding the conditions that made this possible is essential to preventing such offenses of history from ever happening again.[10]

9   Editorial Board, "Shinzo Abe's Inability to Face History," *Washington Post*, April 26, 2013, accessed January 1, 2014, http://articles.washingtonpost .com/2013-04-26/opinions/38843096_1_defense-spending-china-south-korea; Craig Dale, "A More Militaristic Japan? Shinzo Abe's Party Now Controls Both Houses," *CBC News*, July 22, 2013, accessed January 1, 2014, http://www.cbc.ca/news/world/story/2013/07/21/f-vp-dale-japan-abe-election .html. Note the final section, "History's Lessons."
10 Fujiwara Akira, *"Nankin jiken o do miru ka"* [How to See the Nanking Incident] (Tokyo: Aoki shoten, 1998), 7–13, quoted in de Bary, Gluck, and Tiedemann, *Sources of Japanese Tradition,* 1289–90.

READING 4

MUSEUMS AND MEMORY

Memory is life. . . . It remains in permanent evolution. History, on the other hand, is the reconstruction, always problematic and incomplete, of what is no longer.[11]

—FRENCH HISTORIAN AND HOLOCAUST SURVIVOR PIERRE NORA

In January 2013, 75 years after the Nanjing Massacre occurred in China, former Japanese prime minister Hatoyama Yukio visited the Nanjing Memorial Museum. The memorial museum opened its doors on August 15, 1985—the 40th anniversary of Japan's surrender—and remains both a memorial site and a museum. Renovated and expanded in 2007, the site now boasts four main sections including an expanded memorial/exhibition hall, the Centre for the Memory of the Victims, and the Peace Park. One of the memorial hall spaces is built upon the site of the "Mass Grave of Ten Thousand Corpses" while another space includes over 30 sculptures displayed inside and outside the buildings. Approximately five million visitors a year now visit the memorial hall.[12]

Han Yuqing/Corbis

Former Japanese Prime Minister Hatoyama Yukio and his wife bow as they mourn for the Nanjing Massacre victims.

When Hatoyama visited the site he was only the third Japanese prime minister to visit the memorial museum since the end of World War II. To date, no Japanese prime minister has chosen to visit the museum and memorial while in office. He bowed silently before a tombstone dedicated to the memory of victims and apologized for the atrocities carried out by the Japanese army during the invasion of China.[13] Several months later, in a speech he delivered at the City University of Hong Kong, Hatoyama said, "As a Japanese citizen, I feel that it's my duty to apologise for even just one Chinese civilian killed brutally by Japanese soliders and that such action cannot be excused by saying that it occurred during war."[14]

Jakub Hałun

Formal state visits to museums and memorials are often the responsibility of political leaders, both current and

A monument of a woman holding a child stands at the front of the Nanjing Massacre Memorial Hall.

former. Jeff Kingston, director of Asian studies at Temple University Japan, noted: "In the eyes of the Chinese public, [Hatoyama's] visit is very valuable and undermines those in China who argue that all Japanese suffer from amnesia about wartime misdeeds."[15]

---

11 Pierre Nora, "Between History and Memory: *Les Lieux de Mémoire*," *Representations,* no. 26 (Spring 1989): 8.

12 Zhu Cheng Shan, ed., *The Memorial Hall of the Victims in Nanjing Massacre by Japanese Invaders* (Chang Zheng Publishers, 2010), Museum catalog, 7.

13 Elizabeth Yuan, "Former Japanese Prime Minister Slammed as 'Traitor' at Home," CNN.com, January 18, 2013, accessed May 22, 2014, http://www.cnn.com/2013/01/18/world/asia /japan-hatoyama-china. Japan's first statement of apology for its wartime behavior occurred in 1972.

14 Kristine Kwok, "Former Japanese PM Yukio Hatoyama Apologises for Atrocities in China," *South China Morning Post,* November 14, 2013, accessed May 22, 2014, http://www.scmp.com /news/china/article/1355427/former-japanese-pm-yukio-hatoyama-apologises-atrocities -china?page=all.

15 Yuan, "Former Japanese Prime Minister Slammed as 'Traitor' at Home."

READING 5

SOLDIERS AND RECONCILIATION

Is it possible to reconcile with a past soiled with violence and brutality? Is it possible to reconcile with oneself after playing a role in such deeds? One association of former Japanese soldiers spent over 40 years dedicated to answering these questions.

For decades after the war ended, these former imperial soldiers gave public testimonials across Japan and around the world of the violence they committed during World War II. While none of these former soldiers specifically mention participating in the Nanjing Atrocities, in retrospect they recognized their conduct as soldiers was an expression of their education and culture of ethnic superiority against Chinese. This climate, fostered at an early age, carried over to their lives within the military and their misconduct as soldiers. It was their hope that through telling about their experiences during the war, greater reconciliation efforts between China and Japan would begin.

These former Japanese soldiers' experiences at the end of the war were not commonplace. In 1945 approximately 700,000 military and civilian male employees in the military were captured by Soviet troops as they advanced into China that August. This does not include Japanese civilians, including women and children, who were also caught. While many of them were civilians living in Manchuria, some were Japanese soldiers who were being held by Soviet troops on suspicion of committing war crimes. The civilians largely returned home, but for the next five years the Japanese soldiers were held as Soviet POWs, enduring harsh conditions and forced labor in Siberia.

In 1950, 1,109 of these men were extradited as war criminals to China during the early years of the People's Republic of China. Most (969 men) were sent to the Fushun prison in northeast China while the remaining went to the Taiyuan War Criminals Management Center. Unlike their time in Siberia, the Japanese POWs were now treated with greater care. They were fed rice and were allowed to participate in cultural and sporting activities and given ample free time—all under the watchful eyes of Chinese guards. Their internment in China was not completely devoid of politics. The Chinese believed the Japanese POWs had participated in war crimes during World War II and initiated a long-term "crime recognition campaign" or "re-education" program to rehabilitate these men. This included reevaluating their relationship with the Japanese emperor, reevaluating their role in fighting for "his" cause, voluntarily confessing their wartime deeds, and committing themselves in their subsequent years to promoting pacifism. Many critics of this campaign argue confessions in confinement are dubious and go so far as to accuse this process as "brainwashing."

Forty-five of the higher-ranking Japanese POWs were tried for war crimes and prosecuted in several military tribunals in China from April to May 1956.[16] The rest were unexpectedly pronounced exempt from prosecution, immediately released and free to return to Japan. Despite 10 years of imprisonment, many of the soldiers later shared that their reception in Japan was indifferent and uncaring. One Japanese government official greeted them upon their landing and handed them a small amount of cash, a blanket, and some clothes. Some found their way home only to discover their wives had remarried. Others came face-to-face with their own graves or discovered that their names had been removed from the village registry, thus disavowing them of any family inheritance.

Yet upon their return stories of their years in rehabilitation began to trickle out. The former soldiers decided to join together to form the Association of Returnees from China, known by its Japanese acronym as *Chukiren*. Committed to an antiwar mission, Chukiren's ultimate aim was fostering

Sino-Japanese friendship and forging future diplomatic ties between the two nations as a response to their experiences in China. In 1961 another section of this association was formed, Veterans for Japan-China Friendship, and in 1988 the Pacifist Soldiers and Civilians group was formed—all branches of the same spirit, to repair and reconcile relations between Japan and China by specifically addressing Japan's wartime aggression.

Professor James Dawes of Macalester College learned of the efforts of Chukiren and in 2013 published the book *Evil Men* based upon interviews with surviving members. Along with photographer Adam Nadel and a Japanese interpreter, Dawes set out to answer several difficult questions about perpetrator behavior and the ability to recover or reconcile after committing such violence. In exploring their stories Dawes probed into the political and cultural features common to genocide and mass violence. This included examining the psychological and organizational processes shaping these men's ability and decision to commit atrocities during war. If these could be identified, he asked, were there methods available to reverse such processes? Dawes notes:

> It takes time to take men who tremble at the thought of killing another and turn them into people who are eager for it, take men who can't even hold their bayonets without shaking and turn them into men who calmly and deftly twist their blade to slip it in, just the right way, through the ribcage. You must methodically humiliate the victims until they seem like they deserve humiliation. In other words, the mortification of the enemy during wartime—nonlethal practices like ransacking homes, or beating and verbally abusing people—are not accidents or mistakes or things that somehow get out of hand. They are deliberate parts of the training process. A person who has been shamed, starved, hurt, beaten, or humiliated begins to seem pitiful, begins to seem like she deserves to be shamed, starved, hurt, beaten, or humiliated. It makes it easier to kill. . . .
>
> But there is always, also, system and planning. Blame the victim, desensitize, and combine professional incentives with threat and punishment. Atrocity is a plot of incremental escalation.[17]

In excerpts of Dawes's interviews we discover the wide range of memories and reflections still present in these former soldiers' minds:

Sankakura-san: They [the superior officers] made us watch and learn. They would stab at bodies until you couldn't make out the body—the form anymore. . . . And then, you know, you'd get used to it, for the first time, second time, third time—and by then you're used to it, so now you're thinking. "I'll do this and my record will improve."[18]

Kubotera-san: Ahh, if you disobeyed an order on the battlefield, they said you got the death penalty. And then, well, even if you didn't get the death penalty, you'd be court-martialed, and nobody would consider doing something dishonorable. Well, anyway, I was greedy to become private first-class, so that was part of it too. . . . [If you disobeyed] your advance to a higher rank would come to a complete stop. . . . I wanted to be promoted. . . . [19]

Kubotera-san: And then in this pit . . . ah . . . there was this mother and child. And well . . . When I think about it, this was extreme cruelty. . . . Because [my platoon commander] shouted, "Private Kubotera! Shoot them! Ah, I did not expect that. But I could not disobey a platoon commander's orders, so ah . . . well . . . I shot them. . . .

This—was cruel. The mother—finding a mother and child and shooting the child . . . because it was so common, it's unthinkable. However, your platoon commander's order was His Majesty the Emperor's order, and that's how we were taught. Well, ah . . . I obeyed, and I pulled the trigger, but this—when I think about it now, this kind of cruel thing, even if I were to be killed, I wouldn't want to do it.

Ebato-san: But they'll [Japanese commanders] make it so you respond reflexively to the orders of those about you, like a robot or a slave. . . . And other than this corporal punishment was this bullying. And this was [unclear word], endlessly. . . . They [the old soldiers] thought out endless punishments and ways to abuse the new guys. That was the recruitment training, and the result of that was, well, uh—the individual personality was completely killed, and you follow *only* your superiors' orders. That kind of robot. The kind that could, on the battlefield, if the order came down from a superior, kill the other races with cool and composure.

out ideas—without thoughts—that your body would do in a flash
what you're told. You could say we became that kind of person. So
we went to the army . . . the body trained by this recruit training
would simply jump over one's reason—and then you commit the
crime.[20]

Chukiren was voluntarily disbanded in 2002 due to the age of its members.
Its legacy, however, remains. The years of shared stories inspired new associations to emerge, made up not of soldiers but of young Japanese inspired
by their efforts. On the same day Chukiren dissolved, the Society to Carry
on the Miracle at Fushun (SCMF) was established. Currently the society has
10 chapters with hundreds of members in Beijing, Sydney, Berlin, London,
Vancouver, and Japan. Their continual efforts to reflect on the responsibility
of Japan for their wartime past has led the association to pursue antiwar
peace activities and remains as a testament to the decades of reconciliation
efforts of the Chukiren soldiers.

---

16 The trials were in Shenyang (Mukden), Liaoning, and Taiyuan, Shanxi.
17 James Dawes, *Evil Men* (Harvard University Press, 2013), 66–67.
18 Ibid., 68. The term *san* is one of honor and is used to refer to Japanese males in more formal
    settings.
19 Ibid., 69.
20 Ibid., 81–82.

READING 6

APOLOGY

Over the years Japanese political leaders have issued a number of general
apologies for the Imperial Army's conduct during World War II. Despite
these apologies, the Chinese people and Sino-Japanese relations have yet
to be fully normalized, and tensions remain. Often the criticisms revolve
around the actual language used by Japanese public figures to acknowledge
the destruction and terror waged on behalf of their nation during World
War II. What weight do different terms carry under such important circum-

stances? Are there different levels of responsibility expressed in using terms such as *remorse* versus *apology?*

The first Japanese prime minister to issue a public statement in regard to Japanese responsibility for war crimes committed in China was the 1972 statement made by Prime Minister Tanaka Kakuei to the people of the People's Republic of China.[21] He said, "[We are] keenly conscious of the responsibility for the serious damage that Japan caused in the past to the Chinese people through war, and deeply reproaches itself."

By the 1980s the frequency of public statements by Japanese political figures increased. In 1984 Emperor Hirohito said to President Chun Doo Hwan of South Korea during his visit to Tokyo, "It is indeed regrettable that there was an unfortunate past between us for a period in this century and I believe that it should not be repeated again."[22] One year later at a speech given at the United Nations, Prime Minister Nakasone Yasuhiro said, "Since the end of the war, Japan has profoundly regretted the unleashing of rampant ultra nationalism and militarism and the war that brought great devastation to the people of many countries around the world and to our country as well."[23]

On the 50th anniversary of Japan's surrender on August 15, 1995, Japanese prime minister Murayama Tomiichi offered a far more extensive official statement on this important anniversary. *(See Source 1: Speech by Japanese Prime Minister Tomiichi Murayama on the 50th Anniversary of the War's End [close reading].)*

> The world has seen fifty years elapse since the war came to an end. Now, when I remember the many people both at home and abroad who fell victim to war, my heart is overwhelmed by a flood of emotions. . . .
>
> Now that Japan has come to enjoy peace and abundance, we tend to overlook the pricelessness and blessings of peace. Our task is to convey to younger generations the horrors of war, so that we never repeat the errors in our history. . . . I will continue in all sincerity to do my utmost in efforts being made on the issues arisen from the war, in order to further strengthen the relations of trust between Japan and those countries.
>
> Now, upon this historic occasion of the 50th anniversary of the war's end, we should bear in mind that we must look into the past to learn from the lessons of history, and ensure that we do not

~~stray from the path to the peace and prosperity of human society~~
in the future.

During a certain period in the not too distant past, Japan, following a mistaken national policy, advanced along the road to war, only to ensnare the Japanese people in a fateful crisis, and, through its colonial rule and aggression, caused tremendous damage and suffering to the people of many countries, particularly to those of Asian nations. In the hope that no such mistake be made in the future, I regard, in a spirit of humility, these irrefutable facts of history, and express here once again my feelings of deep remorse and state my heartfelt apology. Allow me also to express my feelings of profound mourning for all victims, both at home and abroad, of that history.

Building from our deep remorse on this occasion of the 50th anniversary of the end of the war, Japan must eliminate self-righteous nationalism, promote international coordination as a responsible member of the international community and, thereby, advance the principles of peace and democracy. At the same time, as the only country to have experienced the devastation of atomic bombing, Japan, with a view to the ultimate elimination of nuclear weapons, must actively strive to further global disarmament in areas such as the strengthening of the nuclear non-proliferation regime. It is my conviction that in this way alone can Japan atone for its past and lay to rest the spirits of those who perished. . . .[24]

Three years later in 1998, Prime Minister Obuchi Keizo referenced two of these public statements in his declaration:

Both sides believe that squarely facing the past and correctly understanding history are the important foundation for further developing relations between Japan and China. The Japanese side observes the 1972 Joint Communique of the Government of Japan and the Government of the People's Republic of China and the August 15, 1995 Statement by former Prime Minister Tomiichi Murayama. The Japanese side is keenly conscious of the responsibility for the serious distress and damage that Japan caused to the Chinese people through its aggression against China during a certain period in the past and expressed deep remorse for this. The

Chinese side hopes that the Japanese side will learn lessons from the history and adhere to the path of peace and development. Based on this, both sides will develop long-standing relations of friendship.[25]

21 Tanaka was drafted in 1937 and served in Manchuria during World War II, reaching the rank of senior private by 1940. One year later he contracted pneumonia and never re-enlisted.
22 "Japan: Ritual of Reconciliation," *Time*, September 17, 1984, accessed April 12, 2013, http://content.time.com/time/magazine/article/0,9171,950151,00.html.
23 Times Wire Services, "In U.N. Speech, Japanese Leader Rejects Militarism: Nakasone Apologizes for WWII," *Los Angeles Times*, October 24, 1985, accessed May 22, 2013, http://articles.latimes.com/1985-10-24/news/mn-12688_1_japanese-leader.
24 "Statement by Prime Minister Tomiichi Murayama 'On the Occasion of the 50th Anniversary of the War's End' (15 August 1995)," Ministry of Foreign Affairs of Japan website, accessed July 14, 2013, http://www.mofa.go.jp/announce/press/pm/murayama/9508.html.
25 "Japan-China Joint Declaration On Building a Partnership of Friendship and Cooperation for Peace and Development (26 November 1998)," Ministry of Foreign Affairs of Japan website, accessed May 14, 2013, http://www.mofa.go.jp/region/asia-paci/china/visit98/joint.html.

READING 7

WHAT IS ENOUGH?

In 1997 on the 60th anniversary of the atrocities in Nanjing, author Iris Chang published *The Rape of Nanking: The Forgotten Holocaust*. While scholarship on the event grew steadily over the years in Japan and China, scholarship remained thin in English-speaking countries, even after six decades.

In the United States Chang's book quickly became a bestseller. The author, Iris Chang, found herself catapulted into the public eye and began speaking widely on the topic. Public awareness and outcry around the lack of acknowledgment by the Japanese government rose exponentially. The groundswell of public outcry was particularly large among Chinese nationals living abroad who had worked tirelessly for years to bring more attention to Japan's responsibility for the atrocities committed. Given the popularity of for recognition on behalf of all victims of Japanese wartime aggression.

In an interview conducted one year after the book's publication, Iris Chang and Japanese ambassador to the United States Kunihiko Saito sat in conversation on a nightly PBS news program hosted by Elizabeth Farnsworth to discuss the issue of Japanese redress and apology for acts committed during World War II. The transcript of the conversation is below:

December 1, 1998

Elizabeth Farnsworth: President Jiang Zemin of China went to Japan last week in the first ever state visit to that country by a Chinese leader. Almost from the beginning the past intervened. China wanted a written apology from the Japanese prime minister for his country's actions in China during the 1930s and during World War II. Prime Minister Obuchi did offer a verbal apology, but a written statement expressed deep remorse without apologizing. Officials from both sides played down the disagreement, but as he left Tokyo, Jiang Zemin urged the Japanese to reflect on the past as a way to strengthen ties between the two countries. Now we get two views on the role of history in relations between Asia's two most powerful nations. Kunihiko Saito is Japan's ambassador to the United States. And Iris Chang is author of "The Rape of Nanking, The Forgotten Holocaust of World War II." Mr. Ambassador, from the point of view of the Japanese government why was there an apology and why did it take the form it did?

Kunihiko Saito, Ambassador, Japan: . . . The Prime Minister expressed feelings of deep remorse and offered apologies both to Korean President and President Jiang. And the ways or means to do so may have been different, but, in substance, there is no difference. He offered sincerely a sense of remorse and expressed sense of remorse and apologized.

Elizabeth Farnsworth: Iris Chang, is that how you see it, remorse and an apology, both to Korea's president and to China's president and both equally?

Iris Chang, Author, _The Rape of Nanking_: No, that's—I'm afraid that's not how I see it. Japan had promised a written apology to

China several weeks ago, and it was a surprise to many overseas Chinese people, as well as, I'm sure, the people of China that written apology was not offered when Jiang Zemin finally did visit Japan. And if it's true that both—that an apology for South Korea is the same as the apology for China, I don't understand why it couldn't have been put in the form of a written apology.

Elizabeth Farnsworth: Why is a written apology so important?

Iris Chang: Well, I think it would send a signal out to the international community, as well as to China, that the Japanese people are genuinely interested in coming to terms with their past. And the resistance to having a written apology, I think, just adds to the distrust that already exists between the two countries.

Elizabeth Farnsworth: Mr. Ambassador, we should explain that the Korean president was in Japan in October, and there was a written apology to Korea for Japan actions during the time it had colonized Korea. Why not a written apology in both cases, if both cases are somewhat equal?

Kunihiko Saito: Well, as I said, in substance, I don't see any difference between these two treatments.

Elizabeth Farnsworth: In other words, the verbal apology is just as important, that's what you're saying?

Kunihiko Saito: Oh, yes, and I wasn't aware that Japanese government ever promised a written apology to the Chinese government. I wasn't aware that Chinese government demanded a written apology from Japanese government. In fact, when Prime Minister verbally said that he wished to express his deep sense of remorse and further apologies, President Jiang said that he welcomed these good remarks. And I really don't see that our two governments had differences of views over this point.

Elizabeth Farnsworth: So, Mr. Ambassador, do you think the press just made too much of this, and that it's been not treated properly in the U.S. press?

Kunihiko Saito: To be frank, I think that is a case.

Elizabeth Farnsworth: How do you respond to that?

Iris Chang: Well, I have to say—in all honesty—that the Chinese people are in deep pain for the fact that they don't believe that a sincere—unequivocal and sincere apology has ever been made by Japan to China. And I think that the measure really of a true apology is not what a person or a government gives grudgingly under pressure. A measure of a true apology is what one person feels in his heart when he makes that apology.

Elizabeth Farnsworth: Explain something, Ms. Chang. Fifty years later there have been various statements by Japanese leaders in 1972 and 1985 to China expressing remorse, expressing apology. Why did this become such a huge issue at this moment in this meeting when Asia has an economic crisis, there are ecological issues, there are so many things between them, why, at least in the press in this country and in the press in China—I looked at some of the press from China—it was a big issue there—why is this happening?

Iris Chang: Well, I think it's because the Japanese government had delivered an apology to the South Korean government, a written apology, and the Chinese government had expected the same a few weeks ago. And I think that the reason why it became an issue was because that expectation was pretty much dashed during Jiang Zemin's visit, which was, I think, certainly a loss of a golden opportunity for Japan to properly show its repentance for the crimes committed by the Japanese Imperial Army across Asia. It's not something I think that's well known in this country, that more than 19 million to 35 million Chinese people perished because of Japan's invasion of China, and also the fact that Japan had enslaved hundreds of thousands of women, Korean women and other Asian women, as sex slaves for their imperial army. And these war crimes have really left a deep and gaping psychic wound in China and also in other Asian countries.

Elizabeth Farnsworth: Mr. Ambassador, how do you explain why this became—if not in your view truly a big issue at the meeting between the two leaders—an issue in the American press, an issue in the Chinese press? I know that, for example, I read in a translation of one Japanese newspaper article saying it became an issue because the Chinese government uses it to push for concessions from the Japanese in other areas; is that a possible explanation?

Kunihiko Saito: Oh, I don't think so. In the first place, I don't think that was a big issue between our two leaders, and there is completely false notion which seems to persist somehow that Japan has not apologized for its conduct before and during World War II. In fact, we apologized on many occasions, including a joint communiqué issued in 1972 between China and Japan when we normalized relations with China. And in the most comprehensive way Prime Minister Moriyama stated in 1995 that Japan is aware of the sufferings and damages caused on people of Asia countries, particularly Asian countries, and expressed his deep sense of remorse and offered sincere apologies. I don't really understand why some people in those countries refuse somehow to admit that Japan has recognized its responsibility and offered its apologies.

Elizabeth Farnsworth: Iris Chang, you've been talking a lot and working with people who have survived the atrocities that were committed in Nanking during the war, which you document in your book. What do they say about this?

Iris Chang: Well, most of them believe that Japan has just never given an apology that they find acceptable. And the fact that even now there is so much discussion about how to word the apology, whether the apology should be in writing, it really raises some doubts in the minds of many of the victims that Japan has really properly shown enough repentance for what happened.

Elizabeth Farnsworth: What would be enough?

Iris Chang: Well, I think what would be enough is a—first of all, for Japan to honestly acknowledge some of the basic facts of these kinds of atrocities, which many revisionists refuse to do, and definitely a written apology, reparations made to the victims, the—I think—inclusion of this—of Japan's wartime aggression in school textbooks in Japan. I think—

Elizabeth Farnsworth: So it's not all about the past. It's about a desire that Japan incorporate this in the present in their teachings?

Iris Chang: In the present so they could learn from the lessons of the past. And I think that people don't believe that Japan has properly apologized or atoned for what happened because these apologies don't come spontaneously and naturally. You see, I think that if people have a true desire to apologize, they would do so gladly and repeatedly. There wouldn't be all this parsing of words, and, you see, what I'm curious to know is can the ambassador, himself, say today on national TV live that he personally is profoundly sorry for the rape of Nanking and other war crimes against China, and the Japanese responsibility for it?

Elizabeth Farnsworth: Well, my guess is it's probably not what the ambassador's role is, but, Mr. Ambassador—I'll let you respond to that.

Kunishiko Saito: Well, we do recognize that acts of cruelty and violence were committed by members of the Japanese military and we are very sorry for that. And we understand that the memory of those who suffered lasts long, and I personally think that this is a burden which the Japanese people will have to carry for a long time. As to the incident in Nanking, we do recognize that really unfortunate things happened, acts of violence were committed by members of the Japanese military, and I'd like to point out that Japanese school textbooks mention—all of them—when I examined about 20 available textbooks—all of them mentioned this incident in Nanking. So it is—again—a completely false notion that the Japanese tried to conceal the past history from the younger generation. Instead, we make conscious efforts to teach our younger generations about what happened before and during World War II.

Elizabeth Farnsworth: We have time only for a brief response from you. . . . Did you hear an apology?

Iris Chang: I don't know. Did you hear an apology? I didn't really hear the word "apology" that was made. And I think that if he had said genuinely, I personally am sorry for what the Japanese mili-

Courtesy of Judy Katz

A monument at the Nanjing Massacre Memorial Hall depicts the state of fear and dishevelment faced by Chinese civilians during the war in Nanjing.

tary had done during World War II, I would have considered that an apology. But it's—I think that would have been a great step in the right direction. But, again, there are words that are used such as—words like "regret," "remorse," "unfortunate things happen." It is because of these types of wording and the vagueness of these expressions that Chinese people, I think, are infuriated.

Elizabeth Farnsworth: Thank you both very much for being with us.

Kunihiko Saito: Well, just one more point—[26]

The transcript and the broadcast ended abruptly after Kunihiko Saito's comment.

---

26 Elizabeth Farnsworth, "I'm Sorry?," PBS; Online Newshour (December 1, 1998), accessed August 21, 2013, http://www.pbs.org/newshour/bb/asia/july-dec98/china_12-1.html. The original is no longer hosted on the PBS.org website, but a copy made November 7, 2013 is archived at The Internet Archive, https://web.archive.org/web/20131107011256/http://www.pbs.org/newshour/bb /asia/july-dec98/china_12-1.html.

HEALING HISTORICAL WOUNDS

There is not one cure or step to take in forging new relationships between two nations who share a past of violence, war, and atrocities. In 2002 the Harvard Asia Center hosted a specific conference on World War II in East Asia to initiate one possible step. Some of the most prominent scholars in East Asian history gathered together from China, Japan, Canada, Europe, and the United States. In framing the context of the event Professor Ezra Vogel stated:

> It would be naïve to think that a work of scholarship can by itself greatly advance the healing process between the two nations. But there are political leaders and media spokesmen in both countries who recognize the need for people in their nations to work together. We hope that our progress toward a more objective common understanding of the China War will encourage and assist them in their efforts. . . .
>
> By any standards, the China War is one of the most neglected periods in modern East Asian Studies. Some scholars have begun to take an interest in how the history of that war is viewed and interpreted. There have been studies of the diplomacy around the China War, of Chinese Communist base areas, of relations between the Guomindang [the Nationalists] and the Communists. But few conferences had been held on the nature of the war itself. My commitment to bringing together Japanese, Chinese, and Western scholars to study the China War stemmed from my sense of the deep sentiments that separated the Chinese and Japanese and my hope that scholars working together to gain objective understanding could contribute not only to scholarship but also to the healing of historical wounds.
>
> Scholars seeking to understand the China War confront frustrating barriers: the lack of availability of crucial materials, linguistic difficulties, and intellectual frameworks that do not easily transcend national and disciplinary boundaries. To transcend these barriers, we need scholars in each country who are prepared

to join scholars elsewhere to broaden the scope of issues we raise, to share our materials and research findings, and to strive to achieve a common objective understanding of what actually happened.

Several years ago in Japan, a conference was held between Chinese and Japanese scholars to examine what happened in World War II. Both Chinese and Japanese scholars present at the conference reported that the presentations became so polarized and acrimonious that there was little real academic exchange. I believed that if Westerners organized such a conference it might provide a more neutral setting that would enable Chinese and Japanese as well as Western scholars to engage in academic dis-cussion. I began to make plans for such a conference.[27]

Vogel's commitment highlights the important role scholarship and the exchange of ideas can play and invite a step in healing the scars and horrors of war. But it is just one of many efforts that must continue to take place. Historian Takashi Yoshida believes the legacy and memory of the Nanjing Atrocities carries other burdens as well. Born and raised in Nanjing and currently a professor at Western Michigan University, Professor Yoshida wrote in 2006:

Nanjing has been a mirror of larger attitudes and geopolitical imperatives. Understand the historiography of the massacre, and you will find that you possess a useful index to society and politics of each historical moment in the decades since 1937. It is no wonder that ethnocentric narratives of Nanjing prevailed at the time of the war, during which Japan, China and the United States all found it necessary to promote mass killing in the name of the state and justice. It is understandable that news reports of the testimonies of Nanjing at the Tokyo Trial appalled many Japanese during the occupation, when the military was entirely discredited. It is no surprise that the authorized PRC [People's Republic of China] accounts at the height of the Cold War blamed the United States for abetting Japanese atrocities in Nanjing. It is, finally, no wonder that the history of Nanjing was rediscovered in the United States in the post-Cold War period, just as the hitherto accepted history of the Pacific War had largely disregarded the experiences of Chinese immigrants.

How will the history of Nanjing be told in Japan, China and the United States 20 years from now? Will it be possible for all of these governments and peoples to share a single narrative of the Nanjing Massacre? I am afraid not. The various authors of Nanjing literature may never agree on a definition of truth, giving readers a wide range of narratives from which to choose their own preferred history of Nanjing. Nevertheless, it has already been possible to many individuals in all three nations to overcome the limitations of ethnocentrism and nationalism in their thinking about Nanjing. Motivated by the ideal of universal human rights, concerned persons may eventually be able to agree on an international history of the Nanjing Massacre whose objective will be to produce a more harmonious future. Such a history would seek neither to exploit, nor to exaggerate, nor to rationalize atrocity. Instead, it would articulate an understanding of events that values human life without regard to ethnicity, nationality, religion, or gender.[28]

---

27 Vogel, *China at War,* xv–xiv.
28 Takashi Yoshida, *The Making of the "Rape of Nanking": History and Memory in Japan, China, and the United States* (Oxford: Oxford University Press, 2006), 182–83.

PRIMARY SOURCES

SOURCE 1

SPEECH BY JAPANESE PRIME MINISTER TOMIICHI MURAYAMA ON THE 50TH ANNIVERSARY OF THE WAR'S END (CLOSE READING)

The world has seen fifty years elapse since the war came to an end. Now, when I remember the many people both at home and abroad who fell victim to war, my heart is overwhelmed by a flood of emotions.

The peace and prosperity of today were built as Japan overcame great difficulty to arise from a devastated land after defeat in the war. That achievement is something of which we are proud, and let me herein express my heartfelt admiration for the wisdom and untiring effort of each and every one of our citizens. Let me also express once again my profound gratitude for the indispensable support and assistance extended to Japan by the countries of the world, beginning with the United States of America. I am also delighted that we have been able to build the friendly relations which we enjoy today with the neighboring countries of the Asia-Pacific region, the United States and the countries of Europe.

Now that Japan has come to enjoy peace and abundance, we tend to overlook the pricelessness and blessings of peace. Our task is to convey to younger generations the horrors of war, so that we never repeat the errors in our history. I believe that, as we join hands, especially with the peoples of neighboring countries, to ensure true peace in the Asia-Pacific region—indeed, in the entire world—it is necessary, more than anything else, that we foster relations with all countries based on deep understanding and trust. Guided by this conviction, the Government has launched the Peace, Friendship and Exchange Initiative, which consists of two parts promoting: support for historical research into relations in the modern era between Japan and the neighboring countries of Asia and elsewhere; and rapid expansion of exchanges with those countries. Furthermore, I will continue in all sincerity to do my utmost in efforts being made on the issues arisen from the war, in order to further strengthen the relations of trust between Japan and those countries.

Now, upon this historic occasion of the 50th anniversary of the war's end, we should bear in mind that we must look into the past to learn from the lessons of history, and ensure that we do not stray from the path to the peace and prosperity of human society in the future.

During a certain period in the not too distant past, Japan, following a mistaken national policy, advanced along the road to war, only to ensnare the Japanese people in a fateful crisis, and, through its colonial rule and aggression, caused tremendous damage and suffering to the people of many countries, particularly to those of Asian nations. In the hope that no such mistake be made in the future, I regard, in a spirit of humility, these irrefutable facts of history, and express here once again my feelings of deep remorse and state my heartfelt apology. Allow me also to express my feelings of profound mourning for all victims, both at home and abroad, of that history.

Building from our deep remorse on this occasion of the 50th anniversary of the end of the war, Japan must eliminate self-righteous nationalism, promote international coordination as a responsible member of the international community and, thereby, advance the principles of peace and democracy. At the same time, as the only country to have experienced the devastation of atomic bombing, Japan, with a view to the ultimate elimination of nuclear weapons, must actively strive to further global disarmament in areas such as the strengthening of the nuclear non-proliferation regime. It is my conviction that in this way alone can Japan atone for its past and lay to rest the spirits of those who perished.

It is said that one can rely on good faith. And so, at this time of remembrance, I declare to the people of Japan and abroad my intention to make good faith the foundation of our Government policy, and this is my vow.[29]

---

29 "Statement by Prime Minister Tomiichi Murayama 'On the Occasion of the 50th Anniversary of the War's End' (15 August 1995)," Ministry of Foreign Affairs of Japan Website, accessed July 14, 2013, http://www.mofa.go.jp/announce/press/pm/murayama/9508.html.

CREDITS

Grateful acknowledgment is made for permission to reproduce
the following:

Excerpts from *The Nanjing Atrocity 1937-38: Complicating the Picture*, edited by Bob Tadashi
Waskabayashi, reproduced by permission of Berghahn Books Inc.

Excerpts from Suzanne O'Brien's translation of *Comfort Women*, by Yoshimi Yoshiaki, copyright © 2000 reprinted with permission of Columbia University Press and Iwanami Shoten.

Ōe Kenzaburō's "Portrait of the Postwar Generation" and Fujiwara Akira's "Nankin jiken o dō
miru ka" ("How to see the Nanjing incident") reprinted from *Sources of Japanese Tradition*,
edited by Wm. Theodore de Bary, Carol Gluck, and Arthur Tiedemann, copyright © 2005
Columbia University Press, with permission of the publisher.

Excerpts from Katsuhiko Kakehi's "An Outline of Shinto," from *Contemporary Japan*, Vol. I,
No. 4, March 1933 reprinted with permission of De Gruyter.

Excerpt from a 1948 article, "Reading Mr. Keenan's Arguments for Prosecution," published by
the Japanese news service *The Asahi Shumbun* reprinted with permission of The University of
Virginia Law Library, which reproduced the article in a digital exhibit.

"The Past," a poem by Ha Jin, reprinted from *Facing Shadows* © 1992 by Ha Jin, by permission of Hanging Loose Press.

Excerpts from *Tiger Writing: Art, Culture, and the Interdependent Self*. (Harvard University
Press). Copyright © 2013 by Gish Jen. Reprinted with permission by Melanie Jackson Agency,
LLC.

Reprinted by permission of the publisher from *Evil Men*, by James Dawes, pp. 49-50, 66-68,
69-70, 81-82, Cambridge, Mass.: Harvard University Press, Copyright © 2013 by the President
and Fellows of the College.

Testimony of Professor Miner Searle Bates at trials from Digitized Transcript of Proceedings,
July 29, 1946, The Tokyo War Crimes Trial Digital Exhibition, University of Virginia Law
Library. Original Manuscript courtesy of the Virginia Historical Society from Mss1 Su863 a,
Papers, 1919-1965.

Excerpts from *Forgotten Ally: China's World War II, 1937-1945* by Rana Mitter. Copyright
© 2013 by Rana Mitter. Reprinted by permission of Houghton Mifflin Harcourt Publishing
Company. All rights reserved.

Excerpt from *Beyond the "Judgment of Civilization" The Intellectual Legacy of the Japanese
War Crimes Trials, 1946-1949*, by Ushimuru Kei and translated by Steven J. Ericson, reprinted
with permission of International House of Japan.

Excerpts from "All Captives Slain," by F. Tillman Durdin, from *The New York Times*,
December 18 © 1937 *The New York Times*. All Rights Reserved. Used by permission and
protected by the Copyright Laws of the United States. The printing, copying, redistribution, or
retransmission of this content without express written permission is prohibited.

Excerpt from "Japanese Retain Hold on Nanking; American and Chinese Troops in Midst
of 50,000 Japanese, Awaiting Surrender," by F. Tillman Durdin, from *The New York Times*,
September 5 (c) 1945 *The New York Times*. All Rights Reserved. Used by permission and
protected by the Copyright Laws of the United States. The printing, copying, redistribution, or
retransmission of this content without express written permission is prohibited.

Excerpt from "Abe's Profane Pilgrimage," by Sung-Yoon Lee, from *The New York Times,* January 6 (c) 2014 *The New York Times.* All Rights Reserved. Used by permission and protected by the Copyright Laws of the United States. The printing, copying, redistribution, or retransmission of this content without express written permission is prohibited.

Excerpt from *The Making of the "Rape of Nanking": History, Memory in Japan, China, and the United States* by Takashi Yoshida (2006) 345w from pp.182-183 used by permission of Oxford University Press, USA

Excerpt from Elizabeth Farnsworth's December 1, 1998 interview on PBS NewsHour with Iris Chang and Kunihiko Saito, the Japanese Ambassador to the United States, used with permission of NewsHour Productions, LLC.

Excerpt from *The Rape of Nanking: The Forgotten Holocaust of World War II,* by Iris Chang, used with permission of the Perseus Book Group.

Excerpt from *Japan's Past, Japan's Future: One Historian's Odyssey,* by Ienaga Saburo and translated by Richard H. Minear, © 2001, used with permission of Rowman & Littlefield Publishing Group.

Reprinted by permission of Waveland Press, Inc. from Kwan *Things That Must Not be Forgotten: A Childhood in Wartime China* (Long Grove, IL: Waveland Press, Inc. © (2000) Reissued (2012). All rights reserved.

Excerpt from *China at War* edited by Stephen R. MacKinnon, Diana Lary, and Ezra F. Vogel. Copyright © 2007 by the Board of Trustees of the Leland Stanford Jr. University. All rights reserved. Used with Permission of Stanford University Press. www.sup.org.

From *The Search for Modern China,* by Jonathan Spence. Copyright © 1990 by Jonathan D. Spence. Used by permission of W.W. Norton & Company, Inc.

From *Women Writers of Traditional China.* Edited by Kang-i Sun Chang and Haun Saussy. Copyright © 1999 by the Board of Trustees of the Leland Stanford Jr. University. All rights reserved. Used with the permission of Stanford University Press. www.sup.org.

Excerpt from "The Tokyo Judgement and the Rape of Nanking", by Timothy Brook, published in *The Journal of Asian Studies,* volume 60, issue 3 (August 2001), reprinted with the permission of Cambridge University Press.

Lao She's "Wang Xiao gan lü," Quoted in Chang-tai Hung, *War and Popular Culture: Resistance in Modern China, 1937-1945* (Berkeley: University of California Press, 1994), 214. Reproduced with permission of University of California Press.

Lao She's "Nü'er jing," Quoted in Chang-tai Hung, *War and Popular Culture: Resistance in Modern China, 1937-1945* (Berkeley: University of California Press, 1994), 214. Reproduced with permission of University of California Press.

Lao She's "Smashing Little Japan," reprinted from Da xiao Riben (N.P.: Ronguy junren shiye xunliansuo, n.d.), pp. 1-2 (abridged). Quoted in Chang-tai Hung, *War and Popular Culture: Resistance in Modern China, 1937-1945* (Berkeley: University of California Press, 1994), 214. Reproduced with permission of University of California Press.

Poem "Funds for Building Warships," by Takamura Kōtarō, translated by Hiroaki Sato, from *Chieko and Other Poems of Takamura Kotaro,* reprinted with permission of the translator.

Interview of Chen Deschou is from the archive of the USC Shoah Foundation - The Institute for Visual History and Education. For more information: http://sfi.usc.edu Reproduced with permission.

"Treatment of Sexual Violence in International Law" reprinted with permission of the Women's Initiative for Gender Justice.

Letter by Dr. George Fitch, 1938, found in a digital exhibit, *The Nanking Massacre Project,* by the Yale Divinity School Library, reprinted with permission of the Yale Divinity School Library.

Excerpt from Minnie Vautrin's diary, 1937, found in a digital exhibit, *The Nanking Massacre Project,* by the Yale Divinity School Library, reprinted with permission of the Yale Divinity School Library.

Excerpt from the diary of Tsen Shui-fang, found in *The Undaunted Women of Nanking: The Wartime Diaries of Minnie Vautrin and Tsen Shui-Fang,* edited and translated by Hua-ling and Zhang Lian-hong, © 2010, used with permission of Southern Illinois University Press.

Letters by Dr. Wilson, 1937, found in a digital exhibit, *The Nanking Massacre Project,* by the Yale Divinity School Library, reprinted with permission of the Yale Divinity School Library.

Letters by Miner Searle Bates, 1937, found in a digital exhibit, *The Nanking Massacre Project,* by the Yale Divinity School Library, reprinted with permission of the Yale Divinity School Library.

Excerpt from letter by Charlene Wang, November 6, 2013, reprinted with permission of the author.

Excerpt from Qiu Jin's "Stones of the Jingwei Bird" from *Writing Women in Modern China: An Anthology of Women's Literature from the early 20th Century,* edited by Amy D. Dooling and Kristina M. Torgeson. Copyright © 1998 Columbia University Press. Reprinted with permission of the publisher.